PRAISE FOR
AT HOME IN THE WORLD

"Many people have the fantasy of leaving everyday life behind to travel for a year. Tsh Oxenreider and her husband actually did it—with three young children! In this candid, funny, thought-provoking account, Tsh shows that it's possible to combine a love for adventure and travel with a love for family and home."

—GRETCHEN RUBIN, *NEW YORK TIMES* BESTSELLING AUTHOR
OF *THE HAPPINESS PROJECT* AND *BETTER THAN BEFORE*

"Tsh is a remarkable example of how to balance the rooted stability of family with the winged adventure of wanderlust. This book takes you country by country and shows you how she's found the best of both worlds."

—CHRIS GUILLEBEAU, *NEW YORK TIMES* BESTSELLING AUTHOR
OF *BORN FOR THIS* AND *THE $100 STARTUP*

"Possibly this book should come with a warning label, something like 'only read this book if you want to upend everything in the name of travel, adventure, family, and love.' Because that's exactly what I want to do after reading it. I've always found Tsh's voice to be warm, practical, and inspiring, and never more so than in this wonderful book. It was a beautiful reminder of how travel shapes us, how beautiful the world is, and how parenting doesn't need to mean the end of adventuring. I loved every word."

—SHAUNA NIEQUIST, *NEW YORK TIMES* BESTSELLING AUTHOR
OF *PRESENT OVER PERFECT* AND *BREAD AND WINE*

"Tsh Oxenreider is the only person I know who makes traveling around the world with her family of five sound not only normal, but downright cozy. Her beautifully written stories and intentional perspective offer clarifying reminders of what it means to belong and be well, no matter where we may go."

—EMILY P. FREEMAN, AUTHOR OF *SIMPLY TUESDAY* AND *A MILLION LITTLE WAYS*

"A welcome counterpoint to the 'burn it all down' travel memoir genre, Tsh traveled the world for a year with her husband, their three young children and her job along for the ride. I couldn't put this inspiring book down, not only because of Tsh's glorious and interesting travel stories, but because of the underlying permission to include our children and our significant others in what we love most about being alive."

—SARAH BESSEY, AUTHOR OF *JESUS FEMINIST* AND *OUT OF SORTS*

"There is a 'normal' way of living we easily buy into—graduate high school with good grades so you can go to college, get good grades so you can go to graduate school, get a job, work until you get the promotion, the house, so on and so forth. This book enlivens risk and emboldens us to find a full path, not a comfortable one. This book will make the wanderer feel right at home and have the homebody strapping on a backpack to wander."

—LISA GUNGOR, RECORDING ARTIST

"This book is one of a kind, and for that it's a must-read. It's not a stereotypical travel memoir from a single person about 'finding yourself,' but rather a family that adventures because they already have. It made me wrestle deeply with questions of belonging, home, family, and hospitality—while giving full permission to be okay with the paradox of having wanderlust and also being a homebody. Read it, then buy five copies and give to friends. That's what I'm doing, at least."

—JEFFERSON BETHKE, *NEW YORK TIMES* BESTSELLING AUTHOR
OF *IT'S NOT WHAT YOU THINK* AND *JESUS > RELIGION*

"Warning: This book may create wanderlust. I loved this un-put-down-able take on a true global road trip, family in tow. An inspirational tale of one family's journey to find their place in the world, and one I'll treasure."

—CLAIRE DIAZ-ORTIZ, ENTREPRENEUR, EARLY TWITTER EMPLOYEE,
AND AUTHOR OF *DESIGN YOUR DAY* AND *THE BETTER LIFE*

"As a homebody with a healthy dose of wanderlust, I've been fascinated by Tsh's around-the-world adventure since the moment I first heard about it. I so enjoyed getting to tag along on her family's global adventures, which were nothing at all like I expected—both more strange and more familiar than I had imagined."

—ANNE BOGEL, AUTHOR OF *READING PEOPLE*

"As a devout homebody I'm used to being shamed by books about travel. Not this time. In *At Home in the World*, Tsh's words will have you longing for home even if you're sitting in your favorite chair. My view of home is forever changed for the better. I cannot stop thinking about this book."

—MYQUILLYN SMITH, AUTHOR OF *THE NESTING PLACE* AND
HOMEBODY EXTRAORDINAIRE

"No one leads us through adventure and family better than Tsh! This expansive story of people, places, presence, and pluck is an absolute page-turner. She went on the adventure I always dreamed of but didn't know was possible. You are going to love this book. You'll close the last page, hug your family tight, and then call your travel agent."

—JEN HATMAKER, *NEW YORK TIMES* BESTSELLING AUTHOR OF
FOR THE LOVE

Other Books by Tsh Oxenreider

Organized Simplicity

Notes from a Blue Bike

HOME
in the
WORLD

REFLECTIONS on BELONGING

WHILE

WANDERING the GLOBE

TSH
OXENREIDER

An Adventure
Across 4 Continents
with 3 Kids,
1 Husband, and
5 Backpacks

NELSON
BOOKS

An Imprint of Thomas Nelson

© 2017 by Tsh Oxenreider

Published in Nashville, Tennessee, by Nelson Books, an imprint of Thomas Nelson. Nelson Books and Thomas Nelson are registered trademarks of HarperCollins Christian Publishing, Inc.

Published in association with literary agent Jenni Burke of D. C. Jacobson & Associates, LLC, an Author Management Company, www.dcjacobson.com.

Thomas Nelson titles may be purchased in bulk for educational, business, fund-raising, or sales promotional use. For information, please e-mail SpecialMarkets@ThomasNelson.com.

Any Internet addresses, phone numbers, or company or product information printed in this book are offered as a resource and are not intended in any way to be or to imply an endorsement by Thomas Nelson, nor does Thomas Nelson vouch for the existence, content, or services of these sites, phone numbers, companies, or products beyond the life of this book.

ISBN 978-1-4002-0560-8 (eBook)

Library of Congress Cataloging-in-Publication Data

ISBN 978-1-4002-0559-2
Names: Oxenreider, Tsh, 1977- author.
Title: At home in the world : reflections on belonging while wandering the globe : an adventure across 4 continents with 3 kids, 1 husband, and 5 backpacks / Tsh Oxenreider.
Description: Nashville, Tennessee : Thomas Nelson, 2017.
Identifiers: LCCN 2016037558 | ISBN 9781400205592 (hardback)
Subjects: LCSH: Oxenreider, Tsh, 1977---Travel. | Oxenreider, Tsh, 1977---Family. | Voyages around the world. | Families--Travel. | Children--Travel. | Belonging (Social psychology)
Classification: LCC G440.O84 A3 2017 | DDC 910.4/1--dc23 LC record available at https://lccn.loc.gov/2016037558

Printed in the United States of America

17 18 19 20 21 LSC 10 9 8 7 6 5 4 3 2 1

*To Tate, Reed, and Finn—the best travelers
I know and my greatest adventure yet.*

I knew when I met you an adventure was going to happen.

—Winnie-the-Pooh

CONTENTS

CONTENTS

INTRODUCTION

There is a false dichotomy spread via the modern travel section of your local bookstore: you either love to travel, and therefore throw caution to the wind by divorcing a spouse or dropping out of college to go "find yourself" on sale in some foreign night market, or you're happily married with kids, which means you have zero hankering to leave the suburbs and the school pickup line. Sitting on my desk is yet another new memoir—fresh on the market and one I cannot bring myself to finish—about a vagabond's quest for the open road with the motive to escape any form of responsibility. Marriage? That's only for the conventional types who love memberships at bulk warehouse stores. Produce offspring? That's even worse—say good-bye to any semblance of independence as you know it.

This makes me sad.

I can dispel this myth. I can shout from the rooftops that you can both love to travel and be happily married with children. You don't have to delay familial commitment out of fear that a ringed finger means no more fun in European bars or on African safaris. Giving birth to new life doesn't mean the death of your passport; kids are remarkably fantastic travelers and can open more doors to cultural experiences than going solo.

Ignore the books that tell you *travel* is the antithesis of *family*. To me, those two beautiful words go hand in hand. They stand together on a crowded city bus, holding on as the tires bounce over potholes, siblings who have each others' backs.

It's not easy. You can bet the saffron in Istanbul's Grand Bazaar that it's far easier to pack when you're single, and it's decidedly much cheaper to move about the cabin. But traveling with family isn't impossible. A love for travel, to explore new places and foods and cultures, to sleep on the cheap in the world's grandest cities, doesn't mean you're not family material. It means you're one of the more honest parents in the car-pool line.

If you've picked up this book in search of another story to justify your hard-held belief that kids and travel don't mix, you might want to move on to another one. Or better yet, buy this and start reading it right now, before declining that marriage proposal out of fear you'll never again strap on a backpack. A solid marriage, well-cultured kids, and travel? Hearty ingredients for a fulfilling life.

If you're holding this book because you're weary of punching your parenting time card yet one more day, I offer you solidarity with a side of hope: I can't tell you how to travel with your kids, exactly, but I can show you what it's like for me to travel with mine. This book chronicles my experience as a happily married wife and mom in her midthirties who never outgrew her wanderlust. Those post-college backpacking years whetted my appetite for more, and once my three kids came on the scene, I couldn't believe my good luck: I now have three beautiful people to whom I can leave my love of travel and a worldview that accounts for the entire planet. Because once they've traveled, they've seen it firsthand. No going back. What a gift to bequeath them before leaving their childhood home.

Parenting and global travel—I can't think of a better mix.

This is my family's story. It's a story about how we spent a rather ordinary nine months in an extraordinary way.

PART I

Traveling makes one modest—you see what
a tiny place you occupy in the world.

—Gustave Flaubert

1

LEAVING

The prayer labyrinth is two hundred feet away and the kids are climbing rope nets on a playground next to a babbling brook. Bare feet are required on a spring day like this, textbook with chirping birds and budding leaves, as is a walk through the village park. After several hours in the car, my legs need to stretch. My husband, Kyle, returns from his loop around the walking trail, so we switch shifts, his turn on the playground bench to supervise the kids and my turn on the dirt. In the distance, the kids take turns on the slide with young locals, a revolving door of squeals and dares, the metal slide proffering a taller and steeper drop than anything found stateside, something more risky, as most good European playground equipment is.

Grass sways in tufts against the early spring zephyr, kelly green and iridescent. I walk across the gravel path and onto the grass, remove my sandals like it is holy ground. The dirt is chilly and there is still a bite in the air, not yet dissipated by the April sun; I have no idea where, specifically, we are, but I know we're in Germany. This is our farewell to the country; we'll soon reenter France a few kilometers away. I walk to the labyrinth.

It's not terribly impressive and looks like it hasn't been used for its intended purpose for maybe a decade. It's a circular concrete interruption in the swath of grass, a winding detour on the way to a makeshift neighborhood petting zoo at the park's opposite end. Cars drive past on one side, heading to the grocery store and dance class; teenagers recline on each other atop the park benches on the other side, examining each other's tonsils with their tongues, oblivious to the fact that this is some sort of sacred prayer space. Ordinary life hums around this ordinary town, and I am here, alone in front of a prayer labyrinth in the Black Forest region of Germany.

I take one quiet barefoot step into the labyrinth and turn left, starting the winding path in and out and around itself in symmetry. I begin the monastic prayer I learned six months ago at the Ignatian monastery in Chiang Mai, Thailand, where a woman named Nora taught me letting go would do me well: *Christ be with me, Christ within me, Christ behind me, Christ before me.* Rinse and repeat.

We have two weeks left of our journey around the world, and it is time to begin the nebulous process of landing the plane. Prayer in a labyrinth will help.

I pray through the circle's narrow path, stop once I reach the center, look up to the sky in gratitude, then sling my sandals in my hand and walk back to the kids. They'd enjoy this German petting zoo on the other side of the park, but I'll need to show it to them now—we will soon drive away from this village and have dinner in France.

I have lived in twenty-two homes in just under forty years; the vast majority as an adult, having spent age two to eighteen in the same house. In my university years, friends joked that if you wanted to get married, you should live with me; almost all my roommates got hitched the summer after moving into my place. It wasn't really my college goal to keep cardboard boxes at the ready in case I needed a new living situation, but this is what happened in my early foray into independence. I'd finally settle into the nooks and crannies of an apartment or rental house, only to hear the squeal of a roommate bursting through the door after an eventful date: "He asked me! And I said yes!" A few months later, I'd drag out the boxes and change my address at the post office again.

In hindsight, this was a good thing—I now know I thrive on change, and five different pads in five years of college saved my sanity and kept me going during the bookish years of study all-nighters and shifts waitressing at the local diner. In the thick of it, though, when the lights were off and I was alone in my twin bed, roommate snoring nearby, I'd wonder, *What sort of jinxed roommate potion did I drink?* It became an annual assumption that I'd need to find a new rent-sharing companion every May, a new place where I could hang my growing collection of gently worn bridesmaid dresses.

I was happy for my friends who found lifelong love so early, but I was also relieved I hadn't. I hoped the person for me was out there somewhere, but in my early twenties, I felt as young as I was. I did the math, calculated how much time I had to enjoy being called *wife* even if I waited a solid decade to marry. When it was my turn to graduate, there were blessedly no suitors on the horizon.

Instead of settling down into family life, I applied for a teaching position that required a move to Kosovo, a war-torn pocket in former Yugoslavia, a country fresh from a genocide spearheaded by the dictator Slobodan Milošević. This was my resistance against registering for tea towels and gravy boats and settling into picket-fence suburbia.

This postgraduate season of teaching English to Albanian teenagers, conserving water by taking weekly showers, and cursing a spotty, generator-powered Internet connection in a tiny Albanian village was, somehow, dreamy. I lived in a second-floor apartment on a nameless street in a village of a thousand people who seemed suspended in time. Cars had rolled in only twenty years earlier, and those same cars traveled these streets. My landlords and employers were an American family helping repair the devastated land and its inhabitants, and I took my cultural cues from them. That year I learned how to sit with my thoughts and go without English-speaking companionship in my age bracket (quite the change from university life, mere months before). I learned how to start a wood-burning stove and felt like Ma Ingalls with a navel piercing. I learned to make do without a clothes dryer, as most of the world does, and I learned to burn my trash instead of carting it to the curb on garbage day.

I also learned home mattered to me more than I thought it did. After a childhood spent under one roof, I blossomed in the hodgepodge experience of college, and was convinced that normal things—like predictable water output from the bathroom sink—weren't my highest priority. I categorized myself an Adventurer, someone who flies by the seat of her pants, who needs the next thing around the bend so long as it isn't settling down. I sought out experimental food from the local hole-in-the-wall café—fish still with its head, rabbit casserole— and shunned any resemblance of a self-initiated menu plan.

But after months of daily work in the village, riding the bus into the capital city once a month to call my parents from an international phone, and sleeping under a borrowed blanket I'd never pick for myself, there it was, an innocent little truth staring me in the face six months into my life in Kosovo: I liked the idea of home. Things like wall colors and candles mattered to me more than I had guessed, and it felt freeing to admit it. I wanted to sink into the unpredictability of a cross-cultural life, yes, but I also wanted a bona fide home. This was a season of refinement, of acknowledging there were multiple sides to me that were equally true.

I was infected with an incurable sense of wanderlust, but I was also a homebody.

I matured into adulthood when I acknowledged this truth.

———

We may not have soul mates in this life, but most of us have my-God-if-I-don't-walk-through-the-rest-of-my-life-with-that-person-I'm-an-idiot mates. Kyle was a like-minded American living a few villages over, rebuilding houses for widows who had lost everything during the horrific genocide instigated by Milošević. We hit it off instantly. There was someone else in the world willing to work a horribly paying job in order to play a small part in restoring a ravaged country to its former, if not makeshift, ancient glory. I wasn't looking for him, but when you find that special someone swimming with Albanian teenage boys in a lake potentially swirling with all strains of hepatitis and you're still attracted to him, you don't walk away.

We were fast friends, and we spent all our time together. We helped widows and the poor; we unearthed smoky, seedy jazz bars in the capital city; we took rickety buses to Thessaloniki and found cheap hostels on the beach. And when we weren't together, in the quiet of my own apartment, I wondered whether Kyle was thinking of me as much as I was of him.

We married two years later and vowed to spend our life thick in adventure. Preferably overseas.

———

God has a sense of humor.

Ten years later, I tuck my youngest son into bed and creep back downstairs to finish the dinner dishes. Kyle tosses toys back into

7

buckets, both of us grateful for this time of the day, when quieter hours bookend nighttime kisses and passing out from the day's toil. Our home is of the typical suburban variety, freshly remodeled with our own hands. When I chop carrots, I stand on trendy distressed wood slats; when I empty the dishwasher and toss the silverware into its drawer, the track silently glides shut like a modern marvel. We don't suffer from an overload of stuff by normal American standards, but I am still nagged by the notion that our closets are too full. I am happy to have these dishes to wash, because it means our family eats well, and the tucking-in ritual means the children have a comfortable place to sleep. I know from our years living abroad this is no small thing for many parents and their children.

Kyle and I—we are still the people who met in Kosovo, and we are the couple who later moved with their toddler to Turkey and lived there for three years. I am the one who gave birth to our second child in a Turkish hospital, where I barely spoke the language and almost left the building with a needle still stuck in my spine.

It's now ten years after we met in Kosovo and two years after we moved back to the States from Turkey, and something is missing. Our inner adventurers hug the walls as shadows, eclipsed by parental and culturally expected responsibility. I still think of myself as a vagabond, and yet these days I only travel for work. I am a writer and Kyle works from home for a small company, but we feel the heaviness of our ordinary life. It is a reasonable weight; we aren't overcommitted, and I am mightily grateful for the years of exploration behind us. But our existence is still heavy with midlife expectations—mortgage payments, schlepping the kids to karate and gymnastics, cleaning the gutters.

Tonight, the air is thick with the conviction that there is no reason for unhappiness. We are in our thirties, doing work we enjoy after having spent most of our twenties traveling, and we are finally settling down to become the Normal People most of our friends became ten years earlier. Over kitchen cleanup and toy redistribution, I admit what I know is true: "I miss the Adventurers. And I think it's time for them to come out again."

Kyle knows what I mean. Now is as good a time as it will ever be to move beyond dreaming and playing with the idea we've quietly cultivated for several years. The kids are all potty-trained, they're astute travelers for their age, and yet they are still young enough to be unrooted.

"Let's do it," Kyle says. I dry my hands with the kitchen towel and find the calendar.

This is our grand idea: we'll circumnavigate the earth in one direction, kids in tow, for an entire school year. We'll show them what it means to get lost in the world. It's a dream we've put on hold, one Kyle concocted a few years ago. I was nursing our youngest, and he bounded down the stairs, plopped down on the couch next to me, and said matter-of-factly, "I have an idea." It was crazy and irresponsible and no right-thinking parent would toy with such an idea. But also, it was fantastically brilliant and I said, "Thank you for bringing it up first."

Two years later, in our kitchen in the Pacific Northwest, we circle a square on the calendar. I like having plane tickets in my name on the horizon, and this is close enough: we are going to stop brainstorming the idea; we're going to do it.

We've been earmarking money for several years for our travel fund, and though we haven't yet reached our financial goal, we do the math and calculate how much we'd need to earn working from the road. It's doable. I research flight patterns and travel gear and create a burgeoning to-do list. We'll continue homeschooling our kids, but they'll carry the heft of their spelling lists in backpacks and times tables on portable tablets.

I reject any speaking opportunities for the next twelve months, jokingly adding, "Unless your event is located on an island in the Indian Ocean or on an Icelandic volcano." Kyle meets with his coworkers the next day, asks if they're on board with his working remotely for the foreseeable future. We make a checklist of things to do in central Oregon before leaving for a year.

We prepare ourselves in the ways we know how. We will never be fully ready, of course, because how do you prepare to circumnavigate the globe with three kids in tow?

Two opposing things can be equally true. Counting the days till Christmas doesn't mean we hate Halloween. I go to church on Sundays and still hold the same faith at the pub on Saturday night. I shamelessly play a steady stream of eighties pop music and likewise have an undying devotion to Chopin. And perhaps most significantly, I love to travel and I love my home.

This is my one rub with the trip idea. All these years, I'd been plagued with longing for a return to my global explorative roots, but I also want nothing more than to curl up in my armchair with a good book. I dream about places unknown, but I also buy throw pillows for the couch and mull over the just-right master bathroom paint color. I want the perfect shade of sea-glass green both in tile above my sink and in water below my boat.

Every memoir I leaf through in the travel section at the bookstore tells stories from people in search of themselves on the open road. Usually they are young and single. The occasional volume carries the story of someone older, often in search of healing after unfathomable grief. Their stories are a pre-travel life that is rough at best, soul-sucking at worst. Nobody seems to embark on a massive journey because their lives are already full of meaning.

I look out beyond the precipice into a year of global nomadism and a pang of guilt gut-punches me: I wonder if it's selfish to uproot us in the name of itchy feet.

There is, of course, the immeasurable good fortune that Kyle is also plagued with wanderlust. This is no small thing. I know lopsided couples, one dying to hop on a plane and the other wanting nothing to do with the idea. The travel itch spills into our children as well, besotted with our DNA. Finn, our preschooler, doesn't know the difference between a county and a continent and is along for whatever ride the rest of us venture. But Reed has an unrelenting interest in Turkey, his birthplace that holds little memory, and Tate misses her life as the token blonde kid in a sea of dark heads, with more stamps in her passport than counties in Oregon. Our entire little collective misses the world, and this counts for something.

This is key, I think, to my acceptance of the For Sale sign in the front yard. If we store our earthly possessions for a year in a storage unit, it will benefit all five of us.

We pencil in a hard date.

The house sells ridiculously fast.

———

Selling the house is just one piece of the puzzle; we must also decide what to keep, where to keep it, what belongings we need for the year, and what travel plans to reserve in advance. Trekking around the world will be more enjoyable, we deduce, if we don't schlep much around, and so we narrow down our list of possessions to only what will fit in packs on our backs. We also need to buy said packs, along with the smallest version of gadgets we can afford—only the ones that will make our travels better.

In all this bustle, the questions churn. Do we bring all the tooth-paste we'd need for a whole year? What about an extra power cord for my laptop, in case mine bites the dust in the middle of nowhere? Will the kids have regular chores? Will they still earn allowance? The answer to all is *wait and see.*

On the cusp of homelessness, there's no turning back.

We make several trips to the local travel gear outfitter and try on backpacks half the size of our bodies, weighing them down with beanbags to simulate a full load. Reed, age six, wavers like a drunk through the aisles, knocking down compasses and water bottles. I worry about his ability to carry all he needs for the year, with his low muscle tone and his penchant for surrendering to exhaustion when things get physically challenging. The only pack that fits our four-year-old is school-sized, with just enough room for his clothes, a toothbrush, and a notebook. Maybe a stuffed animal, if we squeeze.

All three kids are determined to bring their prized blankets, emotional lovies since their infancy, which leads to a simple lesson in economy: our bags, like life, have finite capacity. If something comes in, something else must stay behind.

Some items we insist on, several of them surprising: battery-operated electric toothbrushes, expensive quick-drying underwear, an annual VPN account that will let us watch Netflix from anywhere. The kids' clothing is fairly easy, and we stick to lightweight shorts and T-shirts, a few pairs of underwear and socks, and a thin jacket with the thought that we can buy anything we need as we go (after all, every culture has clothing). I have a hard time narrowing down what I will want to wear for the next nine months, and scour the Internet for capsule wardrobe inspiration; I don't want to be an Ugly American with ubiquitous running shoes and flip-flops. I want to blend in with my surroundings, which will be hard to do, since blending in on the Sydney beaches looks different from blending in at the *marktplatz* in Munich.

We will go to my in-laws for a week to say good-bye, then make a stop in Texas to see my parents before leaving the country. This will be our trial run, and I pack both short- and long-sleeved tees, three pants, shorts, a skirt, two cardigans, a jacket, and a fleece pullover. Everyone has two pairs of shoes except for me—I add another pair to my pack, in case I need to dress up sometime between September and June. We all have swimsuits, and the boys' double as an extra pair of shorts.

Our work is lightweight and portable, and we need little more than laptops, cameras, and a journal. I toss in a pen and wonder how long it'll be until I lose it. Kyle adds his watercolors and sketchpad. I debate bringing my yoga mat, but it's superfluous. It gets tossed into the storage unit with the lamps, bicycles, Christmas wrapping paper, the soccer ball, the winter coats. We pack three tubes of toothpaste because they're on sale.

Schoolwork is a bit trickier. Much of the kids' education will revolve around what we do and see, most of it planned on the fly, and I don't want hefty textbooks to detract from firsthand learning. The hand-hewn stones on the Great Wall of China will teach us more about the ancient dynasties than any map in a book. We decide on electronic readers for our two literate children and a simple learning-to-read workbook for the preschooler, mostly to appease him when he wants to do school like his older siblings. Everyone will have a notebook and pen to record travel thoughts, which doubles as both handwriting and grammar practice and a first-edition souvenir. We load the tablet with history audiobooks and apps for math curriculum and toss in a set of Uno cards for entertainment and for practicing number facts. One set of colored pencils, crayons, and markers for the five of us.

We head to my in-laws' house, and within a week I jettison half the stuff out of my pack.

━━━

The French writer Gustave Flaubert wrote, "Traveling makes one modest—you see what a tiny place you occupy in the world." It's easy to assume that Earth is very, very big and we are therefore very, very small, but it isn't so obvious from the vantage point of our living room as it is from teeming market stalls in Turkish suburbs or stuffed buses in India.

In fourth grade, I made a model of the solar system and noticed the size of Earth compared to the sun. I think of Australia, how its gross domestic product is smaller than New York State, yet how tiny one must surely feel in the miles of open outback.

Our individual bodies take up minute measurements of space, which is a good thing because there are more than seven billion of us. But it's easy to feel bigger than I am, important within my own thoughts and somehow significant in the grand scheme of things. My life matters, of course, and so do the lives of my other four family members. So, too, do the seven billion other lives currently inhaling oxygen and exhaling carbon dioxide twenty thousand times a day. We all matter. And yet we are so much more microscopic than our daily tasks lead us to believe. Tiny.

What a tiny place I occupy in the world.

I want to see a thousand tiny places, smell their flowers, and taste the sauces made by their people. I want to feel the difference between the textures of grit in Sri Lanka and Morocco. I want to meet the woman who bakes the best bread in the smallest town in New Zealand. I want to find the best vantage point to see Bosnia from Croatia. What do the Grand Marnier crêpes taste like in Rouen?

In Paris? There are untold numbers of tiny places and extraordinary people who occupy them. We will perhaps see a hundred of both.

We roll up our clothes in backpacks, test laundry soap embedded on dissolvable paper, get haircuts for the boys, then feel silly checking in backpacks meant for African jaunts on a plane to my parents' home in Texas. We eat barbecue and Tex-Mex, we take the Eucharist at church, we say good-bye to the kids' grandparents, and we head back to the airport.

On a steaming hot evening in early September, we board a westbound plane, where, in twenty-nine hours, we will next touch earth in China. As we rumble down the runway, as the nose angles upward, as we lift into the air, I already miss the lamplight glow next to our couch. I crave sitting there among my books.

PART II

Broad, wholesome, charitable views of men and things cannot be acquired by vegetating in one little corner of the earth all of one's lifetime.

—Mark Twain

2

CHINA

Read travel blogs and books before you head out on a major expedition, and you will find as wide a variety of advice on what to bring as there are cultures and climates in the world. One expert swears by bringing only two pairs of underwear for a year's worth of nomadic living, that the disadvantage of having to wash one daily, drying back at the guesthouse while you're out and about, is offset by the advantage of a light backpack. Another experienced traveler—one likely without small heads to count—threatens that if you choose to rent a car instead of relying solely on public transportation, you'll miss out on the real version of the place. Another tribe of travel writers promises that with enough tenacity, you, too, can make a living from anywhere and live the rest of your days location independent, so long as you live out of a backpack.

Research where to begin your round-the-world endeavor, and you'll find some sane advice: start closest to where you already are and avoid major jet lag on top of the inevitable culture shock. If you're European, take a bus across the closest border with nary a passport stamp. If you're from the United States, begin in Canada, Mexico, or Central and South America. (However, as some Canadian friends of ours realized when they started their round-the-world trek in

Argentina, eastern South America is still five hours ahead of western North American time. No matter how map savvy you are, the world continues to surprise.)

It's not standard advice for this new way of life, this living out of the pack on your back for a year with three small kids in tow, to start on the opposite side of the planet amid almost as opposite a cultural worldview. You won't find many travel experts recommend, "Ah, the heck with it—chuck logic out the window and start your kid-centric trip in a huge Communist country where you can't even read the alphabet, much less ask for an appropriate place to pee."

This is how we start anyway.

There are plenty of guidebooks about the fourth-largest county in the world, and there is more to do there than is possible in a life-time. But easy? Ease into a major shift of your family's daily routine, breakfast options, or sense of privacy? You won't find a gradual entry by starting in China. Tiptoeing down a gently sloping beach into the waters of world travel would mean starting in Canada. Cannonballing into the deep end of an ice cube–filled pool full of swimmers with no sense of democratically promised personal space—that's China.

The only real advantage we have to starting our trip in the land of a billion people is that Kyle and I have already been here. Twelve years earlier, we found ourselves newly engaged and schlepping back-packs through China with friends as part of a research project entitled *Could We Actually Live Here?* That was the question on our minds, combining the stress of choosing the right flowers for a fall wedding with deciding in which foreign culture we should raise a family in a few years' time.

We grabbed lunch in the Beijing airport on that trip, and I remember the hotel's breakfast the following morning: fish and rice, and an eggplant-colored hard-boiled egg called a century egg. Ask me what I am least in the mood to eat when I wake up in the throes of jet lag, and I will tell you fish, rice, and a discolored, fermented, weeks-old egg.

We walked up the Great Wall with our friends, dripping with sweat from the humidity, and arrived at the top at closing time, which meant we stole only a few minutes to look around, then rushed back down to our taxi. The vendors taunted us with their Great Wall–emblazoned T-shirts and paperweights, and we joked that if the original Huns somehow made it over the wall today, they'd never pass the elderly women shoving copyright-violating guidebooks in their hands.

Beyond this, I don't remember much of my first taste of Beijing. Clearer in my mind is our trek outward, into the wild west of China on the other side. There, in Ürümqi and Kashgar and the Gobi Desert, near the border of Tajikistan and Afghanistan, China's landscape becomes more like its Central Asian neighbors'. It is here that I had my first and last sip of fermented horse milk tea. This is where I witnessed the extreme geography of Asia: the tallest mountains in the world lying neighbor to one of its biggest deserts. And it is here that I first slept in a yurt.

Our friends decided it would be a cultural experience to spend the night with a traditional Kazakh family in the Tian Shan mountains of western China. We chartered a boat across the Tianchi lake, hiked several miles over moss-encrusted stones, and met our host family for the evening. She was middle-aged with teenage sons, a workhorse of a woman who silently eyed us while we partook of her culinary know-how. She slept that night with her boys in a makeshift shelter nearby while we slept in their dry yurt. The rain began at dusk and didn't relent till the middle of the night. The heavens poured out so much water that nothing left in my pack could be classically defined as dry.

The yurt was dark but comfortable, and every rug, every bit of the tapestried walls, every teacup and sack of grain was a mystery to me. It resembled a movie set starring an unshaven Brad Pitt wandering the Himalayas. The woodburning stove in the middle kept us toasty through the night, but I shivered with exhaustion as I slept.

The next morning, after tea and breakfast, Kyle strapped on his backpack and trekked up the mountain for a solo walk, searching for quiet apart from the crowd. From my vantage point, mountain goats peeked out from boulders, the green grass shimmered with dew, and below, out and beyond, lay a mirrored-gray lake tucked into the nooks and crannies of low-lying clouds. At the base of the mountain, I sat on a wet log, ignored the group chatter around me, and clicked a mental snapshot, long and slow: this world is huge; it is majestic; it is worth exploring just for the sake of knowing it. Above me, somewhere, wandered a man who felt the same way and who also thought it a good idea to marry me. As I looked up the mountain, I considered it—maybe we'd have kids, and we'd unearth the hidden paths and mysteries of this grand world together.

Robert, our first guesthouse host of the year, picks the five of us up at the airport and drives through Beijing traffic to our apartment, a concrete building planted at the end of a gray alley canopied by a thousand electric wires. This is not his real name, of course, but he gives an English name to his Western guests to make his life easier. The lobby is sparse, and the minuscule elevators lead us to the fifth floor, where ten bikes perch against the scratched, unpainted concrete walls, lined up like delivery boys waiting for their next errand. The apartment door closest to the elevator is wide open, and its innards have been turned into a call center, six dark heads bobbing above makeshift cubicles from which the clattering of keyboards can be heard. The matted office carpet down the hallway is so stained I'm not sure where to step.

Robert unlocks a door. "Here we are."

I know generally how our place will look because of the Internet listing, but it is still disorienting to see it in person. There are two double beds, a couch with an extra blanket, a bathroom, a kitchenette, a washer, and a clothes dryer all sandwiched in a room the size of my Oregon kitchen. Robert tells us he is a native of Beijing and is happy to give us ideas of what to do and see during our week there. Our only two official goals in Beijing are to show the kids the Great Wall and to begin the process of jet lag recovery, and we know the latter is best accomplished with sunshine and fresh air.

He scribbles a list of suggestions in Kyle's notebook, most of which we already know: the Temple of Heaven, Tiananmen Square, a kung fu show. On the left he writes them in English; in the middle he writes in pinyin Chinese, a bastardized Mandarin employing the Roman alphabet, which helps native English speakers pronounce the language. On the right, he writes rapid-fire in Chinese characters, which we can show taxi drivers.

"Is there a place to buy food nearby?" I ask. There is, he says, and he draws a map on another journal page that points the way to a mall with a food court and supermarket down the road. He recommends the twenty-four-hour diner on the ground floor of our apartment building, tells us to try their sesame rolls. Then the only person we know in Beijing bids us well and leaves.

For the first time since we left my parents' house in Austin two days earlier for breakfast tacos before our flight, the five of us are on our own. I feel like a squirrelly teenager away at college for the first time: apparently, I am a grown-up in charge here.

Hunger outweighs any desire to shower away the airplane funk and collapse into bed. So we leave our backpacks piled on the couch and follow Robert's map out the building, turn right, and begin our week-long investigation of our neighborhood nestled in Beijing proper. This is a business district, gray office buildings sandwiched together and studded with shops on their first floors; there is a wide concrete pavilion along the road that serves as the evening hangout spot and children's playground. A yellow-gray haze of smog rests on the tops of buildings, pauses to catch its breath or ours, thick and lifeless. Most of the small shops are now closed for the evening, but we find the mall with the food court. We choose a restaurant where the waitstaff appears friendly enough, and we order with our fingers from the menu. We slurp eye-wateringly spicy soup and bowls of perfectly round white rice scoops. The kids whisper requests for cups of water, and Kyle signals for someone from the staring throng of waitresses. "*Shui*?" he asks with a smile. The woman nods, hurries to the kitchen, then returns with a tray of piping hot water in handleless teacups. We forgot to add the *ping bing* to the shui to indicate cold and bottled. Steaming hot water—this the default, and we will forget it routinely for the next three weeks.

We are in China.

Novelist Anthony Doerr says that jet lag is "a dryness in the eyes, a loose wire in the spine." Two days ago we sat in Austin traffic on the way to the airport. Now we are navigating crowded, pallid Beijing streets, loose-wired spines, death grips on the boys' hands, and wondering aloud to no one in particular if street-stall grapes are safe to eat. I take melatonin capsules and strap on my eye mask at night, force my body to sleep after first forcing it to stay awake four hours longer than it wants. At three in the morning, I hear a sound in the corner of quiet rustling and the rapid shifting of paper scraps, like a mouse. I pull up my eye mask, and Finn is rummaging through the near-empty refrigerator, looking for an afternoon snack. I call him back to his pallet on the floor, where he prefers to sleep tonight instead of the couch. He is soon talking in his sleep: "Wait wait!"

Jet lag is punishment to a body already in culture shock, forcing you to sacrifice desire for the necessary: you may want to find solace from reading a novel in bed, but you'll regret that decision later at three in the afternoon, when your body taunts your poor choice with shaky legs and heavy eyelids while standing on a crowded metro, strangers' armpits too near your nose. The earliest European explorers endured months on a ship with seasickness and a vitamin C deficiency in order to touch Asian soil. Jet lag is our modern-day scurvy.

I question our sanity by our third day here. I'm enamored of the earth's diversity of climates and cultures, and I want a drink of all of it. But China is a struggle for me, with its Communist worldview a battering ram against my overzealous democratic autonomy. I knew this about China before we landed here, so a few weeks before we left I journaled a note to my future self, as a hammer to break the glass in case of an emergency (the emergency being, of course, questioning our sanity and considering a trip to a coffee shop to grab some Wi-Fi and book a return flight home):

> You're in China, which is hard. But you can do hard things. You
> won't be here long. This month is the foundation for the year. Lean
> in to the struggles; give thanks for the easy times. Hard doesn't
> mean wrong. You're on the right path.

I need this note. Instead of an emergency hammer, it is a life preserver. It keeps me away from the coffee shop's Wi-Fi, and tonight we find Italian food for dinner instead. The kids watch cartoons on the restaurant's television, and Kyle and I have a miniature date. I'm grateful for the wisdom of my past self.

We walk back to our apartment, bellies full, and sleeping four-year-old Finn loses a flip-flop in the Beijing night as Kyle carries him in his arms. He's down to three shoes for the year until we buy him another pair. That did not take long.

————

We will only be in the capital city for a week, only to acclimate to the time change, to adjust to this side of the planet. It feels heavier here, the majority of the world's population tilting the earth's axis to the east, and I can feel the wobble in our collective rotation.

Today, in the supermarket produce section, abundant piles of pink dragon fruit sit in baskets next to apples and red lettuce. In the afternoon, schoolchildren in blue skirts and red neckerchiefs run to the store nearest our little neighborhood and leave with cellophane-wrapped snacks and cotton candy–colored drinks. Blonde women in line at the supermarket speak Russian, as does the woman in a power suit next to me on the metro. Several miles away, officials are planning their bid for another Olympic Games.

"Mom, whenever I blow my nose, it's all black," Reed remarks.

"My eyes itch here," says Tate. We're leaving a park for the evening and heading back to the apartment, and the gray sky is only slightly yellower than the concrete skyline.

The five of us are eager to leave the city, if only for the day. We need a literal breather.

There is a large Chinese edifice—complete with an urban legend about visibility from space—so well-known that it's used as the national landmark for the entire country. Tourist trap it is, but it's a solid excuse to escape the sallow city pollution, with its dull, stinging scent of metal and exhaust, and to engage with trees. Before we left for China, we asked the kids what they most wanted to see in our first week. All three independently said the Great Wall. Midway through our week, we hire a van and driver for the day, per Robert's suggestion, and watch as the window's view morphs from high-rises and hordes of businessmen in gray suits to dirt and grass. While the driver weaves through city traffic and then suburban villages, we listen to an audiobook about the wall, about Qin Shi Huangdi, the emperor who commissioned the construction, and about Mongols and ancient dynastic leaders with god complexes and paranoia. Our driver does not speak English, and he smiles and nods at us through the rearview mirror.

The Great Wall is an intimidating barrier of stone and fortitude, a staggering example of what humankind (and a steady dose of slave labor) can accomplish without modern technology. It is our springboard into history, how ruthless dictatorship and a reasonable fear of barbaric invasion leads to an impressive architectural marvel of stone and size. We climb up and down stairs that roll with the hills; it's a stroll down a cobblestone sidewalk twenty-five feet above ground, and I hold the backs of shirts as my children lean out watch holes to check our height. We take First Day of School photos, even though it's not technically the first day of school. Our blonde children pose for other photos with Asian tourists. We then queue for a toboggan ride down the hill, the most enjoyable method of egress for children leaving the wall and returning to the parking lot. The man governing the slide warns the Westerners in line, "No *yeeeehaaaaaw*! Be quiet. No America here."

Finn sits in front of me on a plastic toboggan with wheels and a brake handle, and we glide away from the line of tourists in what could be a pleasure ride on a winding aluminum path through the forest, were it not for the timid woman on the slide in front of us, hand brake pulled and eking us down the hill at such a snail's pace that even Finn is impatient. Tate, our oldest and in the sled behind us, escalates her annoyance at me with every careening, inevitable crash into the back of ours.

The Great Wall is a masterpiece, and the kids sketch it in their drawing books as it fades in the van's rearview mirror. Our driver takes us to a farm-to-table restaurant in a nearby village. There, I sample pumpkin ice cream and the kids eat spaghetti. It's surprisingly delicious. Beijing's countryside is a welcome respite to city life, an exhale to a metropolis pace and population. I call our first field trip a success.

Jet lag is harder to shake than we anticipated. The next day I share a phone conversation with a friend in America while standing on our apartment balcony overlooking a behemoth piazza with weeds sprouting through cracks, strangers' underwear drying outside the surrounding windows. Inside, the kids build a fort out of blankets and pillows on one of the beds. We wash our first load of laundry for the year and toss in the guesthouse's two towels. Kyle stirs oatmeal on the hot plate while the kids wrestle in the fort.

Tate joins me on the balcony and says, "China isn't what I thought it'd be."

"What did you imagine?" I ask.

"I don't know," she admits. "Maybe more red and dragons."

China is one of the countries she was most excited to visit, so I wonder what's playing in her head. Does this year already smell like disappointment to her? Will there be an unavoidable sullying of childhood imagination, where dragons fly Asia's skies and lions dance with zebras instead of eat them on African savannas? I secretly love that she's disappointed, because it means our nine-year-old's childlike spirit is still intact.

We force ourselves to stay awake with an evening trip on the metro to Wangfujing snack street. The asphalt shimmers, reflections from lantern lights swinging above collecting in puddles from the spray of booth operators on either side of alleys, booth operators who pour out buckets of ice melt that keep their edible creatures fresh. These narrow alleys house family-run booths of anything imaginable on a stick: starfish, seahorses, turtles burned to a crisp, impaled scorpions still wriggling for life. These are the original food trucks. Vendors shout their wares, hoping to entice us with charred lizard and raw spiders. Reed panics, begs us not to make him try them. We buy corn on the cob.

At an alley's dead end, a woman painted with a white face, pink eyes, and black villain eyebrows trills Peking-style opera into a distorted microphone on a small stage. Her peacock-like hat sprouts blue and gold triangles; she wears a polychromatic silk robe and flutters a yellow fan besotted with red roses. It is for the tourists, and we listen briefly until we end up with headaches from her shrill voice.

The kids do not normally care for McDonald's, but they are hungry for the familiar and beg for hamburgers. We sit at our second-floor booth, nibbling fries and watching out the window as throngs of bodies inch through Wangfujing—teenagers carrying shopping bags emblazoned with European brands, tourists taking photos of St. Joseph's Church, planted by Jesuit missionaries in 1655. The McDonald's speakers play loud American pop. Reed wonders, out of curiosity, if there are any Panda Expresses nearby.

Tonight I take more melatonin and lie awake, restless on our mattress that burrows deep into my shoulder blades and hips. I pull back a sheet corner and my suspicions are confirmed: it is a slab of plywood covered in quilt batting. On the floor next to me, Finn mumbles something about hiccups, eyes twitching beneath his eyelids. I hear the showerhead drip, drip, dripping from the bathroom.

The next few days wane in the September breeze, warm gusts that blow out the last of summer humidity and foreshadow autumn. We visit the Temple of Heaven, take in a kung fu show, and find American-style pancakes at a trendy café, where the kids begin their schoolwork for the year with spiral notebooks and math problems. We take the metro to Tiananmen Square and watch children fly kites with their grandparents, then bottleneck in line with the other tourists across the street to squeeze through the entrance to the Forbidden City. Tate moans and holds her stomach, asks to leave, swears she will be sick. Concrete blares light from the sun with no shadow for respite; throngs of pushing bodies are everywhere. We swim upstream through the crowd, pass the gauntlet of locals selling folded fans and windup toys on upturned cardboard boxes outside. There is no trash can, and I have forgotten to add a plastic bag to my day pack, a travel habit I cultivated when we lived in Turkey and I was pregnant. Ten feet from us, in the dirt next to the sidewalk, a little boy defecates on a piece of cardboard held by his grandmother.

Still no shade, still people pushing forward and backward.

We hold hands, the five of us, and speed walk to the metro station. Tate keeps quiet, seals her lips shut as sweat bubbles on her forehead. We enter the train, hold on to the rails, and she vomits violently on the floor as the doors close. A sympathetic woman hands me tissues to mop up the mess, and Tate holds out her offending damp shirt from touching her skin, says cheerfully she feels better already. I apologize in English to the people around us. Our metro stop arrives, and we exit the train, wind through our neighborhood sidewalks full of men and women in power suits, then up to our apartment.

The smells of the city, the train, Tate's retching have attached to us. We run our second load of laundry.

———

Seven days in Beijing and we feel our brain fog finally lift. Our spines stiffen, and the moisture returns to our eyes. Our bodies accept that we have switched sides of the planet. I give my past self, the one that wrote me my much-needed note, a mental high five. I made it through Beijing. Onward.

It's the start of the second week of our journey, and it already feels like we've been gone for months. We fly to Xi'an, seven hundred miles southwest of Beijing, the country's ancient capital, and check in to a guesthouse near friends through Kyle's work, Americans who moved from Portland several months ago. This new apartment feels like a palace compared to our Beijing studio, with three bedrooms and a separate kitchen, and there is grass outside the building where the kids can play with other children both native and foreign. They head downstairs while Kyle and I put sheets on the mattresses; then he scrambles eggs in the kitchen, the air wafting a familiar smell of home. I smile and sigh in relief at this smattering of homeyness, then head outside to watch the kids.

The blacktop and patches of grass where the children play are surrounded by identical concrete apartment buildings, a village square in this city of five million people. I join a towheaded mother who is watching the game of tag and introduce myself. Her name is Ashley, she hails from North Carolina, she has four boys, and she reads my blog. They have lived in China for several years now, for her husband's work, and it is a thrill for them when they meet other English speakers. Her boys excitedly shout game rules in both English and Mandarin, gather our kids and their neighbors like mother hens. The children play until dinnertime; Ashley and I swap stories about expatriate parenting and homeschooling and good green bean recipes, and we could be anywhere in the world having this experience, but we are in the ancient city of Xi'an in central China.

We will take the bus in this city, mostly, and our friends explain which bus number goes which direction. On the day we visit the Muslim Quarter in the city center, we board a sweaty bus and show the driver our destination written in Mandarin script. Curious eyes bore through our bodies and faces, shamelessly scrutinize our hair, the shape of our hips, our children wearing only shirts and shorts because it is still hot even though it is technically autumn. An old woman stands next to me and yells at me in Mandarin, pointing to the kids' bare legs and shaking her head. She chastises me the entire ride downtown, pointing her finger at my face. The bus driver pulls over to a stop and tells us to get off the bus; we have arrived at our destination. We instead walk five more blocks, passing three more bus stops before entering the archaic city wall that marks the entrance to the quarter.

This is the original city center, perhaps the center of the entire world at the height of the Silk Road. It is here where the trade routes began, where merchants vagabonded westward, through Persia and Jerusalem, possibly passing a living, breathing Jesus on their way to Constantinople and Venice. Xi'an was once the most vibrant cosmopolitan city in the East, and now it is home to one of the world's oldest mosques. It is also the ideal place to buy art, which is my souvenir of choice, both for future use and because it packs easily in a tube strapped to my pack.

We walk through the covered bazaar, pass booths of wooden frogs, jade necklaces, and political posters of Mao, and stop at a table where a man is selling his oil paintings for a few dollars each. I buy three, scenes of children playing in the snow in front of village pagodas, and roll them into our plastic architect's tube. We walk by a stall where a woman is selling scrolls, tall and thin cuts of silk papered with designs of flowers and trees, and Tate asks for one for her room. For the sake of our bags and budget, we have told the kids they may have one souvenir per continent.

"Are you sure you want this to be your souvenir for Asia?" I ask her.

"Can she write my name on it in Chinese?" Tate asks.

We ask the woman in slow English, and the woman smiles and nods, asks, "What is your name?"

"Tatum," she replies.

"I am sorry . . . I do not understand," the woman says. (We have inadvertently saddled our daughter with a name that confuses more people than we suspected, something I swore I'd never do due to my own personal experience.)

"Tatum," my daughter says again, slowly. "T-A-T-U-M."

The woman pauses, repeats the letters, picks up her pencil, and scribbles on the side of her newspaper. "What do you think?" she asks. "The letters sound similar to your name. You say it *Te tai mu*."

"Does that mean anything?" I ask.

She thinks for a moment. "In a way, it means 'Caregiver of peace.'"

"I like that," Tate says.

In Old English, *Tatum* means "Cheerful bringer of joy."

The woman dips a brush in her inky black pot and paints three Chinese characters in the upper right corner of a painting of cherry blossoms. She blows it dry, rolls up the scroll, seals it in a purple square tube, and asks for a photo with the blonde-haired recipient. Tate smiles as the shutter actuates.

We walk away holding hands, me and my cheerful bringer of joy, a caregiver of peace.

That evening, we meet Ashley and her boys at a park for an afternoon playdate and let the kids run back and forth on bridges that pass over a massive pond full of koi fish. From the other side of the pond, I see locals stop to photograph our children. Sometimes they will pose next to them, as though we are family friends, and sometimes they ask first. Most of the time, they pull out their phones and steal photos paparazzi-style, cooing over hair and eyes. Our children are objects of beauty, born with blond heads for strangers to freely touch.

We have dealt with this for two weeks, and will still have one more week before we leave China, but Ashley lives here; this is her local park, nearby is her local supermarket, and these are the people among whom her family lives. I ask her, "How do you deal with this without going insane?" My mother-hen instinct is full throttle as I watch a third group of strangers pose with my kids.

"It is incredibly hard," she says, "easily the hardest thing about living in China. My kids have learned to say, 'One photo? One *quai*' in Mandarin." (Quai is the equivalent of "buck" in American English.) "At least they earn some decent money that way."

A Communist worldview means no concept of the individual, in which your rights end where my body begins. Groupthink is the modus operandi; the whole is bigger than the sum of its parts. On our flight from Xi'an to Guilin, in southeast China, Tate and I sit next to a woman whose eyes light up with eagerness as we take our seats. Over the two-hour flight, she asks us about our travel plans, what Tate is reading on her Kindle and may she read with her, too, where we are staying next, and would we like to meet for dinner at a restaurant sometime soon. I'm an introvert and have to take deep, managed breaths to make it to the flight's finale with a courtesy smile still on my face.

It is dark when we arrive in Yangshuo, a small town nestled in the peculiar karst mountains fifty miles from the Guilin airport and our final stop in the country. Our home for the week is a family room in an inn tucked into trees and the cadence of crickets. Yellow lights glow from the front door as our taxi pulls through the entrance, red lanterns sleepily twisting in the midnight breeze. The next morning, we open our curtains and are smacked with the side of a steep hill, one among hundreds and drawn by God the way a child draws mountains, an unsteady conglomeration of the letter *u* upside-down. They seem fake, a clichéd background in a motel room painting of Asia. The sky is not yellow-gray for the first time in weeks, and the pink horizon makes my eyes ache.

Unknown to us when we booked our transpacific flight, it is Golden Week in China, their national holiday that covers seven full days, during which everyone takes a week off of work to travel across the country to visit family. We take a *tuk-tuk* ride into town, where red flags with yellow stars flap in cadence on banners stretched across streets and booths sell plastic light-up trinkets and paper-thin sarongs. We pop into a market to find snacks and only recognize prepackaged chicken feet, shrink-wrapped and glazed with an orange coating. The *thump thump thump thump* of a bass drum from a troubadour pelts my ears. I push my way into a stationery store, buy postcards, borrow a pen and scribble hello to some family and friends, then hand them back to the cashier, who promises to put them in the mail. I wonder if I have just thrown away ten dollars.

Outside the store, irrepressible floods of people halt all semblance of walkability, and the five of us hold hands. My overworked senses beg for mercy.

I think of Ashley in Xi'an empowering her kids, and it frees my mothering instincts to take over in fierce protection of my kids' bodily ownership as they say no to the camera flashes. Reed forcibly poses with locals on holiday in their own family photo, but he shrugs his shoulders and says, "I guess it's okay, Mom."

In China, strangers unabashedly read over my shoulder on the bus when they see me with an English book. Twentysomethings pull my kids onto their laps on the metro. English speakers interject themselves into conversations between Kyle and me, give us their two cents about where we should go and what we should eat, ask why we are there.

We take a tuk-tuk back to the inn and stay there for our final few days in China. Kyle watercolors and I write; the kids work on their school and play foosball in the game room. They swim in the pool while I park poolside in the private backyard, and though there is a school field trip group staying here, as well as gatherings of extended family for holiday reunions, it trumps sharing my one square foot of bodily occupancy on Chinese streets.

Finn climbs trees and names one Steve, and after dinner one night, we stay in the inn's restaurant and play Uno while Kenny Rogers and Dolly Parton croon from the speakers about islands in the stream. *Sail away with me to another world; and we rely on each other, ah ha.* Kyle and I laugh, surprised at this song playing in the southeast China countryside.

Back in Beijing, an English-speaking local made chitchat with us at the diner downstairs from our apartment, where we suspect Tate got sick from the sesame rolls. Kyle asked him if he was a native of Beijing, and he replied, "No, I'm from the south. It's a tiny village of only one million people." I smiled and said, "I'm also from a village of one million people." In North America, a million feels like too many people. In Asia, it is a village of neighbors and friends.

Starting this global trek in China serves well as our starting point on the opposite side of Western civilization, one of the world's oldest cultures providing us with fresh context. When Captain Cook landed on the Australian continent, China had already existed for thirty-seven hundred years. When Gustave Eiffel erected his giant Tinkertoy in central Paris, the Chinese had already given to the rest of the world paper,[1] umbrellas,[2] earthquake detectors,[3] and rockets.[4]

As in China, famous landmarks in other parts of the world will become the bookmarks in our travel log, the check-marked paragraphs between pages and pages of walks down nameless neighborhood streets and jet-lagged descriptions of cheap local noodles for dinner, where the bulk of our days are lived. All cultures teem with creativity, on display both via inconceivable monuments and in the flawless blend of two spices. I want to see the birthplace of all of it, the homes of humble geniuses who make our lives better, more interesting. I am grateful for our time in this country and its people who have stretched me emotionally, mentally, physically.

The best souvenir China bestows on me is on our last day in the country, in the late evening in the Yangshuo inn's backyard. I am floating in the pool with six-year-old Reed during a starlit swim. Timid in the water for years and reticent to swim without a life jacket, he quietly, uneventfully lets go of the edge and swims out to the pool's center, stars shimmering and karst hills shadowing in the rippled water. This is my child, who is labeled by many as developmentally different. He is fraught with sensory issues, and a frequent question mark hovers over him as we navigate parenting waters. He has already tried mango ice cream in Beijing, and now, he is swimming.

"Hey, buddy—do you realize what you're doing?"

"Yeah," he says between exerted breaths. "Yes. I guess I can swim now." And so he can.

3

HONG KONG

As a Westerner, I tend to lump Asian ethnicities together as one mass of people. Of course, they are vastly dissimilar from one another, like peoples in all pockets of the world, and this is the great downfall of the human race: we tend to homogenize those who differ from us (I hear many Easterners think all Americans look the same). Asia is a behemoth continent, and an hour-long puddle jump of a flight within its geographic boundaries whisks us to wildly different social mores. For the first time since departing the United States, there are seat belts in the Londonesque taxi that takes us to our home for the weekend. We are on the twenty-fourth floor of a high-rise, and still more architecture towers above us. Welcome to Hong Kong, the most vertical city in the world.

We are graced with a light show from our living room windows, incandescent squares blinking and neon stripes dancing, a wall of man-made structure. There is no room for sky and stars.

I tuck the children into their new beds and Kyle ducks out into the rain and into a supermarket; he returns with jars of peanut butter and jam, a loaf of bread, some apples, a bag of oatmeal, and a small packet of brown sugar. We will only be here a few days and don't want to overload on groceries, but Hong Kong is expensive, and we cannot afford to eat out every meal. The imports in the plastic bag look foreign and global. Western.

We wake to the sound of city, of industry. Despite its proximity, our transition from Chinese village to Hong Kong—the financial leader of Asia—is jolting. Asian script on storefront signs outside looks similar, but it clashes with the praxis of buying and selling inside. I have walked on Communist sidewalks for only a month, but my capitalist tendencies are sore from lack of use. The commercialism of Hong Kong is a workout. It is a mash-up of old-world British Empire and modern Asian sensibility, and it is one more city to add to the list of cities where I am three years behind sartorially.

We stroll through Admiralty and SoHo and Mong Kok districts, and I am consistently seconds late with my camera as I am witness to a coruscating kaleidoscope of color and fabric combinations. I momentarily abandon my family to chase after an Adonis of a man; I want to document his royal blue Italian suit. Like many cosmopolitan men, he is most likely popping by the bank before his dentist appointment and simply tossed something on before leaving his flat this morning. He sports an oxford shirt and tie, pants cut three inches from the top of his ankles, and leather shoes without socks. In the American suburbs he would look entirely out of place. Here, on the cobbled streets of Hong Kong, he looks just right, quintessentially debonair. From these mean Hong Kong streets I also learn that a man can pull off a button-down gingham shirt, salmon-colored bow tie, mid-thigh-cut khaki shorts, and flip-flops.

Hong Kong is completely cool, straddling the Western world and its preeminence as the wealthiest spot in Asia. She fully embraces who she is. She is the older cousin in town for holidays, whom you awkwardly admire from across the family table. She is quirky; she is fun; she is serious; she is not to be taken lightly. She is into art.

We are here during a large-scale protest against its Chinese-run government, and this makes international news; but the mobs are calm and confident. We walk through protesting crowds, and locals smile, play cards on the curbside, chat in assorted languages with beer and coffee in hand. Several young people knit. It is the hippest protest I've witnessed. Tate asks me if people are waiting for a parade to start. The protests give me brief maternal pause, but the friendly nature of the situation soon evaporates any concern. Our kids barely notice the crowds with a political bone to pick after a month in congested China.

The biggest mistake we make in Hong Kong is not staying long enough, but this is the consequence of planning our trip's first leg in advance, before leaving home. Some travel decisions must be made in faith with the hope that wisdom we collect in Asian street markets will help us make right our early wrongs. This is mishap number one. If in doubt, always spend more time in Hong Kong.

We eat peanut butter sandwiches and cheap noodles for lunch, oatmeal for breakfast, and apples from our packs when we are peckish. We ride a roller coaster on the edge of a cliff that graces us with a two-second view of the ocean, and we watch a panda named Ying Ying munch on bamboo and scratch her back on a tree. We window-shop; we replace the reeking watch Tate vomited on in Beijing. I stop trying to take photos of the fashion-forward scenery and instead I simply enjoy the view: cotton-candy hair, iridescent pants, men in granny sweaters, power suits with short-shorts. We are overwhelmed at all we do not see, cannot do. Then we return to the airport and board another two-hour flight. Onward to Southeast Asia.

4

THAILAND

Your first impression of Thailand depends upon whom you ask. There are beaches; there are brothels; there are noodles; there are durian, a round, spiky fruit that smells like a noxious gym sock. There are rain forests full of banana trees and elephants. Bald monks hug smartphones and Starbucks cups, varying shades of orange fabric draped over their skinny bodies. An aging American man who stayed after the Vietnam War runs a bar with billiard tables for the tourists; he holds fast to his tight-skinned wife, a woman years his junior. A family of six rides a motorcycle; five smoosh together, back to chest, and the youngest rides in a plastic bucket, his mother holding the bucket to the side of the motorcycle by the handle. There are dentists and doctors with degrees from Europe and North America who choose to practice their vocation here. There are almost one hundred English-speaking private schools in the country for expatriate children.

And this temporary home comes with some familiarity.

In 2007 we stayed in the northern city of Chiang Mai for two months. We lived in Turkey at the time, and after I was diagnosed with severe depression, it was suggested that we visit this medium-sized city tucked into the mountains and misty forests of Southeast Asia as therapy. The perplexingly sizable expat population includes therapists and psychiatrists who speak English and can prescribe low-cost antidepressants with aplomb. It is cheaper to fly across five time zones and rent a house for two months than to travel back to the States and deal with health insurance, wait times, and medical red tape.

In those days, our oldest was two years old and I was in the second trimester with our second. We rented a house in the suburbs, a psychiatrist prescribed me medication, and I met with a therapist three times a week. We ate food not found in Turkey, we fed cucumbers to elephants, and we browsed English bookstores meant for expatriate student backpackers. I bought fabric from the night market to bring back to our apartment on the Aegean Sea and sew into curtains and pillows. We took advantage of cheap prenatal care and discovered that Reed was a boy. He was twenty-four weeks into gestation when we returned to Turkey; there I survived on antidepressants, memories of Chiang Mai, and occasional Thai-based therapy visits via Skype for the next three years.

In Oregon, I had subscribed to a private e-mail list for expats in Chiang Mai in search of temporary housing for the Thailand leg of our trip. Perhaps we'd find an expat family's home to house-sit while they visited their home country. We could find a guesthouse if nothing else was available, but there was something endearing about the idea of watching over someone else's bookshelves, frying pans, and soap dispensers. I placed an ad in the e-mail group.

A woman named Muriel needed what we offered; she was returning to the States for medical reasons and needed a house sitter. She lived in the same quiet suburbs where we had lived seven years earlier. It was ideal, except that she was in her seventies and her house didn't have toys. I waited for another offer, but when none came, we replied to Muriel and agreed to stay.

Muriel's house—this will be our home in northern Thailand.

The plane lands in the early afternoon, and we grossly overpay a taxi driver to take us to the house, a savvy entrepreneur who knows the cash value of white-faced travelers fresh off the plane. (*"Where you from?"* Oregon and Texas. *"Okay, I take you because Dallas Cowboys."*) En route, I daydream about dumping the contents of our backpacks into a washing machine. I am eager for coffeemakers and unpacking our toiletries onto a bathroom shelf after our month of nomadically stirring instant coffee into lukewarm water. I want the kids to make progress on their grammar, their math. I want to cook.

Muriel's Thai friend unlocks the front door, shows us the house, hands us keys, and warns us that her car needs servicing and to use it with caution. Tall ceramic vases ensconce top-heavy silk flowers; a knee-high bejeweled elephant sits next to a lightweight rattan couch; breakable empty tchotchke bowls rest on the fragile glass coffee table. Glass shelves encased with doors hold hefty volumes of Amish fiction, figurines of plump peasant children, and collector's plates signifying anniversaries of varying importance (the marriage of Prince William and Kate Middleton; Christmas at Disneyland, 1981). Muriel's final e-mail to me asked us to please make ourselves at home, but to take note that the dinner dishes are a complete set, and if one should break, we are responsible for replacing the entire imported set.

Everything is also pink. Pink dishes, pink vases, pink silk flowers, pink elephant, pink floor tile, pink bathroom walls, pink bathroom sinks, pink marbled kitchen counters. Everything is some shade of pink.

Thai it isn't. But it is cheap. Kyle parks the breakables above the kitchen cabinets and refrigerator, and we take Muriel's car to a nearby big-box store because, oddly enough, the house has no sheets or pillows. Also, we are out of soap. I wander the store that reminds me of a Kmart from my childhood, and I cry because I am so tired and because I cannot find soap I like. Tate begs for expensive turquoise sheets, and we find plastic bowls, plates, and cups to replace Muriel's dinner dishes we would inevitably break. We gawk at duck beak and pig uterus shrink-wrapped in the meat department, snap photos with our phones, and text them to family back home. The store smells like salty ocean and cheap plastic. For dinner, we eat greasy fried chicken in the dining area.

We drive home, stretch our new sheets across the master bedroom mattress, and crawl onto the plastic, rococoesque bed straight out of a gawdy Caesars Palace bedroom. I glance at my nightstand on the left, jump out of bed, and remove the little porcelain girl staring at me with psychotic eyes. I hide her in the plastic rococo wardrobe across the room.

The next morning, while braiding Tate's hair on our bed, the slats underneath the mattress suddenly snap and drop us to the floor, into the center of the monstrous yellowed plastic bed frame. Kyle and I drag the mattress to the other side of the bedroom floor, where we will now sleep until we leave this house.

The crimson-colored velour bedspread pills miniscule balls of fuzz in the nooks and crannies of our clothes (which I will still pull from my pajama pants four months later in Morocco). Geckos scamper across the floors, walls, and ceilings—this is the only thing remotely Thai about our bedroom. I can hear their little feet at night, inches from my body where I sleep.

————

Chiang Mai is the second-largest city in Thailand, the original seat of the Lan Na Kingdom, which reigned in 1296 and for five hundred more years. It's known for its three hundred Buddhist temples, their roofs like pointed pushpins embedded across the city's landscape, nestled between trees and cafés, neighborhoods and back alleys. There is an ancient moat enclosing the city center, drawing a seven-hundred-year-old fence around travel agency storefronts, burger chains, massage parlors, Mexican restaurants, dentist offices, women selling smoothies from blenders on wheeled carts, expensive French restaurants, and coffee shops with free Wi-Fi. Motorcycles are ubiquitous, the chosen cheap travel method of the masses. Second in popularity are *songthaews*, red pickup trucks with benches along the length of their beds and enclosed with tall roofs, the shared taxi system used by both tourists and locals. These, plus tuk-tuks, the three-wheeled motorbike taxis, all vie for space on Chiang Mai roads, their drivers using horns merely to let others know of their presence, not to tell them to move. It's a jarring practice to a Western driver new to these streets.

Chiang Mai is ancient; Chiang Mai is modern. It is Buddhist monks and smoothies from electric blenders. There are five Starbucks coffee shops in the city of fewer than four hundred thousand people, an impressive concentration outside the United States. The city is a popular respite for vagabonds in need of cheap accommodations and Western creature comforts.

It's also home to the second-largest concentration of Buddhists in the world, and its streets are filled with pilgrims during the Songkran and Loy Krathong festivals. At night, the old city center beams a fluorescent glow from carts selling mango sticky rice, coconut soup, knockoff Birkenstock sandals, and flowing sarong-style pants bought only by tourists. From makeshift outdoor corner studios, artists sketch portraits of children in photos to be sent home as souvenirs for grandparents. T-shirts are silk-screened with beer logos, Che Guevara, and the phrase "Same same but different," vernacular used by vendors as an answer to a potential buyer's question about the validity of the brand-name item for sale. A loose translation is: *It is, and also, it is not*. This phrase summarizes Chiang Mai in a nutshell. It smells of familiarity, but it also really, truly doesn't. It feels like home, and yet it always surprises.

———

I wish I were a more adventurous eater. I will eat spices and peppers with poised composure, but I hesitate at unidentifiable meats even when I'm famished. My plate will pile with vegetables and meats and sauces so long as none of it smiles at me. Edible creatures must also be solidly dead, the overriding reason why I avoided scorpions on a stick on Wangfujing Street in Beijing, still fighting for life and blindly swatting their pincers in the air. *Never put things down your gullet that could slash it in final vengeance on the way down*—this is my gastronomic philosophy.

Tonight, I am hungry. A novice traveler could write an entire book solely devoted to the foreign cuisine offerings of northern Thailand, beginning in its French cafés and pâtisseries—scents of caramelized sugar and baked croissants wafting out their open doors reminding you of a Parisian boulevard—and ending with its offering of fish and chips served on the back porch of a neoclassical Georgian plantation home, crickets singing in the night air like a southern summer. A traveler can dine on pineapple pancakes under banana trees for breakfast, green chiles rellenos and margaritas for lunch, and rib-eye steaks with mashed potatoes and pints of German lager for dinner. Our wallets would be empty if we feasted only on foreign food, which is why it is best in Chiang Mai, as it generally is everywhere, to stick to local fare.

Thai food tastes like ocean and timeworn tradition, fields of basil and groves of mango. Streetwise cooks in aprons and flip-flops stir salty tamarind through rice noodles and hand patrons limes to squeeze over their bowls. Paired with glugs of Singha bubbling water, and it is the best three-dollar investment of your life.

There are passion fruit smoothies from street vendors and strawberry ice cream churned along late-night touristy streets; there is the *gaeng khae* soup with chiles and miso from the cheap diner in our quiet suburb, so spicy it makes me cry. My eyes water as it's placed on the table, even after my request for no spice. This is Thai food.

Tonight, we find a hovel of a shop with the plain name of Cooking Love, tucked deep into the side streets in the old city center. Guidebooks and travel writers rave over this mom-and-pop eatery, and here on our first visit, the owner brings our children over to watch the kitchen chaos. The three of them tiptoe on chairs and peer over the Plexiglas shell.

"Hey! A ten-minute date," Kyle jokes. Children are welcome to be children here in Thailand. Their curiosity is well received, and it proffers us a few minutes of adult conversation.

"Don't you wonder about places like this?" Kyle says. "What's this family's backstory? How long have they been running this place? What was the tipping point that made it so popular?"

I watch the mom and son work in tandem in the kitchen, flash-frying vegetables in a wok and stirring milky-green curry in a stockpot. The teenage daughter takes an order from a table of European twenty-somethings. An old wrinkled man with a toothless grin, presumably the owner's father, welcomes patrons at the entrance, takes their shoes, and meticulously places them on shelves.

"I wonder if that guy was the one who started this place," I say, pointing to the elderly man. I picture him young and spritely, scooping bowls of rice and welcoming curious new guests. He smiles and nods at me. I nod back.

"I wonder if the whole family lives here too," Kyle says, just as I was speculating the same thing. I glance at the back of the restaurant, where a curtain hides a mysterious back half, and I imagine a living room and residential kitchen.

Photos of previous customers wallpaper the walls, Polaroids signed, dated, and faded. The four-top next to us speaks Russian, and on the other side are Australians. The cook brings us our orders, and I dip my spoon into the green curry, glide it out between my lips, and close my eyes. The kids eagerly spoon their plates of chicken fried rice, and Kyle buries his chopsticks into noodles. Steam rises from our plates. Our table overflows with bowls and there are leftovers, and our total bill is ten dollars.

I could not lead anyone there, but thanks to Kyle's innate sense of direction, we dine there ten times over the next month, following the scent of its *tom kha gai* like hypnotized cartoon characters. The grandfather eagerly takes our shoes every time, welcomes us to his family establishment as though we are old friends. On our fifth visit, Kyle says, "I'm already sorry for my future self who no longer has this food."

The family that runs this establishment has a special seat in heaven at the right hand of God. I'm sure of it. They welcome us into their home, the most sacred of places, with the taking of shoes and the scooping of rice.

I am overdue for a dip back into the waters of cheap counseling and decide to treat myself to a checkup. The therapist with whom I met for two months during our original visit to Thailand has retired to his home in Michigan, but the center where he worked is still here in Chiang Mai. I've never met with a spiritual director before, but a writer friend of mine back in the States swears by regular meetings with hers, and there are a few available at this center as a service.

This afternoon, I sit in the office of a silver-haired, quiet-spoken woman named Nora. Her office is a simple converted bedroom in the corner of a house-turned-well-being-center. A couch and armchairs are centered around a coffee table, icons and paintings of St. Francis on the walls, and art supplies on shelves. From my chair, I watch her walk silently around the office, gathering a legal pad, pens, sheets of drawing paper. She sits down, smiles at me, and doesn't move. I feel like a teenager on her first job interview, not sure if I am supposed to talk first. Should I have come equipped with a laundry list of concerns? Would she begin by asking about my childhood? This is not counseling, and I have no idea what to expect from an hour with a spiritual director. Do I make the first move? I sit there, smile back, look around the room.

After an eternity of silence, Nora says quietly, "I'm ready when you are." I shift my eyes back to her, and she hasn't moved. She is still smiling at me.

I decide that candor is probably best, that I will never see this woman again after this month. "I'm honestly not sure why I'm here, other than I feel like I could use some spiritual direction in my life." This is the truth.

"Why do you feel that way?" Nora asks.

I sit for a few seconds, because this is a good question. I'm not terribly sure, other than my soul is weary, my usual recipe of prayer and reflecting on passages from the Bible isn't inspiring me, and I sense a gaping, run-ragged hole in my soul where mature wisdom should be. Also, I don't know where my home is, where I might really belong.

Years have passed since I last felt poured-into, I tell her, and I have not bothered to seek it out. I have embarked on this year of travel, at age thirty-seven, feeling less confident than I did a decade ago about what I believe to be true, and how that truth intersects with who I am. I am weary from game playing and formulaic answers, and the evangelical-Christian hat that I have worn daily with every outfit since I was fourteen feels too small, headache inducing. I fidget daily in its discomfort, but I don't know how to exchange it, how it should be resized. Perhaps I can stitch a new hat from scraps I find scattered around the globe, I suggest. Perhaps she could be my milliner, maybe help me find the first scrap, floating somewhere along the sidewalks of old Chiang Mai.

I tell her this, and she only smiles.

Also, I started this year of globe trekking confident that traveling was the right thing to do, but somehow, that confidence hadn't come with me in my pack. I feel fidgety and lost.

She only smiles.

"I need spiritual direction because I feel like I can't find my compass, the thing that points me home. Also, the hat I've worn for over twenty years doesn't fit anymore, and I want to find a new one," I repeat.

Nora nods this time. "You think I can help you find a compass and a hat?"

"I'm not sure. But I'm willing to pay you twenty bucks a chat to see if you can help," I reply.

"I think it's good you're here," she says. "Because we all lose our way every now and then. Sometimes it helps to ask a fellow sojourner if she can see through the fog in front of you."

I consider the fog in front of me, how I love writing but itch to break out of my genre into something new. I love the freedom of nomadic living, too, but yearn for the simplicity of home. I grow restless with the humdrum of small, ordinary life, but know it's in those hours of sorting socks and vacuuming the car where most of life is meant to be lived. I don't think I am made to do daily extraordinary things, to constantly unearth new sights. The loveliness of wandering, of travel, dangles like a carrot on a stick, but it's coupled with the heartache of wanderlust, of knowing that there will always be one more thing to see. Chasing the globe's rotation for more than a few months will do me in. I will come undone. It is not how I am meant to live; I know it.

"You already have the answers you need within you from God," Nora explains. "I am simply here to walk with you and help you unearth them. I can do that."

She lights a candle on the table in front of us and bows her head. I follow suit and close my eyes.

Because we'll be in Thailand for a solid two months, I can meet with Nora at least six times. There are other things to do in Chiang Mai—night markets to shop for cheap art and phone cases, hikes through the hills to the highest point in the country, elephant sanctuaries to visit. But after my first session, I sense an unveiling—these spiritual direction sessions are a primary reason we've been drawn here.

In our third meeting, Nora ends our time together, as customary, with silence, her reading a psalm. To signify our time is over, she snuffs out the candle. The hour is spent as it was the previous two meetings: silence and candle lighting to start, Nora asking me what God is speaking to me today, more silence from me, then an unexpected outburst of tears as I share what comes to mind, usually some sort of frustration with my work as a writer. I pour out details of specific burdens and cultural movements that tie me in knots. Nora is a safe person with thousands of miles between our daily worlds. She will park when there is inward movement, help lift a stone when she senses treasure underneath.

At the end of our third meeting, snuffed candle smoke still rising in the air, Nora says, "Before you leave Chiang Mai, I have a prescription for you. I want you to visit a monastery in town for a day of silence."

She hands me a brochure with a picture of a labyrinth on the front. I open it and find a smiling priest welcoming me to come for the day, the night, or for a week, to hear from God and get away from the city noise. There is no talking permitted on the grounds.

"You live in a world of noise," Nora says. "Your work is noisy. Your home life with three kids is noisy. God speaks to us best in silence, in nooks and crannies when we're willing to ignore the cacophony."

I take the brochure with me, walk out of the living-room-cum-lobby with a tired grin on my face, get in the passenger side of the car where Kyle and the kids wait for me, and thrust the paper in front of him. "Look what I get to do," I say. I wipe the tear smudges from my face and he backs out of the gravel driveway.

———

Kyle meets weekly with a counselor at the same center, so seven years removed from our Turkey respite, this place becomes, again, a home away from home, a resting place. *Selah.* I work with the kids on their schooling at a nearby café during his appointment, reading aloud and correcting handwriting and playing math card games while we sip pineapple juice and watch birds in the garden. Then Kyle and I tag each other, relay-style, and I meet with Nora while Kyle teaches fractions and tectonic plates and how to sketch birds.

Our routine in Chiang Mai becomes a pleasant revolving cycle of parenting, working, teaching, and spiritual direction appointments. We predict proceeding months will once more resemble the chaos of backpacking through China, a nomadic liturgy of packing, unpacking, and checking school notebooks on airplane tray tables, so this otherwise humdrum routine is welcome. The kids enjoy this slower pace of life, and they feel more like temporary residents than nomads.

This morning, I arrive at the monastery armed with supplies for a day of silence—water bottle, snacks, pencil, journal. There will be meals offered in the dining hall at set times, silent, so I need little else.

I check in at the front desk and they nod me through the open-air entrance hall and out into the gardens. Paths twist this way and that, through bamboo enclaves, interspersed by an occasional bench or tree stump for sitting. In the center are six gazebos, each with a simple wood-hewn table and bench. Dormitories outline the monastery. In the far distance lies the labyrinth.

It is astonishingly hard to sit in silence right now. Bamboo creaks; wind rushes through banana leaves; car horns honk on the highway beyond the garden. I wander the grounds, claim a gazebo, and arrange my provisions in organized piles around the table. For an hour, I stare at them. I have thoughts, but none worthy of journaling.

I wonder what my brother is doing at work in Austin today.
These pants need washing.
We need to make travel plans for France.
I could use a latte.

I sit. I listen to traffic in the distance, nod at the other spiritual pilgrims meandering by on the paths, and fidget on the hard bench. The apple on the table, instead of leading me to prolific contemplation, stays an apple, stares back at me. I start to formulate a thought about the morning breeze and its symbolism, wonder if there is a poem there, but then an airplane thrusts overhead and, like a toddler, I shift my attention to the shiny object in the sky. The first hour ekes by.

I go on another walk around the path, return to my base camp, open my journal, and turn to the next blank page. Nora has given me homework—write a lamentation during my monastic day, a poem of mourning in order to fully flesh out a grieving process that needs skin and bones. So far, though, my thoughts are little more than a swirling mental distraction of annoyances and a vague inkling that something muddy wants out.

I know this: I am weary of playing games, of the games I am asked to play in order to succeed as a writer. These travels for a year are admittedly part escapism, a desperate plea for a sabbatical from expectations, pressure, noise. I want to get lost in myself, I want to stop thinking so much of myself, and I want to see in the flesh how many people there are in the world and how many don't know me or, really, care about me. I want to remember my smallness. I want to be a prophet in the wilderness, shouting from jungles and deserts and foreign cities that we are all small, and to remember what a tiny place we each take up in the world. Small might be insignificant, but it does not mean unimportant.

In Chiang Mai, I have already passed by millions of street vendors—all of whom I will never know—and I think of how many more there are in the world. Their daily lives matter, but how am I any different, any more important, than an old woman selling key rings and water bottles at the kung fu show? I long for God to show me where I belong, where my home is in the world, and my smallness in it.

Before I write my lamentation, I read this from pastor and writer Eugene Peterson: "We are caught off-guard when divine revelation arrives in such ordinary garb and mistakenly think it's our job to dress it up in the latest Paris silk gown of theology, or to outfit it in a sturdy three-piece suit of ethics before we can deal with it."[1]

A quiet awareness surfaces, and I sense that it is ordinary. It's for me. I do not need to make it big, or dress it up by sharing it on social media, or deconstruct it with a three-part explanation. I need to capture it, tackle it to the ground as it flies in the wind through the banana trees. My pen grows pregnant with words. The lamentation flows.

The first draft pulses with a respectable anger, and I set the pen down. I can barely decipher my own scribbles. But this feels good, freeing, a bit rebellious. Frustration quivers out my fingers and my body begins to strengthen as a poison leaves. Being on the other side of the world is becoming a bloodletting. I am fraught with self-imposed expectations about motherhood and writing that need to be released, and the crowded buses, the holding of my children's hands through makeshift markets, the sunsets over suburban Thai rooftops are my medicinal leeches.

I walk to the labyrinth, step into the entrance, and start to methodically pray. Turn right, one step in front of the other; then the narrow path snakes and leads back out, then back in closer to its center. There is a plan, a prescribed path to the middle, but how slowly or quickly I arrive is up to me. I can stop midstep if I want, and pause, admire, adjust. These steps, one in front of another, are an expedition of its own. They mimic this year. First, leave your home, your familiarity. Then board your transport. Traverse through China. Step into Hong Kong. Into Thailand, and next, onward to Singapore, Australia, New Zealand.

When I arrive in the center at last, I tear out the lamentation in my notebook, crumple it into a ball, and set it on the waist-high rock serving as the labyrinth's centerpost. I unearth a smaller rock on the ground and paperweight it on top of my offering to keep it from blowing into the banana trees. This rock is an Ebenezer of remembrance. I am free to scream to God my grievances—at least on paper—but when I am done, I must leave them and remember that my Maker knows me, will watch over my offering, and will return with me. I wind back out the labyrinth, faster this time.

Several weeks after my day of solitude, a few days before we leave Chiang Mai and head to southern Thailand, we go out for pizza at a bricked, side-alley café downtown. It swarms with tourists and the air smells of dough, salty sweat, fire-hot wood. We place our order, and from a distance music begins while we wait for our food. It's quieter at first, echoing off the brick walls and neighboring shops, but soon the volume increases until its distorted combination of modern pop rhythm with Eastern heterophonic melody throbs in the asphalt beneath us.

We join the café's other patrons who have left their seats to witness the commotion, and I hold Finn's hand and squeeze our way through the crowd. A parade has begun, floats with sequined elephants and belly dancers and papier-mâché water lilies ensconced around thrones of young women dolled up like princesses. They wave at eager little girls on the street. Buddhist monks, in their fluorescent orange and burnt sienna robes, follow with flowers and candles to release onto the river at the turn of the parade's bend.

Loy Krathong is Thailand's annual holiday of gratitude; it is their version of Thanksgiving. We eat our pizza quickly; then the five of us soldier through teeming crowds to find a spot where we can release a paper lantern into the black sky. Tonight, thousands of candlelit lanterns will be offered into the air, humanity's effort to add flickering pinholes up in the universe. These lanterns eventually run out of wick and wax, and every year the local municipality spends weeks cleaning up the aftermath, but for one evening, thousands of people gather in one tiny place on the planet to release a token of gratitude. It is a sight to behold.

We find a young monk-in-training, no older than sixteen, offering a flicker of fire for the paper lanterns. Our family's lantern, bought a few feet away at a temporary stand, is large enough for all three kids to hold and release together, and so the young monk brings his lighter to our candle in the center, positions the kids' hands around the lantern's bottom edge, and when the candle starts to flicker, he lets go. The lantern is made of cheap, white tissue paper, and it holds my gratitude for this year of exploration, along with a prayer for clarity, for release. There is nothing to alter its course once it is liberated, but it will be beautiful as it flies into the night sky. Our offering is one of thousands, tiny like all the others, collectively a flickering symphony against a black backdrop.

The kids release the lantern and we watch until it disappears from view, intertwining with a thousand minuscule dancing lights.

"Can we get ice cream?" Finn asks. The pizza feels like hours ago, another world away.

⸻

We fly to southern Thailand for our own American Thanksgiving, to the island of Phuket. One of our travel strategies involves creating, as best we can, an endless summer—or at least, enough warm weather so that we can get by with one thin jacket. We will buy sweaters if needed, but we'd like to try to go without. On our country's day for giving thanks in late November, it is 90°F, a warm, windy breeze rustling through the palm trees. We are on the southern coast of Thailand, on an island mere miles from Malaysia.

We have never been to Phuket and have little more than an Internet's inkling of what to expect. The plane lands, and we hail a taxi driver.

She pulls into traffic and asks in English, "Which hotel?"

I show her the map on my phone that pinpoints the whereabouts of our guesthouse, but she pushes it away with a "Pfft!" Impossible, because this is a real neighborhood and not a tourist conglomeration of hotels. She does not grasp the concept, understandably enough, of a real home turned into a bona fide guesthouse.

"Which hotel?" she repeats, louder this time.

"Not a hotel! House!" Kyle calls out from the backseat, where he is crammed with the three kids. He sounds angry, but he's not. He's employing this trick to bridge the dialect disconnect: speak louder; surely they'll understand.

The driver finds us incredulous. "Which! Hotel!" she yells.

We do this for an hour, as she drives through island streets, heading to the destination on the map while shaking her head. I am hot and sticky, and I am not in the mood to negotiate the cross-cultural language barrier.

Our destination isn't a guesthouse, which no doubt adds to the cabbie's confusion. Our instructions are, in complete seriousness, to take a taxi to a local art gallery, walk to the front desk, and ask for soup. We aren't sure what this means beyond its literal interpretation. Is *soup* code for guesthouse keys? Will an art curator at the front desk nod knowingly, slide us a new map as though we're in a spy movie? Will a bowl of soup unlock the code through its ingredients, or perhaps via a bar code on the bottom of the container? It feels very James Bond.

We are taken down a nameless dirt road and finally, we stop in front of little more than a covered booth, something you might see at an American farmers' market. Two women are painting on canvas. Kyle walks up and asks for soup as the kids and I watch from the car. One of the women nods and makes a phone call while I sit on the edge of my seat, feeling the plot thicken. A few minutes later, Kyle emerges with a fellow in his twenties, motorcycle helmet tucked underneath his arm. The local straddles the red motorcycle parked out front and heads into traffic, Kyle motioning our driver to follow him.

"That guy's name is Soup," Kyle says as he gets back in the taxi. "He'll lead us to our guesthouse."

Thanksgiving Day, we walk the sleepy streets of our beach village, again in search of good food. We have only a few days left in Thailand, which means our season of delectable cheap food is drawing to a close. We are also homesick, so it feels especially important that we feast like kings, to cobble together a Thanksgiving dinner from local cuisine while our extended family gathers together twelve thousand miles away. Soon we will enter Singapore, where nothing is cheap, and then Australia, where even less is cheap. We spend the afternoon on the beach, sun-kissed and sand-caked like it's the Fourth of July, and now we are on the prowl for a turkey-and-stuffing equivalent out of yearning for the most quintessential of American holidays.

It begins to rain and the sun has set, so we need to settle on a spot. We duck into the closest establishment with its lights on, a beacon in the dark pumping John Cougar Mellencamp from the house speakers.

Kyle asks the owner if we can sit outside on the empty patio, at a table tucked underneath an umbrella big enough for the five of us to escape the rain. She nods and ushers us outside, lights a candle at our table. We take menus and cross our fingers, hoping for a decent-enough Thanksgiving banquet. Instead of more noodles and curry, we read the selections: steak, ribs, mashed potatoes, glazed carrots, and rolls. Chocolate cake. Creme brûlée. The kids squeal with glee.

We chase meat with mojitos, which tastes nothing like home, but it doesn't taste quite like Thailand, either. It is an ad hoc meal, food with no particular home, a conglomeration of Western barbecue and Eastern spices, seared and charred. It works well enough. It echoes how I feel right now, one foot in Asia and one out the door. We eat in the dark, in the rain, in flip-flops. Our waitress brings us cake with lit sparklers and sings to us in broken English "Happy Birthday" to pay homage to our national holiday. Tonight, we are satisfied to be together in the world, as a family, on a dot of an island in the Indian Ocean in Southeast Asia.

"I wonder what our next house will be like?" Tate questions, sighing with a full stomach.

"I get the top bunk if there's a bunk bed!" shouts Reed.

Back at the guesthouse, toothbrushes are packed in our bags, shirts are rolled up next to socks, and we are ready to move on. Thailand has brought me some peace.

5

SINGAPORE

Asia wanes. We have been here three months and the air is constant: hot, sticky, garlicky. I rummage through my pack again and again for my tank tops and shorts, wonder why I've bothered packing jeans and a pullover. On our last day in Chiang Mai, we visit a local clinic for yellow fever shots so we can enter Africa in six weeks. I am ready for new sounds, new smells, but Thailand gives way to Singapore, a few more days in Asia.

It is 90°F in Singapore, year-round. There are two seasons: dry and rainy.

Part of Singapore's lure is its airport. Changi Airport is regularly voted the best airport in the world by travelers, a destination on its own. There are free movie theaters, swimming pools, art stations, video game portals, nature paths in outdoor gardens, world-class playgrounds, a butterfly sanctuary, and sleeping rooms. A staff of thirteen gardeners tends to the five hundred species of plants, including seven hundred rare orchids. The airport's website lists the best places to take a selfie during your layover. Because of the airport—and this is no overstatement—I want to go to Singapore.

Truth be told, though, I am admittedly weary of Asia's cacophony, of the crowds and lights clamoring for attention. There are a few blessed pockets of quiet I've found throughout the continent, but they're hard to find, and they're outnumbered by the resonant masses of people and cities. I miss the monastery.

The five of us play in the airport for a few hours after we land. The kids zip down slides and Kyle and I sip coffee, share our eagerness with each other—in three days, we will set foot on a new continent.

Asia lays the groundwork for our year of travel, and it has not been easy. We are Westerners, and certain social mores feel familiar to us: queuing in line, assuming the store hours are the same as those printed on the door's sign, leaving strangers alone in their parenting choices. It has been good for our sea legs to swim in these waters, but we are ready to float for a little while. I want to catch my breath. I want to be in the West.

We leave the airport for our weekend home—a hostel—and catch another taxi. I haven't stayed in a hostel in over a decade, the last of which I slept in a large group bedroom in Dublin, Ireland, where I was witness to unsavory acts best left unsaid. It would have never occurred to me to bring children to a hostel until a friend suggested I try one out if I couldn't find a guesthouse. We would barely be in Singapore, and it felt lavish to spend money on an entire house when we were about to head to the most expensive country of our trip. There are family-friendly hostels, my friend said.

Our bare-bones room is listed as "family-style," which means there are enough beds for six people, most of whom would be strangers if we were traveling solo or as a couple. As a family of five, odds are slim one extra traveler would knock on our door, and we are willing to pay for the extra bed if that were to happen. We rent our blankets and pillows from the front desk, along with towels for our clan, grabbing only three because they're five dollars apiece per night, and we take the elevator to our floor. Even the hostels are skinny high-rises in Asia.

Kyle unlocks the door. The room is a brilliant white with naked concrete walls. Air ducts cut through the ceiling, but it is otherwise a cube of minimalism—white beds to match our white linens, white desk and chair, white window frame. There are two sets of bunk beds with curtains around each bed to create individual minirooms. One set is twin and the other is queen, leaving almost no walking space between our sleeping quarters and private bathroom. The room feels more like one giant bed with occasional juts of concrete sliced through to divide sleeping arrangements. The air duct sighs, then exhales cold air with a loud hum that morphs into a noise that matches the white walls. I can no longer hear Asia outside. I look out our window and see the throng of traffic below. These are the most comfortable beds we have had thus far, and I sleep hard and dreamless.

In the morning, we play bus roulette, see where the wind takes us. Our phone apps tell us where to go, and we hop on a city bus and get off at Fort Canning Park. The highest elevation in central Singapore, it rises not quite two hundred feet above sea level. It is a green respite in a neat and tidy concrete city full of old trees and nineteenth-century cannons, fortified walls, and Gothic gates, a reminder that Singapore was once a European occupation. Though we've already walked miles and miles throughout Asia, we spend the morning walking even more, pretending this park is a forest. The kids play games through the sally ports, hidden doors in the forts that once allowed spies to come and go undetected. We watch older couples speed walk down the paths in matching jogging suits.

For lunch, we find a nearby café called Eat Play Love, where families dine on Western food and then afterward, children make crafts at the community art table while parents sip cocktails and coffee. Our kids glue cardboard, use scissors, and wind yarn around their fingers for the first time in three months.

Lunch takes hours, and afterward, I sense the need for a serious break. I'm trembling, weak, overstimulated. We take a bus and head back to our hostel for mandatory quiet time, where everyone in the family is required to stay on their beds with curtains drawn and do whatever they want so long as they don't talk. It's mildly successful. At the end of the hour, my head still spins, my muscles ache, and the kids are all talking at the same time in an echoey concrete room with no rugs or art to cut the reverberation. I feel my insides spiraling downward, wonder if my outsides will soon follow suit. I am swimming in cacophony.

Kyle is cut from different fabric than I. For twelve years, we've traveled together, worked side by side on business projects, and run a household together. But we are very different people. I like to think of myself as flexible, that I'm good at going where the wind blows, but when I need to adapt to unsavory conditions that test my senses, my body and brain overload.

Kyle, however, is the epitome of adaptability. He makes small talk with taxi drivers as they take convoluted routes and tell about their family exploits. He lets people wrangle for priority in front of him as he queues in line, because why fight it—this is simply how it is done in their culture. He deals with a sensory overload of flashing sights, pungent smells, and dissonant sounds because, well, it's Asia. That's what one does when traveling in Asia. Kyle is the masterful cross-cultural explorer. He also knows me better than anyone, and knows when I am about to shatter.

"Kids, let's go out. Tsh, you stay here," Kyle says. Right now, there aren't eight more beautiful words in the English language.

Kyle is the parent who pushes our kids to try hard, new, risky things. He's confident in his conviction that the heavy backpack is good for our six-year-old son's muscle tone, no matter how much Reed flails in theatrical fatigue every time we walk through an airport. He doesn't flinch from the symphony of childish whining during hours of wandering foreign metro systems. Kyle is the parent to meander through Singapore sans agenda with the three kids.

I insert earbuds, start my sleep playlist, turn down the lights, and read a book. Twenty minutes later, I strap on my eye mask and take a long nap, hugging the white linens and spreading out starfish-style on the queen-size mattress.

Several hours later, Kyle returns with coffee. It's instant, and it's from the hostel's break room, but it is caffeinated, and that's what matters right now. He is the yang to my yin. He anticipates my needs, my moods. I thank God that we met on a dirt road in a Kosovar village fifteen years ago.

Outside, the sun sets, and we pack our bags for the ninth time in three months. Finn asks if we can keep his construction paper and cardboard creations from lunch yesterday. They're cumbersome and oversized, too big for any of our packs. I hesitate.

"Yes, we can keep them," Kyle says.

The next day, we board a plane to Australia. We shoulder our packs, each carrying our weight. Kyle carries an extra paper bag, one containing masterpieces of crayon and cotton ball.

A Market Street in Asia

Lambent lights peddle in lines and squares
Hawking janky batteries and meat-on-sticks,
Some still writhing in final gulps of life.
I tread in a sea of dark-headed waves
With noodle dough jump rope swung between men,
Thwapping in cadence to calls and crows.
Playthings rat-a-tat on wilted boxes, mine for eight quai.
The melon, the meat, the additive music
Pulses me onward, sagacity my sails.
As for me, coruscate shops and sales pale
To earthy mettle, sullied soles, and raw, sticky-still bark.
Light wanes behind me.
Onward.

PART III

The greatest reward and luxury of travel is to be able
to experience everyday things as if for the first time.

—Bill Bryson

6

AUSTRALIA

It's a strange phenomenon, listening to Bing Crosby croon about a white Christmas while driving in the summer on Highway 1 along the Queensland coastline. It's Christmastime, but it's not winter, and it's anything but white. You're stopping for ice cream on the way to the pool, or you're letting your shorts dry on the clothesline while your kids jump on the backyard trampoline. But there's also a Christmas tree inside, Santa-shaped cookies are baking in the oven, and Bing's there, singing about his white Christmas.

We arrive in Australia from Singapore in early December on a cheap, region-specific airline with stellar ticket prices because they don't serve water on the flight. Or rather, they do—for five dollars per bottle. Had I known we'd be unable to slake our thirst for an eight-hour flight, I would have snuck contraband water in our backpacks. Thankfully, this is an overnight trek, so the kids mostly sleep while I try to ignore my thirst. Five hours in, I cave and crack open a bottle of water.

Our first layover is Sydney, then Gold Coast (with the delightful airport name Coolangatta, named after a schooner that wrecked there in 1846); then we catch a northbound train to Brisbane, where we spend the night in a dingy, fluorescent-lit motel near the airport so we can catch an early-morning flight north to Cairns. This means that we fly almost four thousand miles south, then hop a train, and another plane, and trudge another fifteen hundred miles back north. It is the equivalent of flying from Los Angeles to New York in order to get to Dallas. Convoluted itineraries often save enough money to make voyages possible.

It is a jolt, landing in Cairns. The previous twenty-nine hours were spent moving our bodies through airport terminals and train stations, restlessly sleeping and refueling with foreign fast food with jet lag as a familiar friend. We traveled at night, so when we walk up to the car rental desk in Cairns on a bright Friday morning, the woman behind the desk is an alarm clock of cheer. I need coffee.

"Good morning! May I have your confirmation number?" she asks with a smile. Kyle reads her the combination of numbers and letters.

"Ooh, I see that you're American. Whereabouts you coming from?"

"Well, we're from Oregon, but we've been in Asia for several months now," Kyle answers.

"You don't say!" she says as her fingernails clack the keyboard. "I spent some time in Portland a few years back. Beautiful part of the world, that is."

My ears perk, both at the name of a familiar place and at the opportunity for a breezy conversation in my native tongue. "What were you doing in Oregon?" I ask.

"Oh, some family lives there. Let's see . . . We went to the big science museum, and drove to the coast and then the mountains. My goodness, was it spectacular." She prints papers, shows us where to sign, hands us keys.

"Where are you staying in Cairns?" she asks. We tell her the name of our place, and she draws our route on a map. A yellow highlighter squeaks our itinerary to the other side of town. "All right, mates, seems you have all you need, but give me a ring if you need anything. Have a fab time in Queensland!"

The five of us walk through the parking lot to our sedan, arms heavy with backpacks dragging behind us like stubborn dogs, eyelids heavy from the glare of a happy sun. We buckle up in a black sedan, inhale the smell of new car, and fidget with the console buttons to connect the Bluetooth signal to my phone. Familiar bands start playing—Portugal. The Man and Lord Huron. Kyle and I look at each other, wide-eyed.

After three months in Asia, all this feels strangely close to home. Kyle pulls out of the parking lot and heads down the left side of the road, a habit already cultivated from Thailand.

For the first time in our lives, we will celebrate Advent, St. Nicholas Day, and Christmas at summer's apex. It's the heat of the yuletide, and we're sweating to the carols. When we planned this portion of our trip in Oregon, we looked at the map and calculated our general whereabouts for December, realizing we'd be near a culture that recognized the Christian holiday. We have spent a fair number of Christmases in Muslim-majority cultures, and while it's nice to escape the Western commercialism that's taken over the season, it's hard on the kids and conjures aching nostalgia in me. During those holidays abroad I missed "Jingle Bells" and "Hark! The Herald Angels Sing" piping through the grocery store speakers and wishing a merry Christmas to the cashiers.

This is not essential, and grateful for the chance to travel, we were more than willing to forgo a familiar culture during Christmas. But when we first announced to the kids we really, truly would be traveling for a year, the idea was made more palatable to them knowing we could celebrate Christmas in a culture that felt like home, even if it was midsummer.

There's something about this holiday that evokes a longing for home and belonging more than any other time of year. I am curious, however, if it's our long-held familial traditions that make us wax nostalgic, or if it's our customary calendar rhythms. Do we tend to ache for customs of hot cocoa by the fireplace because we've gone through the swelter of summer and the decline of fall? Or does Christmas itself imbue us with sentimentality? We will better understand our human longing to be home for the holidays in six weeks' time, when we leave Down Under and trek back up the latitudinal ladder. Africa is looming.

Of course, a summertime Christmas is only strange to us because we hail from the Northern Hemisphere. In the past, Aussie friends have asked me if singing carols through the snow and curling up by the fireplace to watch Jimmy Stewart is a commercialized cliché, or if it's a literal thing Americans do. In reply, I asked them why Australians don't use local palm trees instead of fake evergreens for their holiday tree, or why they haven't written summertime carols. Their answer: There are, indeed, Australian carols, and a few people do decorate alternative Christmas trees, but for the majority, Christmas is more about the magic, the dreaming, the pretending of a faraway winter wonderland. Santa's from the cold, after all.

This is Christmas four days after a summer solstice: it's home with cognitive dissonance. We wear swimsuits on St. Nicholas Day.

I had been to the northeastern state of Queensland, Australia, before, both times on work assignments. I knew the first time I stepped into Oz that my clan would soak up the flora and fauna; the Australians' love of water; their casual, sunglasses approach to life. From their beer (lager) to their dress (casual), to how they embrace a laissez-faire take on time, most Queenslanders I had met before seemed—well, an awful lot like my people.

They prefer the great outdoors and wearing flip-flops (which here are called *thongs*), they're proud of their beer and ice cream, and they employ an inordinately sizable amount of local vernacular in their verbal cadence. My swimsuit is a *cozzie*, a *bather*, or *togs*. Kyle wouldn't be caught dead in a *budgie smuggler*, but I'm still not sure if he wears *boardies*. It takes me several weeks here to learn that my backpack wardrobe also contains a *singlet, strides*, a *cardie*, a *flannie*, a *wind-cheater, sunnies, grunders*, a *frock, sandshoes*, and of course, *thongs* for wearing in the *arvo*. A *dag* I wasn't, nor was I a *bogan*.

Reed says a few days after our arrival here: "I like Australians. They almost speak English."

We're here for six weeks, and it's Christmas, so we're giving ourselves carte blanche to enjoy good things. Good things sometimes show up in life cloaked as guilty pleasures—dark chocolate, well-crafted mattresses, a forgotten show now on Netflix—and like this entire trip, being in Australia feels like luxury. Luxuries, even relished frugally, feel like an homage to an overabundant lifestyle after my decade-long inclination toward thrift.

Ten years after our start of global, nonprofit employment doing important work in hard places, we struggled with letting ourselves enjoy things. Several years ago, when we lived in Turkey, we spent one Thanksgiving in Paris because it was the cheapest international flight out of Izmir. We spent weeks agonizing before buying the tickets. *What will people think? Should we overcompensate for going to a fancy place by staying in the sketchy part of town? Perhaps eat Thanksgiving dinner at a cheap café as penance?* (Spoiler: there are no cheap cafés in Paris.)

This is still my default way of thinking about luxuries. After earmarking travel money for years, we no longer feel guilty about this round-the-world trip as a whole, but it is still mostly an exercise in frugality. And here we are now, in Australia, right after affordable Southeast Asia. It's one of the world's most expensive countries.

Part of our ability to enjoy Queensland our first week here is through a work assignment. I'll be writing several pieces for the North American division of Queensland's tourism board, which means our job as a family is to learn how to frugally enjoy northeast Oz, home to some of earth's most stunning land and seascapes. We will experience some touristy sights and excursions, so guilt-free and in the name of work, we dive in.

⸻

Australia is home to Uluru, the world's largest monolith and named by white settlers as Ayers Rock, planted squarely in the continent's center, where 35 percent of all the land is effectively desert. Alice Springs, the closest town, is almost three hundred miles away and a five-hour drive through the Outback, where the second most common fatality to drivers, after heat exhaustion, is a collision with a kangaroo or a camel. The continent-cum-country is largely sparse and uninhabited by people, but is home to 5,700 different animal species, 80 percent found nowhere else in the world. Scientists aren't sure whether there are 100,000 different insect species, or twice that number, but odds are good that many are fatal, because Australia has more things that will kill you than anywhere else on the planet. Ten of the world's deadliest snakes live here, and five of the most lethal creatures in the world—the inland taipan (the most venomous land snake on the planet), the Belcher's sea snake (one hundred times more toxic than the taipan), the cone snail, the box jellyfish, and the blue-ringed octopus—reside in the northeast state of Queensland, where we begin our visit.

There are two significant natural wonders to see in this corner of Australia, and a man named John will show us one of them this morning. He is a local Aboriginal guide in the Daintree Rainforest, the world's oldest at some 135 million years.

"My childhood home is just down the street here," he says after we walk through the entrance to the national park. "I went to school a few kilometers away with all my cousins and siblings, and my grandparents' grandparents lived in the same village where I still live."

John is about fifty years old, stocky, with thick hair; he is wearing khaki shorts, a polo shirt, and hiking boots. I'm mildly disappointed he's wearing Western clothes instead of native Aboriginal attire, then kick myself for even having that thought.

Our kids are entranced by him and his cheerful disposition. "Kids, kids, come over here, and we'll first walk around the campfire three times before entering the forest. This place is sacred territory to my people." He is as excited as a giddy child on Christmas to introduce us to his homeland. We walk in a bungling line around the smoky fire; I cough and feel an extra trickle of sweat trace down my back. The smoke smells sweet, like earthy tea, and wafts into the trees, disappears.

John asks the kids to choose walking sticks from a nearby cluster of trees; then we gather around him for a short homily to the woods. "As we enter the forest, stay silent and listen to the trees. They have stories. They knew the dinosaurs now buried in the dirt by name." I look to my children, and Reed, the literal one, raises a perplexed eyebrow.

"That means these trees are really old," I whisper in his ear.

"The Daintree tells us the story of the world," John continues. "Well, the part of the story that doesn't involve us humans. Nowhere else in the world can you see still-living examples of all eight major stages in evolutionary history, all right next to each other. This forest, my friends, is the ultimate natural history textbook." He closes his eyes and we watch as his antennae perk, listening to his native soil. The kids are quiet and find John mysterious, like an eccentric uncle. I bow my head, offer a quick prayer of thanks to be here.

Later, I read UNESCO's description of the crowning of the Daintree as a World Heritage Site, verifying John's assertion. Indeed, the age of the pteridophytes, the age of the conifers and cycads, the age of the angiosperms, the conclusion of Gondwana (the ancient super-continent before it split into today's continents), the origin of songbirds, the mixing of continental biota between Australian and Asian plates, the extreme effects of the Pleistocene glacial periods on tropical rain forest vegetation, and the most important living record of the history of marsupials and terrestrial vegetation—all are on display here, inhaling and exhaling together, its scent of sweet decay wafting in the air.

The land is special here; a dance of God's divinity with dirt. We are here to witness it.

As we start our walk with John, I recognize the good fortune that I'm a lax, germs-won't-kill-you sort of parent. Even with this child-rearing tenet, it takes all my strength here in the Daintree to resist strapping a child or two to my body with duct tape. We're a family of hikers, of natural-water swimmers, a tribe that romps in the dirt—a walk in the woods should be innocuous enough. But this is the Daintree. It is boundless and wild.

We bend around a curve of a well-trodden path, and John points to an innocent-looking fern and says with cheer, "See that? Don't touch it—it'll paralyze you from the neck down."

There are prehistoric leaves that mimic paper accordion fans; idiot fruit, the seeds of which produce a poison similar to strychnine; and six types of wild ginger, some of which provide water for desperate vagabonds while the rest contain poison. There is an innocent-looking willowy shoot waving through the breeze, about four feet out of the ground, with transparent cilia along its body.

"When I was about—oh, this guy's age," John said, pointing to Reed, then back to the plant, "I touched this. Nightmares and shakes every night for years. Strange ones too. To this day, about once or twice a year, that part-a my body'll go numb for no apparent reason. Or it'll tingle this way and that. And then that night, sure enough—psychotic dreams. Yeah. So kids—don't go touching it."

I glance at my six-year-old, who wouldn't have been tempted to touch the plant ten seconds ago. John says, "Onward—this next tree's a doozy that'll put hair on yer back."

I pull the three kids to me. "You guys, do not go ten feet near that plant, do you hear me? Or you will not go to college because of the inevitable medical bills and psychiatric care for which you will be forever indebted to your father and me." This is the whispered voice I reserve for waiting in unpredictable passport control lines or visiting their great-grandma's house-of-breakable-tchotchkes.

"But Mom," Tate says, "the path is only a foot wide. Kinda impossible."

"You'll figure out a way," I reply.

John points to plants and trees used as combat weapons during World War II and in ancient Aboriginal homeopathic remedies and beverages. More than twelve thousand species of insects dwell among this dirt and trees, symbiotic with the white-lipped tree frog, colossal blue Ulysses butterfly, and cassowary. There are stories about every single tree we pass, myths about trees inhabited by ancestral spirits or childhood tales passed down from John's great-grandfather.

As our hike ends, he gathers the five of us around a cluster of rocks. Here, he explains, are the mothers of the artistic tools used in indigenous artwork; paints concocted through years of sediment infused with iron oxide; clay and ochres in shades of brown, red, yellow, white. John's ancestors have dabbled in this medium for thirty thousand years. He taps the rocks on a flat boulder, crushes bits into rock powder, dips his fingers in a nearby stream, mixes the powder and water with his fingers into varicolored paste, and swathes our arms with dots of burnt sienna and white.

"It's a blessing and honor that the rain forest welcomes us here," John says reverently, holding his palms upward. "Let us remember to tread lightly on her and all her family, and to go forth in peace."

He is a friar in hiking boots, a deacon of the forest.

We come to a picnic table under a thatched-roof awning, where a friend of John's is percolating traditional bush tea over a campfire.

"Come, sit down for a bit of tea and damper!" his friend says.

"What's a damper?" Tate asks.

John and his friend look at each other. "Well . . . it's a damper. You know, like a biscuit."

The kids look at me.

"Cookie," I say.

Their eyes brighten and they run to the table, then stop at the rounded mounds of baked flour. Tate picks one up, takes a timid bite, gives a polite smile and nod.

"Well," says John's friend, "it's more like bread."

"I'm okay for now," Reed says, not touching his damper. Finn devours his and eats Reed's. I take a few dutiful sips of tea and swallow the taste of steeped twigs and leaves, breathe in its smoky aroma. Kyle chugs his tea and takes seconds.

I have just taken my children on a walk in the forest, an outing we partake in weekly in the Pacific Northwest. There, we brush past ponderosa pines. Here, we plod through prehistoric plants. The Oregon soil we cross is ripe with our familial ancestry, yet here the rain forest dirt percolates with our cradle, our origin. These roots spread wide and deep. I watch as the leaves swirl humbly in my cup.

We say thanks and good-bye to John, then head back to the park entrance and hop on a bus for a five-minute ride to a more modern path through the rain forest: a suspension bridge through trees to a swimming hole called Mossman Gorge. We dip our bodies and float in bone-chilling freshwater, buried in the veins of the world's oldest patch of creation. Underwater stones scrape John's painted dots off our arms, flecks of rock powder dissolving into the gentle waves that make room for us this afternoon.

I glide on the water's surface and watch goose bumps rise on my legs, then submerge my ears and hear the gurgling life underneath. I listen to my kids squeal at the thrill of the gentle current pulling them where it wants. I gaze at the sheer splendor of the leaves above me, leaves seen nowhere else on this planet.

Sometimes, even when I'm standing on a remarkable slice of terra firma, I'm besotted with wanderlust, my heart thumping for the next unknown place and my mind wondering what's next. But right now, in this rain forest, floating in crystal waters after a walk on ancient, sacred soil with my flesh and blood, I want to be nowhere else. Nowhere. This, right now, is home. I can hear God through the rustling of the prehistoric fan-shaped leaves, the scurry of alien insects on the bark, the familiar laughter of my children slipping on stones in the water. Everything here is unfamiliar, but it's familiar. We are transient, vagabonds, and yet we're tethered.

About Australia, travel writer Bill Bryson says, "This is a country that is at once staggeringly empty and yet packed with stuff. Interesting stuff, ancient stuff, stuff not readily explained." The Daintree Rainforest has one more unique quality: it's the only natural UNESCO Heritage Site that bleeds seamlessly right into another one next door. Packed with stuff, indeed.

Today, we will snorkel in the Great Barrier Reef next door. The kids have been eagerly waiting for this day since before we left for China, and while they're passable swimmers, they've never snorkeled. I'm confident they'll love the boat ride out to the reef, but I'm curious how they'll fare with the wet suits, unwieldy fins, suffocating masks, and tiresome snorkels.

A wet suit is the most unattractive, unflattering garb ever invented, which I'm reminded of because the kids roll with laughter at Kyle and me when we hand them their assigned suits. A few minutes ago we arrived at a platform out in Agincourt Reef, one of the 2,900 complex systems that make up the entire 1,400-mile reef. As soon as the boat parked, there was a mad rush to get in line for wet suits, so Kyle and I ran to the line while the kids waited at a picnic table on the platform.

We demonstrate the process of squeezing our adult bodies into still-damp wet suits, and I feel like I'm stuffing a watermelon into a pair of girl's panty hose. The kids find this uproarious.

"We look like spies!" Finn says when we're all dressed.

"Yeah! Let's go look for a hidden jewel and plan a heist!" Tate replies.

Kyle takes a photo of them with devilish spy glares, finger guns poised. They continue their imagined life as spies while I gather our handful of masks and fins and look out into the rippling aquamarine waves. The sky and water are monochromatic. It is a canvas of blue, textured by shadowy-small waves.

An expert snorkeler I am not, but I know enough to show the kids how to spit in their masks to keep them from fogging, to violently puff when water splashes into their snorkels, and to walk backward in the water so as not to trip on their fins. I check that their life vests are tightly secured, and that the younger two have pool noodles to keep them floating on the surface. Our platform has a floating fence around the permissible snorkeling area, and there are lifeguards at every corner. Still, it feels daunting to release my four- and six-year-olds out into the Great Barrier Reef. This is the constant parental challenge, to push our fledglings out the tree, into the liminal void, a maturing exercise that's exacerbated during travel, when everything is new and nothing is predictable.

I ease into the water with Tate, while Kyle swims in with Reed and Finn. It amazes me that no matter how exotic the location, how one-of-a-kind the experience, the act of swimming always remains the same. During my childhood summers, I woke at the crack of dawn and met my friend who lived on my block for a sunrise bike ride to the neighborhood pool; that early-morning dip involved the same stroke, stroke, stroke as it does now, on the largest reef on the planet. The percussive pulse from submerging my ears into water echoes back the same muffled sounds as my childhood trips to lakes and rivers in Texas. The earth's surface is over 70 percent covered in water, and sometimes I wonder about a drop of water resting on my shoulder, whether it's been to Antarctica or the South China Sea, or perhaps, miraculously, even out my childhood kitchen sink.

This water is cold and clear as glass, and the current allows for simple breaststrokes as I dip my head into another planet. Above the water's surface, it is sun's reflection and waves. Two inches underneath, and I am floating above a kingdom of coral, some four hundred different types in shades of orange, yellow, green, purple. There are staghorn coral, resembling a deer's antlers, clustered in bouquets and offering protection from prey to the smaller fishes. Brain coral, with its folded ridges and grooves. Thousands of minuscule fish swim in a thousand different directions, an aquatic rush hour of scurried dancing. An eggplant-purple giant clam, four feet in diameter, has taken his place on the shallow sea floor, resting vertically, his upward-facing mouth opening and closing with the current. He is the old man of this particular reef, sitting in his favorite recliner, retelling a slow story. I find Nemo scampering through sea lettuce algae.

I resurface every couple of minutes, a mother hen counting her chicks. Tate sometimes comes up to clean out her mask at the same time, grin wide and eyes gaping. She looks at me knowingly, as if we share the secret to the unseen world below us.

"Mom, did you see Nemo? I saw Dory too," she says.

"Did you see the brain coral?" I ask.

"Yeah, that was weird. It looks like a dozen brains were emptied out here from a science lab."

The five of us reconvene for lunch on the platform, plastic plates piled high with shrimp and fish. We are exhausted and exhilarated, cheeks pink and hair matted to our foreheads.

"Mom, did you see the purple and blue and yellow fish?" Finn asks in his high-pitched preschool voice.

"Yes! What did you think?"

Finn shrugs. "Cool."

"This is the best day ever!" Reed says.

"Oh yeah? Why is that?" Kyle asks.

"Because I've never, never, never seen this before. Well, except on TV," he answers.

I think of my childhood: hardly leaving central Texas, content to swim in my neighborhood pool and cruise suburban lanes on my bike. I'm grateful and in awe my children have now seen the Great Barrier Reef. I whisper a prayer that they will still be gleeful over Slip'N Slides and sno-cones.

Hours later, on the boat ride back to land, Finn sleeps on the seat next to me, wiped out from happy exertion. Reed scrolls through the day's photos on Kyle's phone, and Tate reads on her Kindle. I stare out the window. This water holds magic, gives birth to creation where most days nary a human eye is witness. Water is familiar; it is front-yard sprinklers and nearby creeks. And it is exotic, unknown, bearing secrets to worlds beneath worlds.

Our remaining days in Queensland are this: we board a plodding train from World War II upward to an arts village, high in the ancient rain forest; we watch locals hang out laundry and take children to school under the Daintree fan-palm leaves; we examine tiny, chalky Anglican churches nestled in a canopy of rain forest vines next to ice cream stands.

We camp in the countryside near the small town of Port Douglas and swim under stars in a rock-encrusted pool. We hold koalas, pet kangaroos, touch dingoes through fences, ogle wombats, cassowaries, crocodiles. We cross a street, and the tree in the crosswalk's center screeches with rainbow lorikeets, and we watch them darken the sky as they leave in a synchronized dance, a flurry of green, blue, and red feathers. They are Australia's pigeon, and they are breathtaking.

We drive for hours along the Queensland coastline, and the kids call out their holiday wish lists from the back seat. Bing Crosby joins us through speakers. We pull over to a roadside stand for mangoes and a picnic at a beachside rest stop, and Kyle and the kids scurry on boulders along the rocky beach, mindful of the deadly box jellyfish. Tate chats with a young girl about the pet rainbow lorikeet on her shoulder, a nonchalant redhead who might as well have been walking a mutt on a leash. We float on a military-issue duck boat through crocodile-ridden swamps.

Quite surprisingly, we find a Target, and buy new flip-flops for the boys, a new swimsuit for Tate, a few chocolates for St. Nicholas Day. I spot artwork from an Oregon friend splayed on a book's cover in a bookshop in the middle of nowhere. We eat more ice cream and sip flat whites, Australia's contribution to coffee. On the evening before St. Nicholas Day, we toss Kinder Eggs into the kids' sweaty flip-flops at our rustic campsite.

One final afternoon, I unfold a cheap plastic chair under the awning of the campsite's general store, tap into their spotty Wi-Fi, and cross my fingers that a Skype call to our American travel agent won't disconnect halfway through a major credit card transaction. A chorus of kookaburras laugh in the nearby trees, serenading as my hold music. I book our second chunk of flights, to Casablanca, Nairobi, Nice. I recall those vaguely familiar place-names, but they feel a lifetime away.

As I power down my laptop, Kyle pulls up with the rental car, kids in the back seat. "Are you done? We want to drive into town and walk around."

7

NEW ZEALAND

After Queensland, we knew we wanted to visit friends in Melbourne and Sydney, and also make a little jaunt to New Zealand—but the holidays mean outrageous holiday airfare. When frugality is one of your chief traveling considerations, you sometimes have to leave the country, then come back again.

From Cairns, we fly seventeen hundred miles south to Melbourne for a long weekend with friends. This is the first time on our travels that we connect with people we already know, and it is a melding of two worlds—our previous, "normal" life with our current itinerant one. We know Darren and Vanessa because we share fields of work; in fact, Darren is the one who brought me out to Australia on my previous work trips. They are native Melburnians, and their city is so much like our Portland—moody weather but brilliant when it's behaving, indie coffee shops on every corner, bearded hipsters everywhere—that it feels like home. I adore it. We are here only for a weekend, but in every hour I inhale familiarity.

Our friends take us to their kids' favorite playgrounds and to their favorite winery, we crack open a bottle in their backyard while the six children jump on a trampoline, and we join their company holiday party at a city park, where we meet their employees and share a potluck lunch. It would be the equivalent of the Fourth of July in America were it not for the impromptu pickup game of cricket, the Christmas music on the speakers, and the pavlova served on the picnic table (a fruit and meringue-based dessert controversial in these parts, based on the argument concerning whether it hails from Oz or the nearby Kiwis).

We are with people we already know, and right now I'm unaware that we are reaping the benefit from the simple act of befriending people regardless of where they live. Continual good-byes have been a staple in our family. Kyle and I met in Kosovo, and we are used to the risk of hurt. The curse from this is a growing hole in our hearts because friends are always continents away, no matter our geography. The blessing is, well, friends. Wherever we are.

We watch our children play at the park, and Vanessa asks, "So you love being around your kids all the time, then?"

I laugh. "Good gosh, no. Why? Does it seem like it?"

"Well, I would assume you'd have to, to take on a trip like this. Plus, you homeschool. I could never do either of those things."

"This is the hardest part of the trip so far, honest to God," I admit. "I love my kids. But I have been around them for three months solid with no break. I've even been around Kyle that whole time."

Vanessa laughs. "That's veritable sainthood right there."

We fly to New Zealand.

It is nearly midnight when we land, and for the first time on the trip, I pull out my socks. It is biting cold compared to the tropics, where we've mostly been thus far. This is the first time on our trip that the temperature has dipped below eighty degrees, and it's the first time in our lives we dip below the 45th parallel south, halfway between the equator and the South Pole. This week will be the southernmost point on our journey.

We walk out of the airport, and the wind and drizzling rain shock the breath out of me. My teeth chatter. The driver tosses our backpacks into the shuttle van, looks at our paper-thin windbreakers and says, "I hope you've got more than that in your backpacks, mates! We're expecting a cold front this week."

Tonight, we wash our socks and underwear, then dry them overnight in the heat billowing from our guesthouse radiators. It is one week until the summer solstice.

Our plan is to drive southward from Christchurch, the south island's capital, and meander down to Queenstown. We will avoid highways at all costs, and we will stop for wildflowers, well-painted street signs, and hobbit sightings. The drive is three hundred miles, which means we calculate about five hours till our arrival at the next guesthouse. The south island's population is only one million people, yet it's roughly the size of Illinois, which has a population of thirteen million. Surely the traffic here is nil.

This is what's important about New Zealand: its residents, known as Kiwis, are friendly to strangers, the cost of living is startlingly expensive, and the country selfishly holds captive the most staggering creation God has yet brainstormed. We drive away from Christchurch, and everything outside quiets. There is a chill in the air, but I crack down my window to hear the birds. The late morning sun rises above thigh-high golden grass, and our two-lane highway slices through the field. We follow its dotted lines, watch them chase each other beneath our car. They meander to the right and so do we, tucking into a valley and fields of purple lupine.

"Oh my God," I utter. I am not swearing.

Kyle lifts the pressure off the gas pedal and we stare at alien pastures of chiaroscuro shadows, light-carved hills on a flat plain. Clouds dawdle above, their silhouettes below dancing with wildflowers. The scene before us ranks with Tuscany and the Pacific Northwest. I respond the only way I know how—I laugh helplessly.

Kyle whispers, "What in the world?"

The kids exclaim, "Whoa!" and return to their books.

We pull over for roadside lupine again and again, the sun crawling across the sky morphing their colors hourly from iris, lavender, amethyst, lilac, violet, sangria, wine. Cerulean streams and clusters of agapanthus stow away in leggy grass. It smells like sweet spring, tender and hopeful. I take an hour to photograph a stone chapel overlooking the milky green Tekapo Lake, angling to avoid the throngs of Japanese tourists shooting peace signs in the background. The kids impatiently wait in the car. As the sun fades, I force Kyle to pull over so I can capture a local post office's red clock swinging above its front door.

We arrive on our next front porch ten hours after leaving Christchurch this morning.

"Finally!" Tate announces as she heaves her pack through the front door. It is starless outside, pitch-black beyond the cottage's windows. Tomorrow morning, we will see our surroundings. I swing open our bedroom windows and they entangle with vines outside. The earthy smell of garden barrels through our nostrils—soil, dew, musty compost, wet grass—weaving with stealth through the air and hitting the back of my throat. We brush our teeth, change clothes, stock the fridge with our groceries, collapse into bed.

The gold of morning rouses us, and I look out our window from bed.

"Oh my God," I utter. I am not swearing again.

We are carved into a rose garden.

I climb out of bed while Kyle still snores, open the double doors in the living room. I am ensconced by thickets of pinks, yellows, whites; I am standing on a patio thrust into the flowers with a table, chairs, chaise longues. Virescent mountains praise the sky behind the neighbor's house across the street. I head inside to the kitchen and start the coffee; I find my bag and dig out my current book (*At Home*, Bill Bryson). The family sleeps; the coffeemaker murmurs awake.

I have found my elysian fields. I don't plan to leave.

⎯⎯⎯

We are technically in Arrowtown, a tiny bedroom community of several thousand residents outside Queenstown. After breakfast on the patio, we walk to the town's main street, a conglomeration of Old West–style storefronts now holding trendy clothing and bespoke home goods. We stop at the post office (its wooden sign: *Post and Telegraph*) and mail postcards to grandparents. It is a stockpile of stationery and stamps, books by local authors on local places. The standard red mailbox is out front, but inside is a temporary mailbox for letters to Santa. I ask the two women at the desk who in town handles the letters.

"What do you mean?" one says with a wink. "Santa does."

Next door, people dine alfresco at Postmasters, a cottage-turned-café named for its original nineteenth-century inhabitant. On the other side, a man sells ice cream from a stand. I exchange the jacket I was wearing for an apple from my backpack. The weather is warming—not exactly summer to me, but it smacks of spring. I think that airport shuttle driver was wrong.

We walk to the end of the main street, then to the nearby banks of Bush Creek, a tributary of the Arrow River and home of the derelict Arrowtown Chinese Settlement. Stone huts from the 1860s dot the land, a reminder that the town began during the Otago Gold Rush and swelled to a thriving place of residence. Chinese immigrants made their way here, along with Europeans and Californians, then were dutifully persecuted and heavily taxed until the 1940s (New Zealand formally apologized in 2002). Our kids run in and out of the huts, and we imagine frontier life raising a family with fingers crossed in hopes of striking it rich. I am aware of what little Kiwi history I know.

Nearby, an original police camp building stands as a graying wood cabin, parked authoritatively along the river in overstated protection from the original foreigners. Cottonwood trees sway in the breeze, towering above the shanty. They shower puffs of cotton with drops of seedpod on the ground, and the grass is blanketed with tufts of spring snow. The kids sing "Jingle Bells" and toss the snow in the air.

Arrowtown charms, but my mind wanders to our guesthouse. I want to bake in the patio's sun and imbibe the perfume of roses. My body and soul want to pause the sightseeing, to instead soak in glory. I need to stop and smell the roses. We all do.

I think of Vanessa's comment in Melbourne, and I calculate that I have indeed spent more than two thousand hours nonstop with the kids, not counting sleep, spiritual direction sessions with Nora, a few hours at random coffee shops to scramble for work deadlines, and thirty minutes when I had LASIK surgery on my eyes in Chiang Mai. I study my kids' hairlines, scrutinize the freckles dancing across their noses, and marvel that I played a role in creating their bodies. Their quotidian observations slay, make my brain stand on its head. I vie for their moral resolve.

Parenting is hard because of diapers and time-outs, the slog of sounding out vowels and the drama of mailboxes missing party invitations. But it is hardest because it is a mirror. It is life staring me down. It is the echoes of my inner childish voice reverberating from my children's; it is the denial of me going first. It is my flesh and blood unleashed, encased around another personality, another will. It is the continual death of my basal impulses for the exchange of extraordinary. It is fighting traffic for gymnastics class, early-morning sandwich cutting, late-night math drills. It is perpetual togetherness while circumnavigating the globe.

At the guesthouse, Kyle grills and I make a salad. We eat on the patio, and the kids perform a play they've rehearsed in secret. We applaud wildly. Then baths, pajamas, my turn to read a story. The kids climb into bunk beds in the room with blackout shades, hours before the sun sets at ten. I retreat back outside to Kyle, and we open a bottle of wine. I wonder at the sky that resembles early afternoon. We talk about the kids, how they're doing, marvel at their traveling prowess, comment on Tate's confusion with fractions, Reed's challenge with phonics. We laugh at something we read on the Internet. We watch a cat video. I think again about my kids and my mother-heart swells.

Then the two of us change into our pajamas, open our windows, climb into bed, and start *Lord of the Rings* on a laptop. The mines of Moria and the river through Rivendell are right outside Arrowtown.

Three days later, we leave town. It is the first time I sob about leaving a place. We vow to return one day.

To make our week in New Zealand financially doable, we must spend the next half in a campervan, crawling our way back up the south island. In Queenstown, I found a bargain deal that required schlepping a campervan back to Christchurch, and we could make the trek however we wanted. The only two real options were the east or west coast, which in New Zealand is akin to choosing emeralds or rubies. We opt for west because we are West Coasters, and west is best, as West Coasters are wont to say.

After we leave, I read the weather forecast: clear skies east, non-stop rain west. We duck through a rain forest, and a torrent of water pours for two days. The kids play with Lego bricks for forty-eight hours in the campervan, and we drive from campsite to campsite. We make meals of cheese and crackers from the kitchenette. Muddy footprints stomp up and down our minuscule hallway. I paid extra for an Internet router in the van, but it can't endure the weather, so I'm unable to work. Kyle steers our mammoth ride around windy wooded corners through peals of water, and through the downpour and wind-shield patter we shout our thoughts about life post-travel, ideas about where we might relocate, what our work will look like a year from now. We bellow our dreams.

The native Maori tribes of New Zealand christened the islands with the name Aotearoa, which means "Land of the Long White Cloud." No one knows the official origin of this name, but it is birthed from beauty, from gazing at its landscape. New Zealand is one of the least densely populated countries on earth. Here, flowers and sheep and cattle crowd out humankind. Creation reigns. A smattering of men, women, and children are graced with the privilege to walk on it.

This week, we have cheated on Italy and France, on Thailand. Our hearts splinter over a new lover. We board our plane back to Australia with a sigh in our hearts and a promise to rendezvous with her again. Kiwi dirt banked along clouded cerulean water has caked into the tread of my shoes. I choose not to remove it, a souvenir from God's oeuvre. I will let it depart on its own, where it may.

8

AUSTRALIA, AGAIN

Australia feels like returning home. For three weeks, we have permission to take off our sweaty, itchy vagabonding hats because we are house-sitting for friends currently on vacation in Canada. We will hole up in the Sydney suburbs and take care of chickens. Heading here, I suspect, will be like waking up from a complicated dream, where your surroundings seem familiar but still slightly off-kilter. This is a regular home for a regular family, and yet it isn't ours.

The real trick is getting to the house. We'll deplane; then we need to take a train several hours out to Glenbrook, a western suburb hugging the foothills of the Blue Mountains, and then walk ten blocks uphill to our house with heavy packs on our backs. We've held this news as secret from the kids because I know they will be less than thrilled.

I mentally rehearse my news bomb and warm up my cheerful mom voice, and then I spot a stranger holding a sheet of paper among the welcome crowd, *Oxenreider* scribbled in black marker. I glance over at Kyle, and his look of confusion verifies he's seen it too. We have no plans for pickup.

"Um . . . hi," I say reluctantly to this unknown woman. "We're the Oxenreiders?"

"Hello! I'm Beryl, Brooke's mum," the woman replies eagerly, shaking my hand. "But everyone calls me Bez."

Brooke is my friend and writing colleague on holiday in Canada, who has given us detailed instructions how to get to her place. We'll find her parents on the front porch when we arrive, Brooke said, where they would give us the house and car keys.

"Oh, well. Hello! Brooke told me we'd meet you at her house," I say sheepishly. I wonder if I've missed something in my sleep deprivation, lost in translation in the shuffle of travel plans. *Perhaps we were going to meet her mom at the airport after all?*

"Yeah, that's right. But we thought we'd surprise you anyway with an airport pickup. You're probably knackered," she remarks. I am frozen and say nothing, eyes wide. An airport pickup?

"That's awfully kind of you," I say, "but you really didn't have to." My brain is still fully operating in game-face mode, seconds away from telling the kids we need to board a train and walk for miles, pushing through exhaustion. I'm aware I'm still staring, mouth agape.

"Well, we thought about you guys and your kids, and thought you might like a little old-fashioned mum and dad pickup," Bez says. "We know what it's like for our kids to travel with their kids, and we hated the thought of you fighting through Sydney."

"Thank you, but . . . it's not cheap to come all the way out here. We know what gas is like in Australia," I say. (As though she doesn't know this.) "We can't ask you to do this. Please let us pay you."

"Nonsense," she says. "Pete is already waiting at the cars in the garage."

Bez picks up one of our packs and walks. We follow her, deliriously murmuring *thank you* until we arrive at the cars.

"Hello! Welcome to Sydney!" Pete exclaims cheerily. He pulls the packs off our backs, tosses them into his trunk. "Climb in, climb in!"

They've brought not one, but two vehicles to cart us to the

westernmost outskirts of Sydney, more than fifty miles and an hour's drive away. Our eyes are saucers. Kyle climbs into Pete's car with Reed and Tate, and I clamber into Bez's, where Finn has a booster seat waiting in the back seat. They won't let us open our wallets for the parking garage. We pull out on the highway, heading west.

"This is truly above and beyond," I slur, fighting travel fatigue sincere with indebtedness. "We haven't yet had an airport pickup on our trip. It feels . . . nice." I blush at my tinny, juvenile response and gaze out the passenger window. Finn has slumped over asleep.

"We're truly happy to do this," Bez says. "Not sure if Brooke's told you, but our family are big fans of something we call the Westbrook Effect." Brooke has mentioned this, but I can't recall its meaning. She explained it to me months ago as the reason she wouldn't let us pay for our extended stay in her house.

"Years ago, Pete worked for a man named Westbrook. He was from San Diego, and we got to visit him a few times. Every time we did—and it turns out he did this for everyone who came to visit—he'd pull out all the stops. He gave us the master bedroom, the full use of his car, paid for all our meals. He'd clear his schedule to take us all over the city. Westbrook insisted we pay for nothing during our stay, since it was his town and we were his guests. He went above and beyond, making sure we had the absolute best time in San Diego. We loved it so much, his take on hospitality and giving over and above, that we vowed to always do the same as a family. Now, anytime someone comes to Sydney, we pull out all the stops and do what we can to make 'em feel at home. No paying, no feeling weird about asking for something, no tiptoeing around or shushing kids. This is what we always did when our kids were still at home, and now that they're out of the house with their own families, they've kept it up and are still doing it. Westbrook Effect."

We pull into Brooke's driveway behind her car, clean and waiting for our use. Pete and Bez climb out of their cars, open the front door, carry in our packs, give us a quick tour. Pete hands over the keys, insists we make ourselves at home and to not hesitate to call if we need anything; they are just a few minutes away.

Twenty minutes later, after they've left and the kids are entranced with the backyard trampoline, there's a knock at the door. Kyle answers, and in saunters Pete, with two coffees and a paper bag.

"We thought you guys might be a bit hungry and in need of some real coffee," he says. "So this is from the bakery a few blocks away. Hope your kids like grilled cheese." He sets the bag on the counter, gives a quick good-bye, and shows himself back out the door.

I glance at Kyle. "Oh. We're *so* doing the Westbrook Effect, forever and ever."

Three and a half months of nonstop backpacking, and we are giddy at the thought of unpacking. We can buy real groceries without worry whether they'll stay fresh in a backpack for more than a few hours; we can lounge in a real living room to watch Netflix. The exotic and mundane have switched places.

It is December 23 the morning we arrive in Sydney, and we want to finally celebrate Christmas. There is little point in setting up a tree or stockings, but we want to schedule a few cookie-baking sessions, watch *A Christmas Story* with popcorn and cocoa. After a night of sound sleep, we drive to the suburb's center to buy a few gifts at the mall.

We hardly recognize ourselves. We aren't mall people, and we've actually already visited malls in both Thailand and China. Needs for a pharmacy, an English bookstore, clean socks kept pulling us magnetically toward malls the past few months. In today's case, the pull is

Christmas shopping, and it is an odd, disorienting dose of reverse culture shock. "Frosty the Snowman" pipes through speakers, shoppers wobble with stacks of bags on each shoulder, and Santa perches on his throne parked in cotton-candy snow and surrounded by disgruntled elves. Christmas is in the air, and yet the air-conditioning blasts and the crowd is in shorts. I detest shopping in any season and my feelings on the matter are heightened this time of year, but I am determined to find things I can wrap in paper. They must be lightweight and small enough to cram in our packs. I am limited by our backpacks and by the stores' ransacked shelves.

I wander into a department store and am disoriented, like a girl on the wrong aisle who's lost her mom. My current personal belongings consist of a laptop and a converter for electrical gadgets; my current wardrobe consists of garb fit for washing elephants in Thailand, hiking in the Queensland bush, and, eventually, shopping in a Moroccan medina. Brushing past womenswear while George Michael sings about his last Christmas causes dizzying culture shock. The toy section is completely picked over, so I leave.

I find a craft store, disheveled from harried shoppers. An idea has hit me. I find everything I need but Scotch tape, and I ask for its whereabouts.

"Sorry, love, we sold out of Scotch tape weeks ago." The employee walks off. I shrug and opt for green painter's tape from a nearby kiosk, and decide this will work even better.

I find a Target at the end of the mall and shuffle through its remains to unearth a few workable gifts. They're nothing I would buy in our normal life, but life isn't normal right now. I add a roll of pink-and-gold wrapping paper and a tin of obscure-brand chocolates.

Three hours later, we walk through the front door, and I toss bags of leftover Lego kits and multicolored pens on the bed and close the door. I empty my bag from the craft store on the dining table and call out, "Kids! Come here!" I spread out the construction paper, markers, and painter's tape.

"What's this for?" Tate asks.

"We're going to decorate the house. Starting with giving ourselves a Christmas tree," I answer.

The kids slice green paper at sawtooth angles, cut out mismatched circles of red and blue baubles, a janky yellow star. I return to the bedroom and wrap the gifts, then set them under our two-dimensional tree, which Kyle has taped to the wall in an outline of green tape.

We watch *A Christmas Story* tonight, eat popcorn for dinner, and cover cereal boxes with the remaining construction paper to transform them into makeshift stockings. The kids tuck into bed, each in his or her own bedroom—a luxury. Kyle and I sip late-night cups of tea in the backyard under the stars. The neighbor's sprinkler comes to life, sputters its cadence. A nearby kookaburra laughs. It is summer solstice: the longest day of the year.

O holy night, indeed.

Australia, like the United States, is a country of natives overtaken by its European immigrants. Its origin as a penal colony is widely known, having started as a dumping ground for Britain's worst of the worst (meaning, typically, nine-year-old chimney sweeps and Irish women caught stealing butter), and the original Aborigines have struggled to reclaim—and maintain—their identity. Sydney is where this British colony began, and until 1971 the government restricted immigration to white settlers only in order to preserve a British ethnic identity. Since 2005, however, it's estimated that 40 percent of the population has at least one parent born overseas, and as of a few years ago, over a quarter of Australians were born overseas, most likely in Africa or

Asia. It is still a country of immigrants, living among the 3 percent of the population hailing from Aboriginal tribes.

If you weren't born here, statistically you were most likely born in Britain, New Zealand, China, Italy, or Vietnam. But around ninety thousand immigrants are from the United States. This includes my friend, Adriel, who lives in Sydney. She is a native Bendite, which means she hails from the small Oregon town from which we left, and married an Aussie several years ago. I met her months ago when they were in the Pacific Northwest visiting her hometown while we were packing up our life to begin our trek.

Here, they live in a ninety-five-square-foot travel trailer with their two small boys. We invite them to come see us and to park their home in the driveway for a few days.

They have recently relocated to Sydney from Queensland, and with this decision they have taken on a sizable increase in expenses. Sydney has the fourth highest living expenses in the world, and they have channeled their limited funds into a thirty-year-old renovated trailer. With a few refresher coats of paint and a spark of creativity, they have made a tiny home. Two days before the New Year, Adriel and her husband, Ryan, pull an orange extension cord out from the side of their home and plug it into the McAlarys'. (We asked first; they gave hearty permission. See, supra, the Westbrook Effect.)

Their two boys scamper to the backyard to meet the chickens and trampoline, and Adriel invites me into her home for the grand tour. To the left of the door are folding bunk beds for the kids; to the right is a bijou swath of kitchen counter space with a miniature stove and fridge. There is a dining table, which also serves as office, art station, and living room, and behind a kitschy sliding door, their master bedroom miraculously houses a queen-sized bed and corner closet. I flash back to our first guesthouse in Beijing.

We sit in the dining room/living room/office, and Adriel confesses,

"Just a few months here and I've learned so much about myself. I know what I'm like when I don't have a place to call home, how I feel out of sorts. And yet I have a liberation and freedom from the burden of those things that come from a real house. They sometimes get in the way."

Like me, she is in her late thirties and feels misplaced. She is a fellow nomad; her travel trailer is the same as my backpack. I tell her about Kate, a fellow American mother I met in Thailand, who with her husband is taking her ten-year-old son to every continent this school year, including Antarctica. Kate also confessed that stripping away the idea of home feels like swinging midair on a trapeze with no net.

Without a foundation underneath four walls, we identify with everywhere and nowhere. We notice with razor-sharp clarity that grass is generally the same across the planet, and yet each country has its own variety of green turf, its own type of light switch, its own method for storing knives. Adriel calls Sydney home, but she perambulates with her walls every few weeks. My walls change every few weeks too. So do Kate's. So do thousands of other earthlings, scurrying like ants across grass to movable homes, to tents and nomadic dwellings. Some of us have chosen this temporarily; others choose it indefinitely. Many don't have a choice.

I feel at home in the world, and I feel like Alice falling down a rabbit hole. I cannot push a thumbtack in a map and say, "There. That is where I'm from." There is nothing to grab onto, no anchor. A vagabond life provides stopgaps but no permanence. Our friends who have traveled the world before us suggested we keep our house during our voyage; we decided instead to sell. I think of them now and wonder if their wisdom would have insulated me from my sense of free-falling.

Because there is no escape hatch for dwelling on the possibility of home, I wonder if instead I have been given the gift of noticing. Are my senses enhanced, sharpened? Have I honed my discerning spirit, learned to take keen note of the differences in how prices are labeled in markets, how beer tastes on different continents? I feel as though I can smell the exhaust from a car in New Zealand, how it mingles with air molecules in a different formation than in Hong Kong. The Thai speak an octave higher than anyone else I've yet encountered. Australians elongate the cadence of their *e*'s. Finn's left eyebrow arches higher than his right when he's surprised. The southern Chinese have a different accent to their Mandarin than their northern counterparts, though I couldn't pinpoint specifics. I just know they do.

Poet Mary Oliver writes, "To pay attention, this is our endless and proper work."[1] Perhaps I have been given this as a work assignment on our travels.

"Tea?" asks Adriel. "Or beer? We have both. Have you tried Beez Neez? It's wonderful."

Ryan and Adriel are staying with us through the New Year, which means traipsing our five kids to the fireworks display over Sydney Harbor. They know of a good spot, where we will fight crowds, yes, but where we can spread out a picnic blanket or two. Several days ago, they took us to Sydney proper, where Reed splashed in the hot summer waves of Manly Beach for his late December birthday, and where we took a ferryboat down the harbor and witnessed the sun set fire to the top of the Sydney Opera House. It was a relief, a lightness, to sightsee with locals. Sydney is pleasurable, but she is not easy to navigate.

The morning of December 31, a friend of Adriel's calls from our anticipated spot for the evening festivities.

"She got there by ten this morning, and it's already filled to the gills," Adriel whispers with her hand over the phone. "She's saving us a few feet of space, but she says we need to be there by three so she can take a break."

My eyes widen; my heart heaves with the thought of five children parked on a blanket for nine hours until fireworks.

"Still want to?" she asks. I make a face. I mentally replay the Internet video we watched yesterday of last year's harbor fireworks display and debate the merits of wedging the lot of us in three square feet and no bathrooms.

Tonight—the nine of our bodies bedecked with pajamas and glow sticks—we fire up the backyard grill and queue eighties music from our laptops. We cavort on the trampoline and laugh as our neon-glowing heads of pink, blue, and yellow swirl and jostle up and down. The kids giggle, and I bathe in the sound. I sing along loudly to songs from my childhood. We watch the display of fireworks from the comfort of the McAlarys' couch, and we fall asleep at a reasonable hour.

There was a global phenomenon an arm's reach away, and we chose instead to soak in the ordinariness of home, be it a temporary one. Tonight, I log in a day's work of paying attention.

A new year has arrived, and we are squarely in the suburbs to welcome it.

Australia is didgeridoos and dingoes, deadly rain forest weeds and millions of endemic creatures. It is also Santa at the mall and commonplace lawn grass. It, along with New Zealand, is so distant from my native country and my daily awareness that it's easy to forget about this corner of the world. They welcome the day first here, before the rest of us on the planet. They have given us refrigeration, Wi-Fi, and bungee jumping. Australia's citizens primarily speak English, yet they christen places with names like Bong Bong, Boing Boing, Bungle Bungles, Bubble Bubble, Humpty Doo, Headbutts, Tittybong, and Nowhere Else. New Zealand sheep outnumber people six to one and adorn the rest of us with merino wool. Yet the people remind me of Texas, my birthplace—neighborly, proud of their heritage, salt of the earth. They are familiar faces, at home nine thousand miles away from my own.

The citizens of this corner of the world cherish their land. They love their waters. They cultivate both well, carve lightly into the topography, and delight in the natural world's pleasures with aplomb. Representatives of the human race are sparse. Trees that once played with dinosaurs still run wild. Wildflowers frolic in abandon with livestock. People plow the dark soil and paint with earth's rocks.

Asia forces me into the unknown; Australia and New Zealand give me the gift of retreat. Asia taps my Americanness on the shoulder and plays a new song with a novel beat, asks me for a dance. Australia hands me a glass of wine and invites me to take a load off in the chair on the back deck. My wayfaring half has been resurrected, yet my other half, the homebody, still exists among night market stalls and grass tucked at the base of the Southern Alps.

My full body, I realize, was always in my Oregon neighborhood, reading stories on the couch to my kids about faraway lands. I savor mango sticky rice from dubious food stalls in Chiang Mai, and I relish grilled cheese and tomato soup on my dining room table. Our last ordinary days in Australia whisper to me a secret: going into the unknown means returning to the known is a bewitching sweetness. Adventure doesn't always require a sturdy backpack.

We feed chickens; we make soup; we go to the movies. We catch up on work and school. We spot kangaroos crossing the neighborhood road as deer do in Texas. We pay attention for two more weeks. And then, we fold our laundry, repack our bags, and replenish our deodorant stash. It is time to reengage with the planet in a new year.

Summertime Christmastide

Snows of seasonal cotton lie dormant till wind swirls its spell
Kisses ankles of children with ready walking sticks,
Tufts flit down, down, downward again.
Juvenile milky puffs emancipate from its mother branch,
Maypole-dancing down the bole.
December tides of late spring hearken new birth.
Leaves raise hands as celebrants of new life,
A nativity brought for all.
It is summer. Glad tidings to all.

INTERMISSION

For what you see and hear depends a good deal on where you are standing: it also depends on what sort of person you are.

—C. S. Lewis

9

SRI LANKA

Sri Lanka is chaos. Before we leave the Colombo airport, we partake in an unplanned appointment with a uniformed man (military? airport employee?) who has led us to his office and has not spoken for half an hour. The kids are goofing around on office chairs, sitting upside down and swinging their legs; Kyle and I are employing our official everything's-all-right travel faces. We are clueless. Turns out we got bad advice about our visas before our arrival here; they should have either been purchased more than twenty-four hours in advance or at the airport counter in person, instead of what we did— buy them online mere hours beforehand, during a layover in Kuala Lumpur. Crisp American bills suffice as collateral for necessary passport stamps and stickers, and so with a stack high enough on the man's desk and a conniving smile to prevent our eyes from rolling with annoyance, we are allowed into the country, this pear-shaped island southeast of India.

I have never before seen an airport like this. Past the baggage claim, we push our stack of bags on a trolley and walk through a gauntlet of furniture and appliance stores. We are now in a mall. Vacuum cleaners, reclining chairs, dishwashers, electric teakettles—the price is right on household goods in the airport. *Who buys a washing machine after a transoceanic international flight?* I wonder. There really are decent prices on Maytags. Too bad I don't have a house to put one in.

We hail a taxi and have it take us from the airport appliance outlet to the commotion of the train station. We don't know what to expect and we don't exactly have a plan, other than to find a way to our guesthouse. We were told the train is the cheapest and most efficient means of traveling from the capital city of Colombo to our guesthouse in the town of Kandy. We were also told we wouldn't need passport visas in advance.

Turns out it's fine to buy train tickets at the station gate; there's plenty of space in first class at five bucks a seat. There is no place in the station to store our bags while we wait for the train, however, and we are starving after our marathon journey from Sydney. A day ago, we left Australia's capital city at ten o'clock in the evening and arrived in Kuala Lumpur at three the next morning. There, we piled together like bears in a den and slept on the dingy Malaysian airport floor until our flight to Colombo at 10 a.m. I think we've been traveling for nineteen hours, but Sri Lankan time is four hours, thirty minutes behind Australia's, so who's to say?

We keep the weight on our backs and search for food to take on the train.

Outside the station, men sit on curbs munching on corn on the cob and oranges; they stop midbite and stare at us, as if we've stepped out of a sitcom. Toddlers hold hands with grandmothers and uniformed schoolchildren run past us, rushing to a bus stop. Motorized rickshaw taxis slow down and walk with us, honk their childlike horns to announce their availability. Women in vibrant saris of green and gold flash against the sunlight, intermingling with men's plaid wraparound sarongs and polo shirts. The sky is yellow-gray with pollution again; the air smells of factory smoke, curry, and sweat. Passing crowds slow down and stare once more at our flaxen-haired children.

Vendors thrust fried samosas, oranges, brochures for grand tours of the capital city, and fake Rolex watches toward us.

The five of us circle back to the train station, find a tiny attached bakery swarming with customers vying for next in line, and push our way forward for sesame-covered rolls and a variety of samosas. For the kids, I hope at least one of the triangle pastries isn't spicy. We load up on bottled water and pray that they weren't refilled under the tap.

We trudge through the train station, wave at the ticket vendor who recognizes us, toss our bags on the ground, and sit on them. I open the bakery bag and pass out pastries. The kids nibble a feeble corner off their samosas, pass them to Kyle and me.

"No thanks," they each say.

"Aren't you starving?" I ask.

"Yes."

I sigh and reluctantly give them the plain sesame-dotted rolls, and Reed picks off the seeds. Kyle and I eat the five samosas. The garam masala potato filling dissolves in my mouth; Kyle groans with pleasure. They are divine.

Looking at a map, this is an odd stop on our journey. Sri Lanka isn't near anywhere else we are visiting, and neither Kyle nor I know anyone here. We don't know that much about it, either, but when we planned our trip months ago, we noticed it was an even stop between the Australian and African continents, and *huh—I wonder what it's like?* That seemed like a good enough reason to stop, and so, we are here because it's here. It exists. It floats in the Indian Ocean, a teardrop southeast of India, and there probably won't be another time we'll fly across it.

It has not yet been a full day since we were in Australia, where highways felt familiar and smells were commonplace. Now we are surrounded by mystery.

A train pulls into the station and we strap on our packs. First class proffers padded velvet seats, a spitting window-unit air conditioner, and a movie without sound or subtitles, starring B-list American teenage actors. The screen wobbles above the emergency exit, and a few minutes later, the sluggish train departs the station. We pass graffitied concrete walls and piles of trash, a few boys playing dangerously close to the tracks. I see some of Colombo's skyscrapers and the coastline in the distance. The scenery gradually transfigures to stubby shrubs with giant leaves, towering banyan trees, rusted corrugated tin roofs, old women hanging brightly colored laundry, and young men on bicycles. As the train gains speed, it begins to gallop. Our bodies start to wave forward and back, our heads wobble; I feel like I'm on a high-speed carousel horse. My velvet seat begins to shift sideways.

"Mom, I don't feel very good," Finn moans.

"Me neither. You can lay down and close your eyes." He curls up next to me.

Tate looks up from her book. "I don't think I can do any school right now," she says. Reed laughs at the roller coaster ride, sways with the rhythm, and bounces in his seat. He sits by himself and the rest of us close our eyes. I hear Finn snoring. Towns and villages bobble up and down, and I keep my head straight as I pray for a vomit-free journey. Nameless teenagers fight on the screen and shout silent obscenities.

I don't know how we'll find dinner tonight, and I hope for a corner store near our house for eggs and a few veggies—we are nutrient depleted and pastry bloated. It's dark when we arrive in Kandy, and we hail a taxi. He speaks some English and offers a price that sounds extortionate. Kyle texts the German homeowner, who is currently in Europe, to verify the price.

"It's fine," he says. "A little much, yes, but typical for white foreigners."

We climb in, and the driver silently drives the narrow, shadowed streets to our home. Neon lights shimmer on the ground in the puddles where it has just rained. The kids are shells, hollow with exhaustion and whimpering with hunger. My head nods in sleep deprivation.

The van pulls into a driveway, and an old woman stands in the yard to greet us. For thirty dollars a day, it seems our guesthouse comes with a cook available for all our meals. She lives in the other end of the house, across the courtyard, along with her elderly husband, who handles the house repairs.

We remove our flip-flops and leave them outside, then walk inside. The dining table is set with plates and silverware, covered serving dishes, and a pitcher of water. It smells like Sundays at Grandma's house. Maari, the cook, asks, "Is chicken and rice okay, ma'am?"

My eyes water and I nod; I can't speak. We sit down and dish out food. Finn puts his head on the table and falls asleep before he's able to take a bite. Reed cries as he chews, confused with his combination of ravenous stomach and somnolent body. Tate takes a few bites, excuses herself, and finds a bed. It has been thirty-six hours since we left the McAlarys' house in Glenbrook.

Kyle carries the boys to their room, and I find the bathroom, my skin clammy and desperate for a shower. I dig through my pack for shampoo and soap, extract my pajamas, pull back the shower curtain, and scream.

I run out of the bathroom and Maari runs in, confused. She laughs, shakes her head as she heads back to the kitchen, then returns with an aerosol can and a sheet of paper. I hear the spray of the can, and in a few seconds, Maari escorts a colossal, bristly tarantula on the sheet of paper, then out the back door. She shakes him out on the lawn.

"You may take your shower now, ma'am."

That's what she thinks.

I want to follow the kids into desperate, deep sleep. We inspect the folds of the sheets inside and out, I check for bumps between them and the mattress, and Kyle investigates underneath the bed frame on the floor. I peer inside the pillowcases. Lying down feels sybaritic after our day and a half, and my muscles quiver with relief. I strap on my eye mask and pull the sheet over my head, lest a friend of the arachnid's drops from the ceiling in the night and calls my face home.

The next morning coffee, orange juice, and omelets are waiting for us on the dining table.

After breakfast the kids are eager to play, but they're scared of Maari's husband. He's harmless, but he's wrinkled and toothless and smiles at them with affection. I am much more frightened of the yard. We've been warned that in Sri Lanka, cobras are as plentiful as Texas squirrels. Maari warns us of the monkeys; one must be careful of anything inadvertently left outside, because they'll steal anything from oranges in the tree, to a pen dropped from your bag, to shoes left on the patio overnight.

I think of our flip-flops outside.

"Arrgh! Everybody's are fine but mine," Reed whines from the front porch. One of his is missing; the other is torn to shreds.

"Monkey." Maari says, nodding. I pull out Reed's socks and sneakers from the bottom of his pack. I can't remember when he last wore them.

Maari schedules us a driver for the day. This is deemed safer and more affordable than testing out the ambiguous traffic laws as foreigners with a car rental, so an hour after breakfast, the five of us board a derelict Volkswagen van with no seat belts and springs in the seats jabbing through the fabric. The sliding door is bent, and it takes Kyle three tries to close it. I can still see the road through the bottom where it should connect with the rest of the van.

"Kids, if you so much as wiggle your bottoms in your seats, you'll get extra math problems," I say through clenched teeth.

"Where would you like to go?" Rishi, our driver, asks from the front seat.

"How about a tea factory? I hear there's decent tea here," Kyle jokes. Rishi jiggles his head side to side and reverses out the driveway. Here, nodding means no, and tilting your head side to side means "yes, okay," and "sure, why not?" It also sometimes means the opposite, depending whether the person gives you the answer he thinks you want to hear.

The van turns left, and Finn falls out of his seat, toppling against the decaying sliding door. I briskly pull him off the floor and onto my lap, wrap my arms around him, which will do nothing if we crash. I squint my eyes closed and pray for mercy. A seat spring bores into my rear.

―

The first tea plantation in Ceylon, Sri Lanka's original name, was opened in 1867 by a Scotsman named James Taylor. The alchemy of the island's rain, sun, and soil boosted the drink from an exotic concoction from the Orient to a British mainstay, and it is now arguably the most popular drink in the world. Sri Lanka is currently the leading global exporter of tea; 23 percent of all tea leaves worldwide hail from this island. Almost any tea factory here will happily give free tours of their facilities, with the hope you'll buy some leaves as a thank-you.

Rishi takes us to a nondescript factory housed in a metal ware-house. We walk through the front door and are greeted by a young woman in a pink sari, waiting as though she were expecting us.

"Would you like a tour?" she asks. She leads us upstairs to the top floor, where troughs of tea leaves are drying. Machines vibrate the troughs periodically to rotate the leaves, helping them dry evenly.

"This is called withering," she explains.

"How long does it take?" I ask.

"It depends," she says. "We wait until the leaves smell right."

She leads us to the next room, where a cylindrical machine rolls across the leaves and ruptures the cell walls, releasing their juices. The room echoes with a mechanical roar as steel plates rotate in rhythm across round metal tables. Our guide speaks, but I can't hear her. I look at our kids, whose wide eyes are entranced at being so close to factory-grade machinery.

We walk through the deafening room into another, where tea leaves either are spread out to ferment or skip this stage altogether (as it happens, green tea isn't fermented at all; it's this process that turns the same leaves into our black tea), then onto another room where women guide even more whirring and buzzing machines. The whole tea-making process takes about seven steps, and in its finale, the sorted leaves are shipped off to the government, who inspects the batch to ensure it qualifies as official Ceylon tea. There's a reason it's the best in the world.

Our guide leads us to the final tea room/gift shop where we're allowed a complimentary cup of tea and it's assumed we'll buy much more. Reed and Finn take one sip, then return to the windows to watch more moving mechanical parts, so we invite Rishi to join Kyle, Tate, and me. He doesn't speak English, but we raise our glasses and he does likewise; we nod our heads, and sip. There's an understanding with tea. Tate is not quite ten but has already long consumed tea;

having lived her early years in Turkey, she was drinking it as a two-year-old toddler. The taste, the ritual with sugar cubes and miniature spoons, is home for her. I grew to love its taste in Turkey too. She smiles at me, and I wink back. This field trip feels personal, comforting, hospitable. Tea drinking is a liturgy of comfort, and we partake of it everywhere in the world. It's a ceremony of simplicity, nourishment for both the nomads in foreign teahouses and homebodies in their beds. We buy more than we can fit in our packs, and plan to mail some back to one of the kids' tea-obsessed grandmas.

In the evening, Rishi suggests checking out the left canine tooth of the Buddha; it is Kandy's claim to fame, displayed in the town center for all to admire. This isn't exactly on our agenda, but this is the closest we've been to any of the Buddha's teeth, and our itinerary isn't exactly jam-packed. We jiggle our heads side to side. *Sure—why not?*

Kyle wraps himself in Rishi's tablecloth-like sarong because he is wearing shorts, verboten in sacred temples. The five of us walk up the steps to the Buddhist temple where inside awaits Gautama Buddha's tooth. Rishi waits for us outside. I have no clue what to expect. As a Christian, I can appreciate the devotion of the faithful Buddhists, but I've never been big on relic veneration. I'm especially not a fan of sensory overload, particularly in swarming crowds where I'm deluged with musty incense, thunderous chanting in a language I don't know for an observance I don't understand, dim lighting, and no obvious exit sign. We gingerly step through the temple doors. *This is the wrong place for us to be*, I think immediately. I look at Kyle, and the crowd behind us pushes us through. We're stuck.

I hold the boys' hands and we begin pushing our way through. Monks pound rhythmically on drums and the beat rattles between my ears like a tuning fork. Mobs of worshippers and tourists move through like cattle in a stockade, and we have no choice but to join. We inch our way upstairs with everyone.

A shrine of candles in front of a gilded door waits at the back of a large stone room, and the multitudes stare in anticipation. I can only assume that the Buddha's tooth is behind the doors. We stand and wait.

There is no ventilation inside these thousand-year-old walls, and there are only six square inches of space for our bodies. The heat is sweltering. We wait for a glimpse of this tooth. And wait. And wait. And wait. Nothing happens. I stare at the gold-plated doors and my mind wanders about what's behind the doors. I imagine a dining room set, like on *The Price Is Right*. The beat of the drums grows louder as the orchestra of monks marches closer to us. Tate covers her ears and stands on her tiptoes; she can't see anything. The boys can only stare at other peoples' backs centimeters from their noses. There isn't enough room for me to pick them up.

"What's going on?" Reed yells from below. I shrug my shoulders.

"I want to go home!" screams Finn, and he starts to cry. I'm desperate for an exit, but there is no way out of this crushing crowd, the walls closing in. There is nothing to do but wait and watch this door, and endure the continual *boom boom boom* of the drums. I struggle to breathe, pray that I don't faint.

We wait for thirty more minutes as the surrounding devotees mumble their chants. Several tourists hold up their phones to record what they're unable to see. Finn leans his head into one of my sides; Reed leans into the other. The boys try to sleep standing. Tate pushes her way to the front of the crowd so she can better see.

Finally, the gilded doors open. The crowd's chanting grows faster, louder, eager with veneration. A monk emerges holding a golden dome atop a red velvet pillow, and he sets it on an altar. People inch slowly into a queue for a chance to pass by the tooth that was presumably under this gleaming dome and that we would not, it would seem, technically see.

Kyle and I nod, hold tight the kids' hands, call for Tate to come back, and we force our way against the crowd. We zigzag down the stairs and through the halls, collapse out of the temple and into fresh air, and speed-walk to our van waiting for us on the street. We beg Rishi to take us home.

The next morning, the five of us go on a walk through the country's national botanical gardens, not far from our house. Monkeys follow our steps; diminutive brown toque macaques scampering across suspension bridges and hiking paths. They stop when we stop, then start again when we continue walking, like a comical classic movie. Finn takes a hundred photos of them, finds them hilarious.

This morning is our calmest so far on the island, and it is a relief to let the kids run through grass. Locals stare. The boys inch close to a termite hill, and I holler for them to move away.

"Not termite hills," says Rishi. "Cobra houses."

We move to a forest grove, and are surrounded by vanilla vines, cocoa, nutmeg, cinnamon, and coffee trees. It smells like Christmas morning.

Sri Lanka is best known for, aside from Ceylon tea, its enormously high concentration of spices—some of the world's most significant spices hail from this unassuming island. Its rare blend of acidic soil, humid air near the equator, and relative protection from other environmental threats make for ideal growing conditions for beloved staples like vanilla, nutmeg, curry, and cinnamon.

I pluck fallen nutmeg pods from the ground, slide them in my pocket. Their dark seeds are covered in a waxy red coating, like

European cheese. They smell like comfort, pie, a fireplace. I'm hit with a pang of homesickness.

Our flight out of Colombo is in the middle of the night, so on our second-to-last day in Sri Lanka, we gallop back on the train, first-class to the capital city, and watch the same American teen movie. We plan to hole up and catch up on work and school before boarding the plane because we'll soon hit African soil running, and we won't have much Internet access there. We book a guesthouse with a backyard pool two miles from the airport.

At the train station, Kyle negotiates a price with a driver, but he forgets to ask about his type of vehicle. We strap on our backpacks and find our driver waiting for us with his three-wheeled motorized rickshaw with a backseat bench sized for two adults.

I sigh. I'm so tired.

He crams our bags around his feet, behind the bench, and in between his seat and ours, then positions our bodies just so. I prop my foot high on a steel bar so I don't slide off the bench and onto the highway with Finn on my lap. Tate and Reed squeeze in the middle together, and Kyle miraculously sits sideways on the edge. The driver pulls into traffic and speeds up to forty miles per hour, dodging in and out of what would be lanes if lanes existed in Sri Lanka. With one hand I hold on to the rickshaw, with the other I squeeze Finn; I pass the time ignoring my itchy nose and reading passing bumper stickers in English, like *Your love gives me thunder.* The ride takes an hour, and the kids pass the time with skip-counting math songs, their mouths singing inches from my ear. Kyle stares straight ahead, eyes darting with the traffic as if he's playing a video game. He loves this.

When we eventually pull off our bags, we see that the driver shoved Tate's pack against his greasy gearshift, and her doll's face was propped out of the zippered enclosure. The doll's nose and chin are smudged with grease. Tate hides her tears. The driver laughs, asks for more money than was originally agreed.

The guesthouse we booked is already filled with guests, says the owner when we arrive. But he also owns the house next door, still under construction, and hopes we'll find it accommodating until tomorrow morning, when the original guesthouse can be solely ours until our flight. I exert all my physical strength to not roll my eyes in weariness. In the backup house, we toss our backpacks on stacks of shrink-wrapped new tile, eat Indian takeout on the floor, and take cold showers. Before crashing into bed, we unwrap the guesthouse's new pillows from their plastic bags.

Early the next morning, we walk over piles of stone, past flip-flopped jackhammering construction workers in the yard, to our booked house. The backyard pool is full of chemicals and won't be ready until tonight, the owner says. But the cook that comes with the house helps us bide our time with a breakfast of eggs, sausage, and instant coffee, and I thank God that back in Sydney I loaded all our e-readers with books. That feels like a lifetime ago.

We read chapters and chapters that day, suspended in this Sri Lankan intermission. At seven in the evening, the kids begin to swim, and they stay in the cloudy water for three hours. At midnight, we wake them up, toss on clothes, and climb into the four-door car waiting for us outside, a quiet sedan with seat belts. The drive takes two minutes. Sri Lanka remains a mystery.

PART IV

Nobody can discover the world for someone else.
Only when we discover it for ourselves does
it become common ground and a common
bond and we cease to be alone.

—Wendell Berry

10

UGANDA

We sit on covered cushions and faded blankets on a dirt floor in one of the two rooms of this house. The walls are made of the same hardened mud as the courtyard outside the doorless entry. It's as though the house erupted organically from its natural setting, though I know it was fashioned by the hands that live here. I gather with an Ethiopian family—mother, younger sister, and brothers—sit in a corner, and watch as a traditional Ethiopian coffee ceremony unfolds. The eldest daughter, Birhan, roasts green coffee beans over a plate of hot coals, swirls the beans with a stick. Their aroma washes over me, conjures a nostalgic hint of coffee shops back home. I wonder if I've ever sipped an espresso bought in Oregon and made from beans grown a hundred feet from here. It's possible. The family members wave their hands to their noses, inhale the scent of roasting coffee. It smells like home to them too. I copy them. This takes a while—maybe twenty minutes of this aroma bath—and we watch, smile at one another across the language barrier.

Next, Birhan pours the now mahogany-colored coffee beans from the plate into a vessel, and with two hands, pounds in dutiful rhythm with a three-foot chunk of rebar. *Thump, thump, thump, thump.* It's the same sound as the coffee vendor in the old market in Izmir,

Turkey, where we used to live. Every ten seconds, she pauses, checks the status of the beans, then continues.

Once they're ground, Birhan pours the coffee into a *jebena*, a clay pot with a bulbous base and twiggy pouring spout. Water bubbles inside, percolating the beans and spitting partially brewed coffee out the spout, until a roiling boil reaches the pot's neck. I notice another smell: the scent of myrrh burning as incense, leathery and nutty, as one of the brothers brings a bowl with a hypnotic stream of smoke wafting up to the thatched ceiling and sets it next to the coffee. It mingles with the scent of the coffee, which hints of, oddly enough, early summer blueberries. The rich, sweet smoke billows above our heads. Birhan empties the coffee into a bowl, then returns it to the jebena for a second brew. Then a third. Then, at last, it's ready.

Birhan's mother, Tigist, takes over. She pours the coffee over a tight collection of small, handleless cups, letting the brew spill over between them until they're all full. She adds sugar to each cup, then passes the tray around, first to us, as guests, then to her family.

Coffee is sacred in Ethiopia. An invitation to attend a coffee ceremony is considered a mark of friendship, and we have known each other for several years now, even though we just met today. A bowl of popcorn is passed—the mainstay always accompanying the national drink—and Tigist and I raise our tiny cups of brew, nod to each other from across the room, and sip. We toast to a friendship that spans miles, languages, and our different lots in life. We are mothers; we belong to each other. This coffee brings us together.

Two weeks ago, I worked from a coffee shop in a Sydney suburb. A year ago, I worked at a coffee shop tucked in the mountains of central Oregon. On this day, I am in a minuscule village in the Ethiopian Highlands, not far from the origins of my favorite drink, sipping coffee brewed from beans just picked from the tree. I am with friends.

I'm not sure what I expected from Africa when I boarded that plane to Uganda one week ago, but it was not this.

———

Africa is a stranger to me, I think as I sit in my airplane seat. I've never been here before, and have little knowledge of the continent's fifty-four countries. We won't be here long, either—we're meeting friends in Europe next month, so this African stint feels sandwiched, crammed between two longer stays in other continents. I regret this not long after boarding this flight from Doha, Qatar, to Entebbe, Uganda, where the fellow passengers and flight attendants are the most hospitable we've yet encountered.

Now we have landed in Uganda. We join the back of the lengthy visa line in the muggy Entebbe airport, and not two minutes later, a genial woman in an airport uniform sidles next to me and links my arm with hers. "You've got small children! Come with me, ma'am—you can come to the front of the line." The people in line smile and nod at us, as though to say, *Of course! Move to the front.* This is how our African experience starts, with such familial hospitality. This bodes well for our month here.

We will visit five distinctly different countries: six, if you count the days we'll wait in South African hotels for flights. Due to budget constraints, our line on the map takes zigzagging to a new level; we'll touch tarmac in Dubai between both Johannesburg and Nairobi, then again between Nairobi and Casablanca. After this week in Uganda, we will head to Ethiopia, but then we'll fly from Ethiopia to Zimbabwe also via South Africa, then via South Africa again back up to Kenya. None of this makes any sense on a map. I'm nervous about the wear and tear these extra, fairly needless seven thousand miles will wage on our bodies.

From what I've read, Africa is layered, volatile, ancient, misunderstood, huge. It is rife with unfair stereotypes. It's home to 15 percent of the world's population and holds the most countries of any other continent. Multicultural is an understatement. To be in a continent of this size, age, and diversity for less than a month isn't even scratching the surface. Not even skimming it, really. I merely hope Africa's relationship to us will move from stranger to acquaintance.

We get our passports stamped, then head out of the Uganda airport and find Joy and her kids waiting for us.

"Hello!" Joy says. "How was your flight? I bet you're exhausted."

"It was actually not too bad," I say, giving her a hug.

"Um, Mom?" I hear. Reed taps me on the shoulder. "I think I left my blanket on the plane." My heart stops.

"Are you sure?" I ask. He nods.

Kyle takes off his backpack. "I'll be back," he says, and dashes back in the airport.

Before we left Oregon, we debated what to do about prized possessions, the birth-treasures of our kids. It'd be heartbreaking to lose them, but a year is a long time to go without their beloved blankets, especially when the comforts of home are in short supply. We decided to let the kids take them and risk their potential loss.

Thirty minutes pass, and Kyle reemerges from the airport. "The blanket's on its way to Rwanda," he says, catching his breath. "The plane eventually comes back to Uganda, so they'll do their best to get it. The guy was really nice; he said he'd shoot me an e-mail when he finds it." And just like that, Reed's birth-blanket has been lost in Africa.

This isn't Reed's first missing-object incident on our trip. He left this same blanket on an airport shuttle in Hong Kong, and Kyle bolted down an upward escalator to save it then. Reed also left a cherished stuffed penguin in New Zealand, which was then sent to the

McAlarys' house in Australia, but only after we departed for Sri Lanka. (The penguin finally arrived in Texas, miraculously unharmed, five months after our travels.)

Reed's face contorts; he holds back tears. "Bud, we'll do our best to get it back," Kyle says, ruffling his hair. Reed buries his face in my side in embarrassment, and my stomach twists in knots. Losing an irreplaceable item is high on my list of travel concerns.

Uganda is the second most populous landlocked country in the world, and it's also the second-youngest country in the world, with a median age of fifteen. The total dependency ratio—meaning, the percentage of dependents to the working-age population—is 102 percent. I don't understand how that's possible. Uganda is a very young, very crowded country. It's also quite hot.

I sit next to Joy in the passenger seat and watch her weave the van like an expert through lanes swollen with vehicles. Traffic is slow. People walk along either side of the road, men in trousers and dress shirts on their cell phones, women draped in fabrics of cantaloupe and lime colors balancing on their heads giant baskets with bananas for sale. Young men in T-shirts walk with their friends, and stores crowd the road's shoulder with samples of what's for sale inside: living room furniture, women's dresses, auto parts, avocados. The movement of wheels and feet summon a shaggy carpet of red dust. Every other billboard is an ad from the government's health department: "Cheating? Use a condom. Cheated on? Get tested." "Everybody has a role to play—say no to sugar daddies." "Would you let this man be with your teenage daughter? So why are you with his? Cross-generational sex stops with you."

Joy pulls the van through a rusted metal gate and into her driveway. The kids spill out of the van like a clown car, then all dissipate to various corners of the yard, porch, and house. Bodies disappear in seconds, eager to play with new friends.

I know Joy as a fellow writer, but our families have never met. Is it coincidental that the majority of the children we've encountered on our trip have been boys? Ashley's family in China has four boys, and the itinerant family we met in Thailand, traveling to all seven continents—they have one boy. Our friends in Melbourne, Australia, have three boys, and in Sydney, Adriel and Ryan have two young boys.

I have a hunch this unplanned phenomenon isn't without a cosmic purpose for Tate. She's in a volatile, awkward age with one foot in childhood and one in adolescence, and she's growing into a new phase when roots need to reach, burrow deeper into rich, stationary soil. We decided to take this trip now—during her tenth year—because we sense that soon, it'll be much more difficult to uproot her. This is an age of magic for our oldest, but she's been lonely since we left.

It's been five long months since we first touched Beijing concrete, and Tate has blossomed on these travels. Her fertilizer has been carting all her belongings on her back, sharing bedrooms with her brothers, standing on long metro rides, and the loneliness that goes with being the only girl. She is growing into the adult tasks of rolling up her sleeves and taking slow breaths when things don't go as planned. A lack of girlfriends has sprouted adaptability, resolve, mettle.

Joy has five boys and one girl—Hanna—who is around Tate's age. Half a year with no companionship, and my girl is given a girlfriend. They head upstairs and into Hannah's bedroom full of dolls, then close the door.

"Dave will be home from work soon, so I'll start dinner and you can keep me company," Joy says. Kyle settles onto a couch and is soon catnapping while I help Joy slice potatoes. Finn and Reed scurry past the kitchen window; then Joy's twin boys follow seconds later with Nerf guns. No sound from the girls upstairs.

Half an hour later, Dave walks through the front door, so I wake up Kyle and the four of us head to the wraparound porch. Joy opens a bottle of wine and pours it into glasses.

"From South Africa," she says. "It's fabulous." I sip tart hints of grapes, black cherry, tobacco, the salt of the ocean. The yard shimmers jade and the sky shifts from blue to orange. Boys dog pile on one another, giggling.

"How are you guys adjusting to life here?" I ask. They've lived in Uganda less than a year. Previously, Dave's job as a pilot stationed them five thousand miles southeast, on an island in Indonesia, and they'd lived there for eight years.

"Indonesia still feels like home," Joy admits. "And it probably will for a while. I mean, we were there a long time. It's the place our kids know more than anywhere else."

"It'll probably take a while to love it here, eh?" I say, nodding. Expats understand that it often takes time to warm up to a new place after the initial honeymoon period.

"Actually," Joy says, "I already love Uganda."

The sun shifts below a tree and I squint. Pink stripes paint the sky.

"In these eight months, I've simply chosen to love it," she explains, shrugging. "I don't think it's wonderful, and I really miss Indonesia and Oregon. But there's a lot to love about Uganda, so that's the stuff I'm choosing to focus on."

We sip our wine, and I think about how terrible I am at this. I've lived in twenty-two houses and five different cities, and I always, always dwell first on the negative. My cynicism broods over what's missing, why a new home fails to measure up to the one previous. I bellyache about the weather, the traffic, the restaurants; I'm a knee-jerk Eeyore until convinced otherwise.

Joy assures me right away she's not perfect at this, that there is a laundry list of things that make life hard here. "The eggs here have no nutritional value to them—crack an egg and you'll see what I mean. The yolks are gray. The roads are terrible. *Terrible.* Potholes are flat-out canyons in the road. And if you get pulled over, get ready to pay a bribe, since you're a foreigner. Oh, and mosquitoes—you have to watch out for them like the plague. Literally. Well, malaria at least."

I make a mental note: *Find a pharmacy; buy a malaria kit.*

"But man, this red soil . . . it gets under your skin. I promise you, you'll be hard-pressed to find people as friendly as they are here in this part of Africa. People love people here. Relationships are everything. And avocados are huge; they're like a dime each."

The sun falls, and we eat dinner on the porch, fill ourselves with guacamole, and let the kids play in the dark. Then we say good night, and the five of us head to our guesthouse down the street in Joy and Dave's safari van, tires tumbling over potholes. We shower off red Ugandan dust, double-check that mosquito nets cover the length of our beds to the floor, and crank pedestal fans on high. Early the next morning, I meander through the guesthouse's garden and find an avocado tree. Its fruit weights down the branches, big as eggplants.

We drive to Jinja, a town eighty miles east of Kampala and known for its status as home of the Nile River's source. Dave and Joy let us borrow their van for a few days, so Kyle braves gargantuan potholes and muddy-red roads, inching to Jinja at a snail's pace with throngs of vehicles and pedestrians. Motorbikes weave around traffic with fifty empty plastic jugs piled high and strung together on their backs. Monkeys play Frogger across the road, and we swerve every twenty feet to avoid the road's crevasses. We're inching through a traffic jam, and a uniformed man waves us over.

"Hello, sir," he says as Kyle rolls down the window.

"Hello, *Ssebo*," Kyle answers, as Joy taught us to do.

"It seems you were going a little too fast," the officer says with a smile.

"Really? I didn't think so."

"Oh yes, sir," he answers politely. "It's okay; it happens sometimes." I look away from the passenger seat and feel heat rise from my neck.

Kyle nonchalantly shuffles in his seat and digs for his wallet.

"Here in Uganda, this sort of violation only costs you thirty dollars." Kyle pilfers through his wallet, pulls out a twenty. "How about this?"

"Okay, sir, that is plenty. I can take that, no problem." Kyle hands it over, and the officer stuffs it in his breast pocket.

"Have a good day, *Ssebo*." Kyle smiles as he rolls up his window.

"Oh yes, you too, sir," the man says, and waves us onward. I seethe in my seat, wait for the irritation to flow through me before I talk again.

"That sort of stuff makes me crazy," I say.

"I know it does," Kyle says graciously. He is unfazed in these situations, almost relaxed. It was one of the first things I noticed when I met him in Kosovo.

The remainder of our drive to Jinja is beautiful. Red soil gives birth to lush trees and fields of swaying crops, and as we cross the Nile, the sun dips, smears the sky in pinks and oranges. Women walk by balancing buckets on their heads, and they wear dresses in flamboyant floral patterns and skirts in vivid reds, greens, purples, corals. Produce stands dot the road's shoulders next to concrete houses painted in vivid turquoise and yellow. Several houses and storefronts are painted with a sponsored brand's logo; I see a home brought to us by Pampers and a local bank proudly presented by Mitsubishi. Uganda is a country of colors.

Smaller-town Jinja is more tranquil than the bedlam of Kampala, about a quarter of its size and considerably greener, grassier. Its economy is built on tourism because of the Nile, but it's also home to several nonprofits, and an acquaintance's organization, Sole Hope, is one of these. Their headquarters and guesthouse are down a suburban road, which will be our home for the next few days. We ring the bell at the gate, and someone buzzes us in. Kyle parks the van under an awning by the front door.

"Hello, sir. Hello, ma'am! Welcome!" says an elderly gentlemen as we open the van door.

Two younger men greet us and take our bags to our rooms, and the kids squeal at the sight of triple bunk beds. The house is open-air, old-world Mediterranean style with rooms dotted around a central courtyard.

Asher, the American woman who founded Sole Hope with Dru, her husband, gives us a tour of the house. "Here's the kitchen," she says, and we enter a small room where two local women are cooking.

"You're welcome to come in here anytime to make breakfast or lunch—feel free to use any of the groceries. But let these ladies do their magic for dinner. Except for Sundays, we all eat a family meal together."

"Hello, ma'am! Hello, sir. Hello, children," they say to us, smiling. The affable women return to their food and continue singing as they chop.

People come and go; cross breezes waft through open windows. Children wave at ours, then run freely through the front and back-yards. A man works from his laptop on a couch; a woman carries in a laundry basket and starts folding clothes at the dining table; a few twentysomethings chat on cushioned swinging settees in the court-yard. A young guy is asleep on a patio chair, book open on his chest. People seem as if they're home.

Dru finds us. "Hey, would you guys like a tour of the work?"

Their organization works to eradicate the relatively simple health problem of jiggers, a sand flea that burrows in rural dwellers' feet. Sterilized safety pins help dig fleas out of skin, and shoes made from old tires and jeans protect them afterward.

We're introduced to the local men who cut soles from discarded tires, the men and women who sew cuts of denim donated by North Americans and Europeans to make the tops of shoes. Machines whir; power tools clatter; voices laugh and chatter. We say hello, and their work stops for a minute so they can shake our hands, welcome us to Jinja, thank us for visiting. We meet the house handyman, and I notice he's wearing a T-shirt from an organization run by friends of ours in Iraq. A teenage boy is showing our kids the ramshackle wooden play structure in the front yard while two monkeys swing from trees above them. The house dog runs laps around the house, backyard to front. We're asked our impression of Uganda. We tell them we're in love.

Dinner is ready, and we come in for a communal dinner around the table. This house is headquarters for making thousands of shoes, but it's also a waiting room for parents in queue for Ugandan adoptions. Three families are here with their new children, waiting for their date when a judge will give them an official okay to head back to the States as the new parents of Ugandan babies. The young foreigners here are interns, college students spending a semester to learn, help, grow. We toast, break bread.

After dinner, our kids dig out board games in the living room. We sip tea with other adults in the courtyard and watch the pink sky fade to navy. We listen to stories about adoption and trips to the Ugandan countryside to remove jiggers from feet. We share our stories of travel mishaps and working from the road. We all talk about raising kids.

We're strangers, but this is community.

The next morning, the five of us take Joy and Dave's van to a Jinja neighborhood that sits on muddy banks, a slum along the Nile where people live in cobbled-together houses on muddy streets and work mostly as fishermen. We tumble through the marshy roads and roll down our windows. Pop music blares out of blown speakers, chickens scurry through boggy pothole-lakes as we pass, and vendors sell eggs on overturned milk crates. No one pays us notice. We are here at Dru's recommendation.

Kyle slows down by a young man. "Hello—I'm looking for Joel. Do you know him?"

The guy nods, points ahead. "He should be up over there, by the water. Would you like me to run ahead and tell him you're looking for him?"

"Well—sure, thanks," Kyle replies. The young man runs ahead while we finish plodding through the mud and find a spot to park.

A few minutes pass, and a man walks up to our window. He's in his midthirties, about our age, and wears a smartly pressed blue-and-white checked oxford shirt with red pants. His hems are rolled up to avoid mud.

"Hello. I am Joel," he says and shakes Kyle's hand. "I hear that you are looking for me?"

Kyle explains we are friends of Dru and that we've heard he gives the best tour of the Nile River in Jinja.

"Oh yes, of course! I do. Would you like one?" Joel asks. We nod eagerly.

"Let me get my boat ready. Five minutes. I will meet you down there, by the water." He points, then rushes off to make preparations.

We tiptoe around the chickens and head to the riverbank, where Joel is now waiting with life jackets. "Welcome to the Nile!" he says with grandeur. "I hope you enjoy your tour." His skipper, Nate, revs up the motor and we wobble into his low, narrow fishing boat with a plastic tarp canopy. Tate white-knuckles the sides while her brothers sway back and forth on purpose.

Official Nile tours cost a family our size about two hundred dollars, but Joel says he'll tell us everything he knows for forty. "I don't know anyone who knows the history and biology of the Nile more than Joel," Dru assured us before we left.

We scud along Nile waves in the ramshackle fishing boat while Joel points at different birds, gives us their names: white-breasted cormorant, little egret, great pelican, ibis. He knows the name and story of every bird that perches in passing riverbank trees. He knows why currents sway this way and that, and he knows why farmers with cleared fields along the river grow their particular crops in this particular time of year.

Tate asks, "What kind of tiny bird is that? Some sort of wood-pecker?"

"No, that's a giant kingfisher," Joel answers. The bird's black head and beak look oversized on top of his brown breast and spotted body. "They mostly eat crab, but they use their beaks to remove the cara-pace first. They like fish, too, and they eat them headfirst."

Nate slows the motor, and the boat quiets to a hum. We've stopped at a spot where water bubbles to the surface from below, where there's a convergence of ripples collecting at a bent metal sign, waving with the water flow. A group of East Asian men in suits have left their boat and are huddled together on a small grassy island next to the sign for a photo.

"Source of the Nile," Joel explains. "It's where Lake Victoria flows out and begins the Nile." Our boat skims to the sign. It reads:

THE SOURCE OF R. NILE

JINJA

WORLD'S LONGEST RIVER.[1]

While we wait our turn for a photo, I imagine this same water empty-ing in the Mediterranean, 4,258 miles north of us in Egypt.

Two hours later, Joel's boat returns us to shore sunburned, exhausted, and euphoric. "Thank you so much for taking your children to the Nile," Joel says to me, giving me a hand as I step out. "They ask good questions, and I am glad they're here to see it."

The next morning, the five of us drive back to Kampala to visit Dave's work, join Joy and the kids at their local pool, and let the kids romp one more time in their yard. I go to the nearby American embassy to refill more pages in my passport. Kyle drives to the airport to retrieve Reed's blanket, which has now enjoyed a side trip to Rwanda. We sit on our friends' wraparound porch and graze on avocados sprinkled with pepper and lemon juice. The kids beg for a sleepover with their new friends; Joy happily agrees and shoos the two of us out for a date.

Tonight, Kyle and I dine on pizza and wine on red-checkered tablecloths under mango trees. I do mental math and realize we'll be in Italy in less than two months, probably eating this same type of food under a different type of tree. We whisper to each other the languages spoken around us: *French. Mandarin. Some sort of Indian language, maybe Tamil. Swahili.* The restaurant's patrons are an assembly of united nations. Uganda has gathered quite the global crowd.

"I think I really love it here," Kyle says.

I nod. "Wait—the restaurant? Or Uganda?"

"Both. But I mean Uganda."

The next morning, the kids are thrilled to have had a sleepover with friends, a first on our travels. Joy returns us to the airport, and we hug farewell with our arms dusty red and our eyes wet, promising to stay in touch. We were barely in Uganda. I hardly opened my laptop. The pack on my back seems lighter as I walk down the airplane aisle; my shoulders feel stronger. The plane hasn't departed, and I already want to return here, continue my conversations with all the folks we met, meet even more people who call Uganda home. We touched the red dirt, but we didn't scratch the surface.

11

ETHIOPIA

Geographically, Ethiopia isn't far from Uganda, but the differences are palpable before we even leave the airport. It's much colder here; despite our proximity to the equator, we're far removed from the tropics because of the high elevation. Guidebooks say it's hotter in the southern part of the country, in the Great Rift Valley, but we'll be north for the duration of our short visit, from here in Addis Ababa and onward into the Highlands. We dig to the bottom of our packs for layers. Seven hundred miles northeast doesn't seem too far on the map, but just a few hours ago we were sweating in Kampala.

We check in to our hotel room and pray the heat works, take quick showers to warm up. They gave us a different room from the one we booked, but we are desperate for sleep, so Tate joins Kyle and me on the one king-size bed and the boys share the twin, feet to feet. In eight hours, just after sunrise, we'll meet our new driver and host, who'll take us into the Highlands, to an obscure village even he has never visited. Kyle pulls shut the blackout shades, turns off the light, and I burrow into the blankets. Sleep comes in two minutes, dreamless.

My alarm sings far too soon, and I drag my body into clothes, then wake the kids. Finn's mouth is hanging open and Reed is drooling, deep in slumber. The room is still freezing. We trawl our wasted bodies down to a hotel lobby breakfast of cold pastries, sugared cereal, and instant coffee, which seems a travesty here, origin of Yirgacheffe, one of the world's favorite coffee beans.

It's seven o'clock: time to meet our host for Ethiopia.

Atkeltsion is waiting out front with a local driver and his companion. "*Salam*, and welcome to Ethiopia," he says. "Ready to head out?" The driver grabs our bags and tosses them in the van.

Our host is in his late twenties and speaks English with a flawless American accent. We climb in a van that is the same size as Dave and Joy's, but with more rows of benches and considerably older; it reminds me of our van in Sri Lanka. Atkelt—as our host asks us to call him—has rented this entire van for the weekend; it normally functions as a taxi. The three narrow rows of passenger seats provide scarcely enough room for us to put our legs down. The three kids climb into the back row, and Kyle, who's over six foot two, claims the extra inches of legroom in the front. I'm left in the middle row with our pile of packs.

The van heads north out of Addis with windows open, and I breathe in the dryness of desert air. It is nosebleed dry here, and I'm already parched. The kids ask for water, and I realize we haven't yet bought any. Wind slaps dust from the road into our eyes, and I slide the van windows closed. We immediately start to sweat.

"Atkelt, can we stop and buy water sometime soon?" I ask.

"Oh sure, sure," he says. "Our first town is soon."

I hear a small voice behind me. "Mom?" Reed squeaks. "I'm gonna barf."

I turn around and his limp body sways; his white face drips with sweat. I scramble for a plastic bag, and I pass it back with seconds to spare. Reed vomits what little breakfast he has eaten. The driver tells Atkelt he knows of a place right up the hill, and in a minute pulls over to a natural spring on the side of the road. A pipe juts out of a rock at the base, a provisional public faucet dribbling spring water. Kyle jumps out and holds his hands under the pipe, then splashes cold water over Reed's head and shirt. They climb back in the van. Five minutes later, Finn pukes.

My mothering brain has been devoted these five months to basic tasks: feeding our children, advancing their education, timing the drying of their clothes before packing for the next destination. Even the hunting and gathering of food seems to consume hours of my day. Check in advance the altitude of our next destination? Determine the upcoming climate's effect on our need for plentiful water? Calculate our ability to procure water from the road? Consider whether these roads will prove so dusty that it makes schooling impossible? I don't have remaining brain cells for advanced preparation.

These are rookie traveler mistakes. Addis Ababa, our starting point, was already above seventy-five hundred feet in elevation. We're three hours into an eight-hour trek heading into mountains at a ten-thousand-foot-elevation, we're in a van with bad shocks and no air conditioning with the outdoors too dusty to open windows, the van is uproariously loud, and we have no drinking water. These narrow roads are sinuous, coiling into the sides of hills. We've been in the country twelve hours, most of which were spent sleeping, and we've had no time to get our act together.

We finally arrive in a small town, and Atkelt hops out at a convenience store to buy a case of bottled water. I clean up Finn's face, and we declare a sick day, ban the kids from their lessons on the iPad while we're driving. Tate huddles in the corner, avoiding her brothers' touch. I think of her regurgitative retching fiasco on the Beijing metro, now over five months ago. Four hours down in a suffocating van on serpentine roads, four to go.

We pull back onto the road. "Since we're sitting here, now is a good time for me to tell you a little bit about Ethiopia!" Atkelt shouts.

The van rattles upward, and the sound of its loose parts jiggling, wind smacking the windows, and potholed terrain is earsplitting.

"The first thing to know is that we're one of only two African countries that have never been colonized by a European power," he bellows. "The second is that we use a different calendar than the rest of the world. These two things alone will make Ethiopia feel like a completely different place from anywhere on earth."

Atkelt is married to an American, and his understanding of a Western worldview helped him land this job as a translator and guide for Americans who come to visit. Even though his family has firmly settled in Addis, they travel to the States every few years to visit his wife's family.

"Some say Italy colonized us during World War II, but it's just not true," Atkelt yells. "They occupied us here for a few years, but we kicked them out."

Ethiopia remains the oldest still-thriving civilization in Africa, and one of the oldest on earth. Addis has its fair share of strip malls, but a few miles out of town feels otherworldly. Outside the windows, grasslands are dotted with stick huts, elderly shepherds draped in rough brown cloth traipse through fields with walking sticks, and camels—so many camels. Camels are at every intersection, poking along the shoulders of the main road with their unwieldy, knobby-kneed gait. We are so close geographically to Uganda and Kenya, to the African Great Lakes landscape of wild animals in pastureland, but Ethiopia sits as a crown in the Horn of Africa, soaked in Middle Eastern sensibilities. Because of its history of not (or barely) being colonized, it has a culture of its own, its own geography, its own climate.

The Ethiopian calendar is connected to Orthodox Christian history: Ethiopia uses the Julian calendar instead of the more conventional Gregorian one. This year, 2015, is 2008 here, and the Ethiopian day begins at sunrise, whenever that is, not 12:01 a.m. The first hour is around our six or seven in the morning.

I ask Atkelt if this adds confusion in his family's life. He shrugs his shoulders. "Nah, not really. It's mostly confusing for the visitors." I wonder about specific opening and closing times of shops, how to know when your favorite show airs on TV, or when to arrive at the airport. There are no proper Western answers for these questions.

We're here in Ethiopia for one specific reason. Actually, a specific little boy. Our family began sponsoring a few children after I traveled to the Philippines to write on behalf of Compassion International, and Abubeker is one of these kids. We figured this trip was the best chance we'd have at meeting him together, as a family.

Atkelt has worked with Compassion for years as a translator and guide, but he's never been to Abubeker's microscopic village, where Compassion runs a children's center. There the village kids play after school, receive help with their homework, and find physical and spiritual nurturing. The center is a conduit through which sponsors can support local children, which ultimately results in supporting the child's entire family. It is his family we are making the effort to visit.

Eight bruising hours later, we stop for the night at a hotel still an hour away (Abubeker's village has no sleeping space for guests). There are three twin beds in our room for the five of us, and dinner in the hotel restaurant includes some sort of meat (chicken? goat?) and *injera*, Ethiopia's national sourdough bread made of teff flour. Its spongy texture is moist, and it is fermented, tart. I nibble at it politely. We're also slightly parched nutritionally from a lack of vegetables, since Atkelt has warned us not to eat any while we're in Ethiopia (he says it takes a while to acclimate to the natural bacteria found on produce, and we aren't going to be here long enough to bother). The next morning, we take cold showers in our rusty bathroom, eat cereal in the hotel restaurant, and hop back in the van.

In an hour, we pull up to the center. A crowd of children has gathered, holding signs and chanting a local welcome song. No sponsor has yet visited their village or center, so this entire community has come out and sees us not as Abubeker's visitors, but as theirs. Young boys in soccer jerseys and dress shirts, teenage girls in their best dresses of vibrant yellows, pinks, and greens, all chant in unison and wait for us to open the van door. I see him there, in the middle of the crowd—I recognize him from years of photos sent to us. A pint-sized Abubeker holds a sign as big as him, shy smile and big brown eyes. He is seven, Reed's age, yet he's the size of Finn, our four-year-old.

The five of us are pulled by assorted hands through the courtyard and into a side office, where local volunteers wait, ready to serve us a traditional Ethiopian coffee ceremony with popcorn, the favorite local snack. Children's photos are plastered on the concrete walls like wallpaper, with names, ages, and religions scribbled underneath. More than two hundred kids are part of this sponsor-driven community effort. I sip my coffee and visualize a map covered with thumbtacks scattered worldwide, pinned strings gathered at this village so small it doesn't make local maps—Australians, Europeans, South Americans, North Americans, Asians, fellow Africans, all giving so that families in this little village have more to help their kids thrive. The concept is not foreign to me, but it blows my mind standing here. How many roads converge here?

"This center supplements food staples so families have enough food. Women also learn trades here so they can sell goods," the center director explains as we munch popcorn. "We've got a fantastic algebra teacher in town, so he holds weekly math tutoring here. We're growing quite a lot of math scholars." The staff members laugh at this inside joke.

Tate, Reed, and Finn are summoned to play schoolyard games outside, so we swallow the last of our coffee and head outside. Abubeker plays on the swing set with Finn as if it's after school and they're having a play date. Reed plays duck-duck-goose with other boys, and Tate is surrounded by girls touching her hair and giggling at the sight of it. The English-Amharic barrier is unpassable, but everyone laughs, shouts, plays.

We say good-bye to the crowd of children, leave the community center, and give Abubeker a ride to his house. He sits next to Finn, and I admonish them both to stay seated, to stop horseplaying with each other in a moving vehicle. If there were seat belts, I'd tell them to buckle up. These boys are so much alike.

On the way to Abubeker's house, we stop at a grain warehouse to buy his family a gunnysack of teff, the crop from which injera is made. A sixty-dollar sack will provide Abubeker's family of six enough food for three months. Kyle hops out and negotiates the sale with Atkelt as translator, as camels and droves of local men circle around to oversee the process. Four men heave the sack into the back of the vehicle, and the van lowers by two inches with a thud. Our van's tires bump to his house as seven-year-old Abubeker navigates us to his nameless street.

His four older siblings, two brothers and two sisters, are waiting at the front gate of their shared compound, ready to welcome us with kisses on both cheeks. They lead the way through the dusty courtyard to their two-room home, cramped between several homes identical in size. Abubeker is the youngest in his family by quite a bit; his brothers and sisters seem to be teenagers at least.

Atkelt speaks with the two older brothers, then explains. "They could have chosen to leave home to make their way on their own by now, but they've chosen to stay back for their mother's sake." Their dad is nowhere to be found. Having birthed her first when she was fifteen, Abubeker's mother, Tigist, is remarkably young for having a twenty-year-old. She's younger than I, in fact.

Tigist and I smile at each other as Atkelt prods Abubeker to introduce us. I'm at a loss for words. I shake her hand, then hug her. I marvel at how she wakes up daily wondering whether her five children will eat, and I fret over whether my kids log enough reading time.

The family killed the fatted calf, so to speak, to celebrate our arrival. We sit on covered cushions and faded blankets on the dirt floor in one of their rooms, and a daughter walks around to each of us, pours a pitcher of water over our hands with a bucket below to catch the overflow. It's a ritual I did a thousand times in Kosovo, some twenty-six hundred miles north of here. Another daughter brings out a large round platter and places it in the center, piled high with chicken, various purees of yellow and orange, chili-red sauces, and a sunburst of rolled injera around the edge.

"Abu, show your guests how we show respect for elders in Ethiopia," Atkelt suggests. Abubeker pulls off a piece of injera, dips it in the red sauce, walks over to the other side to feed his mother. He kisses her on the cheek, and his siblings applaud.

We're invited to feast on more injera, made by Tigist and her daughters, and it is infinitely better than the hostel restaurant's. After lunch, we're served more coffee and more popcorn. I'm stuffed.

Kyle nudges Reed and Finn, and they pull out gifts from Australia. Abubeker has never before seen Play-Doh or Matchbox cars, and he's never had crayons or a coloring book of his own. His eyes sparkle with magic and he shouts with glee, happier than Christmas morning. He giggles with delight at the squishy feel of Play-Doh, and the whole family oohs over its Technicolor shade of green.

Afterward, Reed and Finn run outside with Abubeker to play soccer. Tigist shows the rest of us her home, including the communal kitchen across the courtyard, a cavernous hut about twenty feet away that is shared by the other nearby households. A fire pit sits in the center of the stick-built room, and a few bowls, a pot, and some spoons are stacked in shadowy corners. Everything is tidy and ready for the kitchen's next user. I spot a hole in the ground in one of the corners, with a small, twig-made stool fastened over the opening.

"What's that?" I ask.

Atkelt translates my question and Tigist blushes, then squats on the stool to pantomime its purpose. She lifts up her skirt to just below her knees, and I understand. This is a birthing stool. Incense burns at the bottom of the hole following a birth, she says, to purify the air and to waft a welcoming scent as new life is brought into the world. The new mother would remain on the stool the rest of the day, clean her body and get a few hours' rest before the work of mothering begins. I stand speechless, in awe.

A few minutes later, and it's time to leave. Tigist and I hug, and I whisper in her ear, "I will pray for you." I don't know what else to say. I'm exhausted and elated.

Kyle lifts up Abubeker and the five of us hug him; we tell him we love him and his family, and to obey his big brothers and sisters, to keep loving on his mother. We thank his siblings for the food and the afternoon, and for letting us be a tiny part of their family life, their community.

We drive back to the hotel, an hour away, and sleep soundly before waking early the next morning for another arduous, eight-hour drive back to Addis Ababa. We remember to bring plenty of water. The kids drift in and out of sleep. Kyle and Atkelt chat politics, science, movies. I scroll my phone and find an audiobook on Abraham Lincoln I never finished. I plug in my earbuds, slip on my eye mask, and stretch out over our pile of bags. He runs for senator against Stephen Douglas as I watch camels scroll past my window.

Tonight in Addis Ababa, before we wake for an early flight to Johannesburg, I don't mind sharing a bed with two other people in the freezing hotel.

12

ZIMBABWE

There's a bridge over Victoria Falls that connects Zambia to Zimbabwe, the two countries that share a border with the largest curtain of free-fall water in the world. The bridge's original purpose was to attract tourists—to transport them across the bridge via train, specifically—but it's now home to a 111-meter bungee jump. Tourists come visit from around the world to zip line by the falls, or take a sundowner (hiring a boat and skipper to cruise the Zambezi River at sunset), or white-water raft the rapids. I don't think all this is what David Livingstone originally imagined back in 1855 when he named Victoria Falls after the reigning British monarch.

The only real purpose behind the town of Victoria Falls is to serve as the gateway to the famous natural landmark, and as such, it is the epitome of a tourist town. Clive, our guesthouse host, picks us up at an airport so small, there are no Jetways, gates, or even baggage carousels. It's a large one-room house with a counter for checking in and a pub while you wait. It feels like a café with an adjoining parking lot for airplanes.

"Welcome to Zimbabwe!" Clive says cheerfully as we climb into his SUV. He wears khaki shorts and a khaki button-down short-sleeved shirt, khaki socks, and khaki hiking boots. "Here—have some champagne." He passes back two stemmed glasses and offers the kids grape juice. Outdoor a capella singers in native garb welcome tourists at the parking lot exit. It's hard to believe we were in Abubeker's village two days ago.

Clive grew up as a farmer's son in Zimbabwe, but he turned his vocation to tourism when his father had to sell the family farm. "Once Robert Mugabe came to power, the Zimbabwean dollar became more valuable as kindling for the fire than for actual currency," he explains. The country currently uses the US dollar, and Clive uses his own thatched-roof home as a house for tourists when they come to Victoria Falls. He makes a profitable living doing so.

Initially, we hesitated making the effort to come here. It's appallingly expensive to get here, for one, and it's not cheap once you're on the ground, either. Only a few airlines fly here, and they all come via Johannesburg, South Africa, which is, for us, an incredible distance from where we already were in East Africa. Going to the falls for the weekend from Ethiopia is like going from Washington, DC, to Caracas, Venezuela, for a little three-day foray.

But we have no idea if we'll be back on the continent with our children; so we booked a flight and guesthouse. We can only be here four days. It's all we can afford.

Clive's house is Colonial-style Africa: thatched roof, wood beams, plastered walls, a bank of windows facing the backyard. Sleeping porches dot the upstairs veranda, and every room has ceiling fans. This is the largest kitchen in all the guesthouses we've had, and it includes a dining table for eight. The living room has one wall of books, the other wall a collection of local wines and coffee, free for us to sample. I already mourn our fleeting three-night stay.

We meander out to the backyard. "Hear that?" asks Clive. "That's the falls. When the birds aren't chirping, you can hear them from here. During the wet season, it's so loud it rattles the windows."

It's a faint white noise; I barely noticed it until Clive pointed it out. But now, I can't ignore it. It's hard to fathom we're this close to another one of the world's natural wonders.

We have no time to waste, so Clive drives us to the falls the next morning. At the entrance to the Mosi-oa-Tunya National Park, a rhythmic song of continual rain reverberates as background music. Water mists our cheeks and shoulders, and the temperature is ten degrees cooler than at Clive's house three miles away. We walk through the entrance, past the stands where waterproof ponchos are sold, and head downward to the trail.

The air radiates a cool, damp humidity and our legs are freckled with water; we tread gingerly to avoid slick puddles and sloping slants. The water pounds louder with every inch closer we step; it mimics a ba-*bump,* ba-*bump* heartbeat as the Zambezi River pulses over the edge, 355 feet down to the basin. We still can't see it yet, but its rhythmic call is deafening.

Here I am, seeing Victoria Falls for the first time.

It begins as a simple mist in the air, like a stroll on a rain-drizzling day. But I look up, and there's not a cloud in the sky. The sun penetrates its heat and light through baobab leaves, but it's still sprinkling. If I were wearing glasses, like Tate is right now, I'd continually have to wipe off my lenses, fruitlessly, until they were finally pocketed as useless. Everyone remarks on the non sequitur of cloudless sky with the thundering boom, growing louder and louder as we wind down the slick walkway, closer. Then, a bend in the path, and I see them—the falls.

There's nothing quite like standing on a part of the earth that feels like the edge of it. A gash in the planet's skin has created an outpouring of water so big that it's impossible to see when it lands—a swirling mix of clouds and fog, spray and foam. Kids scream with delight at the sight of it and the up-pour of water now in their hair and skin. I keep walking, gingerly. Parts of the path have guardrails, set back just enough to observe only the top of the falls, but there are many more parts of the path without a barrier. I inch slowly, slowly across the slippery stones and grip my offsprings' hands as though their lives depend on it (because they do).

And so I am witness to the top of the falls, where the Zambezi performs its downward kamikaze into a boiling pot, the name given to the foreign pool at its base, still so difficult to reach that researchers disagree on its true depth.

The deeper I move toward the falls, the wetter I become, until I'm finally at the meat of it all, its widespread body open for witness, and I'm wholly doused. I wring out the hem of my shirt, though it's pointless.

Kyle turns, says, "I'm gonna run back to the entrance and buy some ponchos." They're of no use by now, but without them we feel like unseasoned travelers. The kids laugh at the hilarity of looking as if we all jumped in a pool fully dressed. I cover myself with cheap yellow plastic and don't look any less ridiculous.

The late Lord Curzon of Kedleston, viceroy of India at the turn of the twentieth century, once said about the falls, "Such is the density and fury of the spray-storm rising into the air like the smoke of some vast cauldron, that the spectator within 100 yards of the cataract can see nothing at all, and gets little beyond a drenching for his pains."[1]

Our pains are happily drenched.

We keep walking the path around the falls and discover a white, gleaming statue of David Livingstone, a monument to his "discovery" of the falls. Locals had already named the falls *Mosi-oa-Tunya*— "The Smoke Which Thunders"—generations before, but the British explorer romanticized the notion of exploring deepest, darkest Africa and finding a suitable route from west to east. Bumping into the falls was his happy accident. The Zambian town on the other side of the falls is named Livingstone, and the original 1904 Victoria Falls Hotel on the Zimbabwe side pays homage to his imperial Victorian British era. Livingstone wasn't exactly a savior to the land. He loved it—or so they say—but he brought with him disease and a prejudiced perspective of God-ordained domination. Nonetheless, he is revered around here, at least by the booming tourist industry.

Clive spoke of the falls this morning as if we would soon behold his religion. "There is something magical about them; I can't explain it," he said. "It's the sound, the feel of the air, the sheer size of the falls compared to your body. I go there to meditate. I sit at one of the benches for hours at a time, just to think."

Victoria Falls was fashioned over time, after millennia of erosion smoothed away stones and the earth shook forth its gashes. God carved out of the earth yet another home for magnificence, a hidden repository. It's just water falling, but Victoria Falls is *the* waterfall. It is the ultimate drink of the earth, kowtowing in obedience to the curvature of dirt and rock.

Travel writers and explorers have long bemoaned difficulty in adequately describing Victoria Falls. Most toss in the towel, declaring with poetic license, "You just have to see them to really understand." Words fail. Guidebooks move on after a paragraph's description to list best nearby hotels to stay at and restaurants to try. Who am I to think I could do better? Tonight in my journal, sitting on the back porch of Clive's thatched-roof home, listening to children snore upstairs in open-air rooms, I find myself able to do little else.

During my sessions with Nora in Chiang Mai, I discovered a dependence on poetry. I knew its antidotal powers in my real life, when work via the Internet and hours staring at a screen required a forced clean break to something utterly different. I kept a book of poetry on my nightstand back home and would read a few pages every night before bed. I didn't think there'd be much of a need on the road, however, and as I sit here in Clive's backyard, having seen another of the seven natural wonders of the world this morning, I wonder why on earth I made such an assumption. Perhaps I thought our entire trip would be poetry in itself, that all the sights and smells and sounds would be enough beauty. Reading and writing poetry might break me.

Turns out, poetry is becoming a lifeline on the road. I need to read it, and I need to write it. Reading it reminds me I'm not alone in my witness of the indescribable, the unprocessable; writing it forces me to slow down, to grasp what I'm really gathering on this journey. That lamentation I wrote at the monastery was ointment for an open wound. Reading and writing poetry afterward have been bandages. They're protecting my soul from deeper infection as I heal.

I scribble in my journal a terrible, ramshackle poem about the falls, but at least it gives substance to my being here. I close the journal, pad into the kitchen, and brew some rooibos tea I find in a drawer, then wander into the living room as I wait for it to steep. I peruse the dusty collection of books on the shelves and pull out a book of poetry, wipe off its spine, and settle back outside with my cup of tea. A trumpeter hornbill flies overhead, greets the purple evening sky. I sip my tea.

I flip through pages and read a poem about the falls by a Scottish poet named Muriel Spark, published in 1948. In it, she writes that the sound of the falls begins as the hint of a sigh; then, "the cry becomes a shout, the shout a thunder."

That's it, I think. That's the sound of Victoria Falls, the drainage of water over rock into earth's deep. They frame the resonance of the falls and do an adequate job at the impossible. But these words—the sigh, to a shout, to a thunder—that's also my insides right now. We left to travel the world without a home, so we're walking the earth's paths without a safety net. In China, this was a sigh. I didn't know where to call home, but I knew it wasn't there. In Australia, currents gained speed, and my murmurs were cries; it felt good there, and I remembered that even *this*—the hum of that refrigerator, the chores of backyard chickens—this wasn't really mine, either. It was familiar, yet unfamiliar. It felt like home, but it wasn't.

And now, Africa. Africa is a cry that's become a thunderous shout. Here, people commune with the land and with their neighbors. Isaiah, Joy's gardener in Uganda and their next-door neighbor, is her sons' kindred spirit, their older brother; he watches over the kids as much as the flowers and grass in his custody. Joel considers it his honor to invite foreigners into the family of the Nile, to escort them up her glorious channels in his fishing boat. Abubeker's siblings raise their little brother and watch after their mother; they invite us into their family for the day. Clive cherishes his beloved Victoria Falls, makes his home available so we can experience them. Africa is a community of strangers, but they extend hospitality like a family of humanity. Perhaps we will leave here more than just acquaintances of the continent.

The next morning, we pack up to leave. Our flight isn't until the afternoon, and Clive invites us to stay as long as we need. I assign schoolwork for the kids, and I sit with them on the back porch and work while they work on their math and writing. Kyle sips a beer out front with Clive, who's waiting for a friend to arrive.

"When he comes, he'll have papers for me to sign. He's selling me a house. Would you be willing to sign as our witness?"

"Sure," Kyle says.

A few minutes later, Kyle signs official Zimbabwean documents as a third-party witness to a real estate transaction. Then they set aside the papers, and the three of them sit for several hours, sipping beer and discussing the merits of Buddha, Muhammad, and Jesus until it's time for Clive to drive us to that café-pub with airplanes parked next door.

13

KENYA

Frugality is our mission in Nairobi, since we'll only be here one night. We just left Zimbabwe and are spending another small fortune and a sizable chunk of our travel budget here in Kenya, so the cheaper our quick, overnight stay in the capital, the better. Nairobi's traffic is notoriously bad, so staying close to the airport to minimize our commute is also ideal. Pamela's house is perfect.

We don't know her yet, but Pamela listed her house on a booking website, and it's barely big enough for all of us while still cheap. John is our driver, a colossal man with a jovial belly laugh. He's picked us up from the airport and has immediately won the kids' affections by laughing at their terrible jokes.

"What's brown and sticky?" Reed asks him while we wait for Kyle to run back in the airport to search for, to no avail this time, Tate's hat from the Johannesburg airport she's just left on the plane.

"What?" John replies, squinting into the noon sun and searching for Kyle outside the airport.

"A stick," Reed answers.

"I don't—oh. Ha! That's funny. Yes, that's a good one!" John says. He laughs for ten seconds, a high-pitched snicker the antithesis of his gargantuan frame. I instantly love anyone who appreciates my children's quirks.

Kyle returns and shakes his head, ruffles Tate's hair and tells her she'll find another hat somewhere. We climb into John's vehicle. It's another safari van, but this time it actually makes sense.

We pass through Pamela's neighborhood security gates, and John remarks, "I've never been in this neighborhood before. In fact, I don't think I knew it existed."

This is because his typical clientele, whom he customarily transports from the airport to a five-star hotel and then on to their destination, probably travel on a slightly higher budget than we do. He turns off the ignition and hops out to help bring our bags inside.

"Hello! Welcome to Nairobi!" Pamela waves and smiles, runs gaily out her front door as though she knows us.

"How was your flight?" She shakes all our hands, including John's. "Come in, come in. Hello, children!" she exclaims in a delightful singsong Kenyan cadence, hugging each of them.

We walk into her home, and Pamela explains that she is an event planner, and as such, likes to make sure all details are just so.

"Please, use all the food in my fridge," she says, showing us a kitchen smaller than my bedroom closet in Oregon. "I just bought eggs and yogurt, and there is pasta over here in the cabinet." She leads us to the bathroom and shows us how to finagle the quirky turn of the shower nozzle and where she keeps travel-sized soaps for guests.

"Where are you staying tonight?" I ask her, now that I realize we're staying in her actual home and not a second guesthouse.

"Oh, my mother lives a block away," she says. "I just crash at her house whenever I have a guest here. It's okay, actually, because I have a wedding to run tomorrow and have to wake up early." She pours us cups of tea and asks us to sit, asks questions about the details of our travels thus far, where's been our favorite place and what's been surprising. She asks about our plans for tomorrow.

"Oh, you will love the Maasai Mara!" she exclaims, clapping her hands. "I used to go there on family vacations every year when I was a child. Lovely memories." I already wish we could take her with us.

She stands up, gathers her keys and sunglasses. "I want to hear all about it when you come back! I'll see you soon, okay?" Pamela says good-bye, walks out the front door and down the concrete path in her yard, then turns left to walk to her mother's house. There's no dining room table in her diminutive cottage, so we eat pasta for dinner on the hallway floor. The kids find this a special treat and ask if we can do this all the time.

Our flight itinerary the past few days has been excruciating: from Victoria Falls, we flew to Johannesburg, then waited two days for our flight to Nairobi by way of Dubai. We've been moving for seventeen hours, and yet John insists on an early departure the next morning, since the drive is long and it'll get hot. Early the next morning, we push through exhaustion and load our bags into John's van, ready for another lengthy, jerky ride in another rickety van.

John makes his living guiding tourists on safari through the Maasai Mara National Reserve, a dedicated space in Kenya where wildlife roam free. It's where Karen von Blixen-Finecke, also known as Isak Dinesen, set her memoir, *Out of Africa*, about her life on her beloved Kenyan coffee plantation from 1913 to 1931. It's where Kenya makes the bulk of its tourism revenue. It's not cheap to go on safari here, which is why John is unaccustomed to taking visitors to one of Nairobi's sketchy neighborhoods parked on the flight path. We've been given a sizable discount because a friend of ours in Oregon, a former resident of Kenya, works for a socially responsible safari company, and they've invited us to see their work.

John drives through Nairobi traffic and tells us about his childhood in the city, how he and his wife and kids recently moved to its outskirts to be closer to his mom, who is in poor health. "I spend half my time guiding safaris, and half my time feeding my mother," he jokes.

We push our way through traffic and out of town, and begin our zigzag through the Kenyan countryside. John tells us most of his clients miss this drive. "They prefer to fly a private jet to the Mara, so I drive this by myself, then meet them there," he explains.

An hour into the drive, he pulls over to a wide shoulder with a scenic overlook and a restaurant teetering on the edge of a cliff, held in place by support beams.

"This is the Great Rift Valley," John says as we gaze over the edge at an immense vista of rolling hills around flat plains in shades of umber and sepia. "And there is where we'll be going today." He points to a spot far in the distance, past hazy skyline and the burnt sienna valley. "And notice that satellite dish, right there in the middle," he says, pointing next to a small white dot in the center of the vast land-scape. "When we get there, we'll be halfway to the Mara."

John leads us to the restaurant and introduces us to staff behind the counter. We order a quick breakfast of scrambled eggs served on stainless steel plates and chase it with a slurp of British tea in plas-tic cups. For three more hours the drive remains fairly blithe and breezy, and as we pass the satellite dish, a giant white man-made dome interrupting the bushland topography, I give thanks that this ride is smoother than Ethiopia's.

The van turns left, and here it is: a long, craggy, interminable road with no end in sight. John veers sharply to the far right of the road to avoid a pothole he's memorized, then yells at us through the cacoph-ony of cheery kid chatter, "Roll up your windows or you'll eat dust!"

Thus ends the breeze and thus begins the second leg of our drive, a two-hour traverse so shaky I pop a part of my back that's been stiff for two weeks. Even with the windows rolled up, for the next two hours I continually flush out my eyes with drops and brush off dust collected on my pants. Ethiopia coached us to stare straight ahead to avoid carsickness. John drives and drives, flying through and skidding over washboard gravel for two hours, and then, finally, a sign: Masaai Mara National Reserve. A baboon sits on top of the sign, picking at his fingernails, ignoring us.

We turn right, drive twenty more minutes, then reach our safari camp and tumble out of the van, sweaty, disoriented, and caked with layers of dirt. We are in the epitome of the middle of nowhere. This camp is parked in the middle of the East African savanna, a manufactured conglomeration of tents and gathering spots with little more than hippos and acacia trees as neighbors. Camp staffers unload our van and bring our bags to a covered check-in desk, and I wonder, *Where do these people live? Here?* We are miles from anything manmade beyond this camp, several hours' drive from any sensible living quarters. And yet, as a woman on staff explains to us after handing out water bottles and wet washcloths, they manage to bring in several hours of Wi-Fi a day, they generate their own electricity, and there will be three catered meals per day. There is a pool. I can't imagine how they've carted in the water for it. I silently speculate how much this place costs regular visitors who don't benefit from our discount.

The camp has several tented hotel rooms scattered on the property, each with a balcony overlooking the Mara River. Two young men on staff show us our room, and I squint my eyes to imagine Karen Blixen here on safari with her Swedish husband, Bror, only without our benefit of electricity and running water. Canvas walls roll up on all four sides and flowing mosquito nets smother four-poster mahogany beds.

After dinner down at the dining hall, I muster enough strength to take a shower before crawling into bed. I'm shaking with fatigue. I slide between the sheets, and I discover old-school toasty hot water bottles gurgling at my feet. "If you open the walls at night, you'll hear hippos playing while you sleep," a luggage carrier shared earlier. All night, hippos grumble outside our balcony while we sleep in the dark, dreamless. I wake up shivering in cold morning air, looking through the bed's mosquito netting at our canvas walls and dark wood floors. After weeks of sleeping on ten uncomfortable beds in Africa alone, in one night I feel as if I've caught up on sleep last seen in Australia. This is heaven.

Last night we told John we preferred to sleep in this morning, even though we'd miss key animal-sighting opportunities, so we arrive at the dining hall for breakfast minutes before closing. Everyone else has already gone out to the savanna. We gulp coffee, devour eggs and sausage, and run out to John's van waiting for us. He laughs at our tardiness.

His safari van is officially locked and loaded for its intended purpose: the roof is buttressed up like a convertible van with shade covering. This means there's room to stand on our seats, our heads popped out the top like meerkats with cameras around their necks. John drives us away from the camp and heads into grassland, tracing wheel ruts left by thousands of other off-road vehicles. Safari hat provided by John strapped firmly under my chin, coffee-colored linen pants procured from Sydney, I have officially channeled my inner Meryl Streep.

Kenyan safari guides, like John, aren't locals who've slapped a logo on their vans and recruited naive tourists out to the wilderness; they're licensed by the government, navigators who have taken classes on flora and fauna and can answer any wildlife-related question lobbed their way. As he drives, the kids pepper John with questions, their expert on call about why hyenas prefer to lie in puddles on the path, why elderly elephants go rogue, why hippos are the most dangerous animal in Africa. John knows the answer to everything.

We come to a herd of zebras and Reed asks him, "How can you tell the difference between the boys and the girls?"

"Well . . ." John hesitates, looks at me. I smile. "Well, you just can."

"But how?" Reed insists.

"They have different parts."

"Like male and female humans?" he asks in boyish soprano.

"Yes," John says, sighing. "Just like humans."

"Hmm . . . weird," Reed says. "It doesn't look like it. They just look like plain zebras to me." He zooms in his camera lens and John howls with laughter.

John weaves seamlessly through the savanna as he talks, having memorized these obscure bush paths over years of work. He knows where to find a herd of topi, silently munching on a grass lunch. He knows of an elephant family that likes to hang around a particular cluster of trees, and drives us twenty feet from a mother and her newborn before she rustles her ears, huffs through her trunk, and tromps toward us. John shifts in reverse and spins the wheels before we zoom away backward, our guide laughing. Nearby, giraffes mimic trees, indifferent and moving only leaf-chewing jaws. A herd of warthogs traipses by our van, en route to their next feeding. Crocodiles loiter open-eyed along the waterfront, behemoth in size and still as statues. Hippos splash in a slough of water. And after miles of searching, John finds us a pride of lions, sleeping underneath a tree, ten feet from our tires and indifferent to our presence.

None of the animals pretend to give us notice, in fact. We are human observers of our own nature documentary.

"Can we get out and take a family photo?" Kyle asks.

"Afraid not, no," John says. "Kenyan law says no one but a licensed safari guide can exit a vehicle on the Mara."

We head back to Nairobi tomorrow morning, and we want to surprise Tate, who will turn ten. Her birthday—the day we'll do nothing but drive in dust for five hours. When we arrived at the camp, I asked the front desk woman if it were possible to order a small birthday cake as our dessert. Tonight over dinner, I still haven't gotten word from the safari camp, and I wonder if they've forgotten. It's after eight o'clock in the evening, and Finn is sound asleep, drooling facedown on the table. We've finished our meal in the communal dining room, and we're desperate to head back to our room and crawl into bed.

I hear a faint beat of drums, and in the distance I see a faint glow of torches perforating inky night sky.

The sound grows louder and the light bounces closer, taking a few steps forward then reversing backward, then side to side, then another step forward. These drums and torches are dancing. I hear a murmur of rhythmic voices. As the fire glows brighter, so does the volume of drums and voices, locals chanting a song in cadence with bobbing torches.

"What's going on?" Tate asks.

"It sounds like a battle's about to start," Reed observes. "Or maybe a concert."

Closer and closer, a mob of singers heads into our open-air dining room, led by a man in a white chef's hat wielding a chocolate cake in one hand and machete in the other. Guests at the other tables around us whip out their phones and start recording. They're heading straight to us.

Tate's face beams scarlet and she glares at me, mortified, with eyes big as saucers. The song ends, and the mob promptly begins a new one, another Swahili incantation. Two minutes pass of chanting and bobbing around our table, swaying with flame-lit torches and drumbeats. Finn hasn't moved, and drool has collected on the table under his lips. He snores.

The chef places a chocolate cake in front of Tate, and I notice it's sized for a full-scale birthday party. A woman lights ten candles with her torch, and the serenaders croon, "Happy birthday to you, happy birthday to you, happy birthday dear *Tah*-toom, happy birthday to you!" Tate blows out her candles and the surrounding audience bursts into applause. The chef hands her a machete half her size, and she carves the first slice, then hands the knife to Kyle to finish. Finn is immobile, drool now dripping to the floor.

We pass out cake slices to the surrounding diners and staff, eat our own share, and save an extra slice for Finn. Earlier this morning around four o'clock, Kyle had woken up Tate for a sunrise hot-air balloon ride and father-daughter breakfast on the Mara. Tonight, she is serenaded with torches, dancing, a cake, and song. I tell her that for my tenth birthday, I visited my dad's office in downtown Austin and his secretary gave me a blank legal pad of my very own. And for her eleventh birthday, we will probably order pizza and watch a movie on Netflix.

It's early the next morning, and we've left heaven and are driving back to Nairobi with John. When we pull into town, at sunset, he joins us for dinner at a roadside diner, drops us off at Pamela's for one final night, then heads home to care for his mother. We have another flight tomorrow.

I wake up in the middle of the night in Pamela's bed, disoriented and overwhelmed with sensory overload. Her next-door neighbor's sewers have flooded her yard, and the stench is so foul, it's as if we're wading in Nairobi's sewage pipes. Kyle opens the front door and finds the yard impenetrable, with all but a few inches of Pamela's walkway floating with raw sewage. We try, impossibly, to go back to sleep.

Pamela calls the house in the morning: "I am so, so very sorry. Please let me refund you your money." We insist against it, and leave a small tip on the kitchen counter as an assurance, and as an offering for what chores must inevitably be on her horizon.

John arrives early this morning, and he and Kyle gingerly carry our luggage over their heads to his van, one piece at a time. Tate,

Reed, and Finn each take turns aboard Kyle's back, and I pray none of their shoes touch ground—I imagine the putrid smell on their soles lingering on our long-haul flight up to the top of the continent. I tiptoe across Pamela's walkway, balancing between the few dry spots left, and pray for mercy for both me and her.

Several hours later, during our layover in Dubai, I receive a text message from the housing service we used to book Pamela's place, letting me know we've received a refund of thirty-five dollars, the cost of one night's stay at Pamela's house. A few minutes later, I get a text from Pamela herself: "In case you are wondering, I moved to a new house today. I'm settling in well already, and tomorrow I think I'll paint the walls purple. It was nice to meet you!"

14

MOROCCO

Casablanca is bone-chilling. From the feel of the moisture of the train cabin's window, so is Fez. Our friends told us we might want to rethink our original plans of staying in a tent in the Sahara Desert this time of year; they said it'd be so cold we'd scarcely leave the tent. February in the desert is no joke, especially with thin windbreakers and no hats, gloves, or wool socks. We skipped the Sahara idea, and are now heading onward to our friends' house in central Morocco after our flight into its largest city.

After an eighteen-hour serpentine flight to Morocco from Kenya via Dubai, our old friend Nick looks like a wavering mirage in the desert at the Fez train station tonight. He's wearing a thick wool coat and winter hat, and we stand shivering in our paltry jackets. Nick graciously lets us sit in silence while he expertly drives us home through the city's shadowy streets; then we walk through the door and in sleepy stupor, I hug Erin, another old friend. The five of us collapse in their beds, barely knowing where we are and quivering with chilled limbs and fatigue. I slide on my two pairs of socks under pajama pants. Normally I detest wearing socks to bed, but desperation has trumped the luxury of bare feet against sheets. It's midnight, and we've been traveling for twenty-two hours.

I close my eyes, and one minute later, it's the next morning. I wake to the smell of coffee and home, and sure enough, I pad sleepily downstairs and there's my friend Erin, slicing fruit for her young boys and waiting on a French press. I haven't seen her in the flesh in almost a decade. During these six months of travel, we've either known absolutely no one or been with friends we've made only in the past few years—even when we're graced with companionship on the road, there are far more days when it's been just the five of us. Now I am standing in the kitchen of one of my bridesmaids. We've known each other since high school, and Nick is an old friend of my brother's. The four of us have all known one another since before we were married. I hug her again, much longer this time.

Nick and Erin now live in Morocco, and because we lived in Turkey before they moved, our paths haven't crossed in a long time. They are a sight for sore eyes. They are part of our soil.

We've wanted to visit Morocco for years, but this morning we're infected with a bad case of travel weariness. My muscles ache, my brain feels as if it's running on autopilot, and the boys wake up happy to be in a regular house with childhood rooms and toys. Erin is a professional cookie decorator and she knows how to knit; Tate has wanted to learn how to do both. Kyle wants to just sit. It's cold outside, coffee is ready, and Nick has started a fire. We're in Morocco, but we could be anywhere.

We stay here in their house. All day.

We want to explore Fez, but we want to see old friends more, and so today we do what old friends do: we drink coffee, we drink gin and tonics, we order pizza, we watch questionably downloaded American television, we bake cookies, and we talk. We talk future plans and cultural frustrations, mutual friends and their whereabouts, work glories and woes, and of course, kids. We catch up on life from the past few years. We talk about Texas, how we're all from there, and how it no longer feels like home.

Tonight, sleep comes like a tsunami. I wake the next morning in the same position that I drifted off to dreamless sleep, and I head back downstairs.

"Good morning! Ready to see Fez?" asks Erin.

I feel much more like myself after a day of lounging and another night of sleep, and for some reason, I woke up this morning hyper-aware that in three months, we will be back in the United States. Heck yes, I want to see Morocco with old friends. I want to wander the old streets of Fez.

The Medina of Fez is yet another UNESCO World Heritage Site and was first built in the ninth century by refugees fleeing current Spain. Today the area has a population of more than 150,000 permanent residents, is home to the world's oldest university, and is the largest car-free urban area on the planet. It is fortified by a five-mile diameter of thick walls that were originally built to withstand attacks, but now they serve as a border between ancient and modern.

We follow Nick and Erin through the medina's blue-tiled entrance, an archway through the fortified sandstone walls pricked with tiny holes, like shortbread. White satellite dishes dot the tops of the ancient buildings beyond, and Arabic chatter murmurs in the background. Medina simply means *city*, and this was, literally, the city of Fez a thousand years ago. Men stand and chat outside their connected stores, showcasing piles of spices in burlap bags and displays of plastic toys in cellophane bags. A vendor sells a mound of conch shells from a moving cart; he yells his price as he passes by.

"Snails," Nick explains.

We keep walking, and vibrant oranges and limes line the walls, waiting in stacked crates to be sold. A butcher displays skinned lamb carcasses hanging in his window. Young men doze on piles of rugs, and an old man chips away stone with a chisel, carving something written in Arabic. Smells waft around us, swirling through the air: cigarette smoke, roasting chestnuts, piles of paprika, raw fish. Upstairs, old women hang laundry, stretched across to their neighbors' windowsill, while children ride plastic tricycles around potted plants on balconies. Travel writer Nigel Tisdall called this medina in Fez "the original live/ work neighborhood."[1]

We maze through narrow streets, turning right, left, right again, each one the same dusty caramel color and packed with shops and cafés.

"Do you ever get lost?" Kyle asks Nick.

"All the time," he replies.

Tate slips next to me and says, "This reminds me of Turkey." I give her a knowing smile and nod. There are startling similarities between this and the archaic, still-standing *pazars* in our former residence. We'll be there in two months, and walking through this Moroccan medina whets my appetite, makes me strangely homesick.

We turn a corner, and Nick leads us to a narrow restaurant, asks a waiter if we can sit on the top floor. We climb up a cramped spiral staircase so dark I debate using my phone's flashlight app, and when we reach the top, the sun sprays through walls of windows and bores into our eyes. We take a seat at a table long enough to seat nine. Rooftops of the medina splay before us, reds and ochres; pointed minarets pierce the blanket of lower-level apartments and shops. Nick and Erin order a spread of food, and we sip mint tea from tulip glasses while we wait. The warm liquid travels through my limbs. Morocco is cold.

Rather abruptly, the sky darkens and the sun tucks behind clouds. Gusts of wind begin to clang windows and shutters surrounding us, and at a window facing ours, a woman hastily gathers her drying laundry and bolts the shutters closed. Our windowpanes rattle and clang against their frames. Kyle and Nick try to seal shut open windows, but they're delicate, breakable antiques. We watch them knock against the wind.

We agree to second rounds of tea, and Tate reads a book while the four boys chase one another around the terrace.

"Do you come here often to eat?" Kyle asks, admiring with his fingers the walls plastered in blue-and-green painted tile. "I would."

"No, but we should," Erin answers. "This is some of the best comfort food in the world. You'll see."

Soon, waiters emerge from the narrow stairway with arms covered in tagines, Moroccan earthenware pots with cone-shaped dome covers. They're set in the center of the table and the waiters lift the lids. Steam wafts in our faces, and I breathe in the scent of Sunday afternoon. Chicken, beef, and lamb bubble in cumin-infused sauce next to carrots and onions, and next to them towers of flatbread totter high on plates. Julienned potatoes, fried, bob and bubble in a red sauce.

"This smells exactly like pot roast," I say.

"It tastes like pot roast," Erin says, eyes hungry. "Dig in."

We fork chunks of meat and potatoes, scoop carrots onto the plates in front of us, and drown rounds of flatbread in the red sauce. Our kids devour their plates and hungrily ask for seconds. The fall-apart meat and succulent carrots taste like relief, like home; I want to swim in the sauce, submerge my face and breathe in. This rooftop in Fez smells like a fall childhood day in Texas.

We toast another round of mint tea after we eat, when the startling sound of breaking glass pierces our ears and wakes us from our food coma. A delicate terrace window has succumbed to shattering, leaving a wake of glass shards scattered on the balcony. Full-force gusts of wind bellow through, hint at more destruction on the horizon. We pay to remove our offspring from the crime scene and give our hearty thanks to the chef.

Bellies full and the wind much calmer on the ground, we stroll slowly again through the Medina labyrinth, eyeing oysters piled high on carts, more roasted chestnuts, more leather bags, more metal trinkets. Another butcher displays a camel head in his window. Carpet salesmen try to entice us with more mint tea. A *muezzin* beckons followers with a call to prayer, competing with the roar of scooters squeezing past our entourage. Nick and Erin lead us to their favorite art shop, and we bargain for watercolor scenes of Morocco, a cheaper alternative to the renowned rugs.

Tate whispers in my ear as I flip through paintings, "Can I pick out a painting for my room?" Along with her scroll from Xi'an, she's also collected a batik print from Kenya. I go ahead and nod, bending our souvenir rule.

"Wherever my room will be," Tate explains, "I want it to look like this year."

Tonight after the kids go to sleep, we toast manhattans in Nick and Erin's living room and watch *Saturday Night Live* reruns. We laugh at actors who remind us of college friends and reminisce about late-night drives through Austin streets.

"Remember when Corey and John and all those guys showed up to Kerbey Lane wearing random clothes they found in Jeff's mom's closet?" A fond college memory of mine, since I was there working my waitress shift and feigning acquaintance with friends who'd arrived in embarrassing flowered dresses and white blazers.

"Or on that train in England, when the drunk guy sang 'Rhinestone Cowboy' when he heard we're from Texas?" Erin adds. I had completely forgotten that one.

"How about all those nights in your apartment rewinding the kissing scene in that Drew Barrymore movie with Michael Vartan?"

Kyle chimes in. "Remember when Nick picked me up so I could surprise you with the news that I'd moved to Austin?" I stop and remember. His move to my city after our time in Kosovo signified serious commitment. My heart flutters with this memory. I love that we're in the Moroccan apartment of friends who played a part in that. These people are an extension of family.

Whenever I leave a place and move on to a new one, I carry a peculiar loyalty about where I once was. Ethiopia was a challenge, but when we arrived in Morocco and Nick and Erin asked about it, we could only sing its praises, as though it needed our defense. I think back to Sri Lanka, and the whirling-dervish monkeys no longer agitate me in my memories like they did when I was standing in that park next to them. I even brush off China's pollution with a shrug, now that I'm months past breathing it in.

I'm fairly indifferent to my home state of Texas when my quotidian days are lived out among its traffic and concrete sprawl, but I pine for her live oaks and cicada-singing evenings when they're nowhere to be found in central Oregon winters. Or tonight, in urban Morocco. I never feel more Texan than when I leave Texas, and I never feel more American than when I'm abroad.

I am years past and miles apart from my childhood, and yet those roots cling for life to me, no matter how hard I try to shake them free. I can be in my Turkish neighborhood, minding my own business, and a smell will waft through that transports me instantly to the swing set at the park next to my elementary school. Without warning, my heart will ache for five minutes on the merry-go-round. Or I can be in Morocco, swapping memories of late-night college shenanigans, and I'll crave a midnight run for chips and queso more than I can stand it.

As I fall asleep in Nick and Erin's bed, bags packed in the corner for an early-morning run to the train station back to Casablanca and onward to Europe, I connect dots between places and people. When my heart pangs for Austin, it isn't the salsa or the flip-flops weather, the live music or the hipster culture. It's the people. When I hear *Austin* I picture faces and names, Thanksgiving in my aunt's backyard, being poolside with my cousin while we watch our kids swim.

Africa has been Joy and Dave, Asher and Dru, Abubeker, Atkelt, Tigist, Clive, Pamela, John, and a million kids. It's their love for neighbors, their families, their guests. It's drums and flaming torches for tenth birthdays. Africa is old friends like Nick and Erin.

Morocco has been a surprising balm in the middle of our journey, a slight taste of home. For months, we've surveyed the most majestic creatures on earth, the oldest civilizations still in existence, some of the planet's most extreme low and high elevations. We've walked through fields of purple lupine in New Zealand and dusty desert mountains of Ethiopia. We've sampled the questionable pizza preferences of Thailand, Uganda, Kenya, and Morocco. I've lost track of various local interpretations of all the tea we've sipped.

But I am drawn to these countries' couches and stovetops. I keep scrutinizing their different types of light switches and windowsills. My fondest memories, so far, have been sunset conversations with my friend Joy about parenting, listening to John's childhood stories, learning about Atkelt's life in Addis Ababa married to an American, and watching my old friend Nick haggle prices in Arabic in the medina.

North Africa is completely different from its eastern continental counterpart. It's much more similar to our Turkey than to Joy's Uganda or Clive's Zimbabwe, and it's whetted our taste for what lies ahead, farther on in our journey, back home. Or at least, what we used to call home.

Africa is red dirt, camels hugging highway shoulders, blushing skies, waterfall drizzle, intricate glass tiles on the wall. But really, it's people. It's hosts serving postmeal popcorn, kids laughing in the grass, grown men laughing at terrible kid jokes, neighbors loving neighbors. Africa is shared community. It's one billion people on the planet. It is the welcoming family of humanity.

Cradle of civilization, indeed.

Early-Dawn Expotition

It's just you and me, boys,
An expotition of the finest.
Banded mongoose scatter beneath our breakfast,
Ringtailed, spry as both of you.
Let's gather our provisions,
White noses and pink cheeks
Let's witness beasts of the field.
Thundering zebras, sharp-serrated crocs,
The cape buffalo, droll and brown-wigged,
Wandering warthog, a jackal with caught rabbit.
Let's find the lion ogling his thoughts,
Juvenile mane frisking gold-tipped grass.
We will forget our camera. How about that?
And so, this early-dawn expotition,
This morning, just us,
Stays with us, in cameras inside.
We really saw the lion.
Just us.

PART V

To live is to be slowly born.

—Antoine de Saint-Exupéry

15

FRANCE

Outside of the United States, there is nowhere else I feel more at home than Europe. In fact, I often feel *more* at home in Europe. My favorite day's agenda anywhere mimics a life in tucked-away European villages—walking to the market for the day's groceries, sipping coffee that isn't in a to-go cup, drinking wine with lunch without judgment. Where, for some mystifying reason, food is much kinder to my innards. I can digest Italian pasta with nary a flinch, and the gelato keeps me headache-free, although I cannot say the same for its American ice cream counterpart.

Europe has always, *always* been my favorite. It's marked my heart, soul, and the pages of my passport. From food to art to history to cobblestone roads that trip me every time, I love it all. I met my husband in Europe. I spent my most meaningful, postcollege, still-young, fresh-faced-traveler days in Europe. I swoon over French and British and Italian and Irish accents. I love Europe's multiculturalism and influx of African and Middle Eastern immigrants. I'm glad Ingvar Kamprad thought up IKEA and Michelangelo said yes to painting that ceiling for the pope. I'm a fan of the Beatles, Sigur Rós, Mozart, and Daft Punk. I even appreciate the vague cigarette smell wafting through cold morning air in eastern Europe.

Europe is, on the whole, my happy place. If I could afford to, if I had legitimate permission stamped in my passport, and if the people I'd miss most were willing to come along, I would live here. This small slice of land has my heart six ways to Sunday.

It's not perfect here. Nor is there one homogeneous, oversize culture called *European*. If I could, I'd take the food and art of Italy, for example, couple it with the quiet, understated personality of France and the orderliness of Germany, the cinematic and literary wit of Britain, and blend it into one utopian, and ultimately dystopian, probably, civilization. Expat friends who live throughout Europe have regaled me with stories about their daily life that, were it my home, would indeed cause me to question my loyalty to the continent. Europe isn't perfect. But she sure is lovely.

We cross the Mediterranean on a short flight from Morocco to the South of France, where we'll live this month. Vagabonding through Africa was scraping across hallowed ground, and it accomplished its main task: we hanker for more. Its resonance continues to shake me. The past month has left us ragged and road-weary, however—irresponsibly behind on work deadlines and clamoring for a kinder routine. It's time for another slow break—as in Chiang Mai and Sydney—to catch up on work and school. What better place than in a plebeian village in the French region of Provence?

We chose Chiang Mai because of its budget-friendly accoutrements and therapeutic resources, and we parked in Sydney because we had a free housesitting gig. Now, in southern France, we'll live among friends. We don't have local French friends, nor do we know expats here who've moved abroad permanently, but here in this village are fellow travelers we already know who've parked for a bit, wanderers who live like us, who know us in context outside our nomadism.

Our flight lands in Nice, on the French Riviera, and we drive west through Cannes in search of a village named Cadenet, population four thousand. The road hugs France's Mediterranean coastline at sunset as incandescent glows of evening lights flicker in high-rise flats. I sit in the passenger seat, searching my phone in vain for inexpensive-yet-French dinner options.

"Between Nice and Cannes, it looks like the only family-friendly option still open is Quick," I say.

"Yeesh," mutters Kyle from the driver's seat. "Yeah, okay."

Quick is Europe's answer to McDonald's, and though we're not beneath this, we had hoped for more genteel cuisine as our first meal in France. We debate stopping by a late-night market for bread, cheese, and fruit, but decide Quick will be—well, quicker. It's late, and we have a long drive to our house.

We walk into Quick, and Finn shouts, "Yay! They have a play place! Can we go?"

"Uh, sure," I say, and they run off. "Wait—what do you guys want to eat?"

"Whatever!" Tate says, answering for all of them. Patrons look up from their hamburgers.

I walk up to the girl behind the counter, smile, and ask, *"Parlez-vous anglais?"*

She returns my smile and says, *"Oui, veuillez commandez là-bas,"* pointing to a box behind me. It resembles a movie rental kiosk seen outside American grocery stores.

I walk up to the box. *"Ici?"*

"Oui."

She returns to distributing fries on trays, and I touch the screen in front of me. *Bienvenue à Quick*, it displays, and below it, a British flag. I tap it, and the screen changes to *Welcome to Quick*.

"Oh, thank goodness," I breathe.

The menu is straightforward and equipped with visual help, and I order burgers, fries, and bottled water, then walk back to the girl. I stand there and smile because I'm not sure what to do.

"I will bring your order to you, ma'am," she says.

"Right," I stammer. I head to our table, where Kyle sits with his eyes closed, halfway to sleep. It's late, and after a day of trains and planes, we still have an automobile to drive.

"Wild to be finally here, eh?" he says, eyes still closed. The kids scream on the playground through the glass, knock on the windows, and wave at us. It's nine in the evening, the diner is half-full for dinner, and it's as hushed as a library.

"Yep," I answer. I feel like I'm shouting.

Food arrives, and I crack the playground door to let the kids know.

"Yay! Guys, food's here!" Finn bellows. People look up from their meals again.

"Shhhhh!" I snap. They run to our table and open their burgers.

"Hey guys," I utter in a low voice, "Hear how I'm talking? This is the volume I want you to use right now. France is quiet, okay?"

"Okay," says Tate.

"Okay," whispers Finn, barely audible.

"I don't know if I can do that," Reed says.

We inhale our dinner and hop back in the car. It's dark now, the sky starless. We drive away from the coastline and head into the countryside toward Aix-en-Provence, our only landscape headlight beams illuminating the road. Two hours till our village. Finn drifts to sleep in the back and the older two stare at nothing out the window.

We pull into the village of Cadenet near midnight. Streetlights evidence spindly routes winding between connected houses, but otherwise, it is dark, lifeless. It's a small town, and our guesthouse owners gave us vague directions via e-mail as to the whereabouts of our house. We know it's just beyond the village, so we drive two minutes north through town to the other side and begin our search. Our headlights pierce fields on either side of our two-lane road.

Back and forth, back and forth we traipse on this farm road, finding nothing. Veering onto a dirt road in hopes that it leads to our house, we find it's dotted with only a few dilapidated farmhouses and machinery parked in fields, ready for tomorrow's work. A porch light quivers on as we turn around in front of a house.

"Go! I don't wanna scare them," I say to Kyle, delirious and tired.

"I don't want *them* to scare *us*," he says.

"Maybe it's that old lady in *Ratatouille* with a shotgun," Reed says from the backseat.

We drive past a derelict shanty, lightless and brooding, and I'm nervous for a moment it's our guesthouse.

Kyle pulls back onto the farm road, driving at a snail's pace. On the left, a row of tall hedges reveals a dirt path with worn tire ruts we've missed in our search. He shrugs, turns the car through the hedge, and lets the car amble in neutral down the path. Our house owners are in Cuba for the week and have left a key on the coffee table for us inside, front door left unlocked. We have no way to call them.

Tucked behind the wall of formidable foliage sits a cottage with a gravel front porch. The porch light is on.

"This is it!" I exclaim. I'm pretty sure I recognize the cottage from its online listing.

We walk in the house, toss our bags on the living room floor, pilfer through them for pajamas and toothbrushes, then crash into beds. I'll see where, exactly, we are tomorrow.

Fingers crossed this is the right guesthouse.

The next morning, I tiptoe through our compact cottage while everyone sleeps. It is simple, two bedrooms and one bath with a catch-all living room, kitchen, dining room. Small, still bigger than Beijing.

I slide open the wall of curtains hiding windows, and I gasp.

Our house is nestled next to a diminutive creek, with rolling vineyard hills outside one window and perfect orchard rows of olive trees behind the front porch. We are surrounded by cultivated land, lying dormant in winter's end. Grapevines are bare and the trees are sparse, budding hints of what's to come in two months' time. Unopened bottles and jars wait for us on the kitchen counter, labels scribbled *olives marinées, huile d'olive, tapenade, confiture d'abricot.* There is a bottle of wine, and next to it, a card written with *Moulin à Huile d'Olive Bastide du Laval,* the same script on the jars and bottles. I walk outside and find a wooden sign with the same name, hanging from the hedge.

We are staying on an olive oil mill.

Our nomadic friends that we're joining have already settled into Cadenet for a week. We've known them for a few years through my writing work, and when they visited us in Oregon the summer before we left, we witnessed how well our kids got along. On their own family European trip, they're currently living in the heart of the village, in one of the row houses. Between us, one family is renting a house in town for easy access to shops; the other is renting a house just outside town for access to land. Our *moulin à huile d'olive* offers a yard for our lot of seven kids; their place provides a place to park in the middle of town. We will share.

They've invited us to our first breakfast in France, since our kitchen is still empty. We knock on their front door, one among many standing like soldiers in sepia-colored plaster, and a collective shout of English resonates through the wall.

"They're here! It's them!" I hear a young boy squeal.

Our friends are Ryan and Stephanie, entrepreneurs with a million ideas and the zeal to accomplish them. They have four kids—Abigail and Caden are the same ages as Tate and Reed, and Johanna and Kepler sandwich Finn in the middle. Stephanie is pregnant with Oliver. I think about lugging my backpack on the Sri Lankan train, late-night interludes sitting at east African airport gates, and marvel at her willingness to backpack Europe thick in the second trimester of pregnancy. They are a boisterously loud and well-traveled clan.

After breakfast, Stephanie shows me around Cadenet. It doesn't take long.

"Here's the bakery; they have really good *pain au chocolat*. Here's the coffee bar, but it's hard to work there with all the cigarette smoke. Here's where they have the farmers' market on Tuesdays. Down there is the post office, but I haven't tried it yet."

Stephanie reminds me of the French custom of greeting with *Hello, how are you?* every time you enter a place, and *Good-bye, thank you* before leaving. We turn a corner and walk into the market, a village grocery shop the size of an American roadside convenience store.

"*Bonjour, comment ça va?*" Stephanie and I say in unison. An aproned woman smiles and nods at us.

I add oranges, apples, butter, yogurt, *rouge d'hiver* lettuce, and a roll of paper towels to my basket, then ogle wheels of cheese on display through glass.

"I haven't had a bad one yet," advises Stephanie.

"*Comment puis-je t'aider?*" asks the woman behind the counter.

"Umm . . ." I mull, then point to one. I shrug and smile, ask *Is it any good?* with body language.

"*Trés bon, madame.*" She shaves off a sliver, hands it to me. I slide it in my mouth. It is a symphony. I close my eyes, give her a thumbs-up and instantly pray the hand gesture isn't offensive. She laughs, butchers off a wedge, and wraps it in paper. We pay, say *merci* and *au revoir*, and leave.

We walk ten steps and head into the boucherie. It smells like chicken soup on a cold day.

"*Bonjour, mesdames!*" a middle-aged man greets us wearing a grease-smeared apron. Stephanie introduces me, and he shakes my hand and says, "*Bienvenue!*"

I point to some bacon, smile, and nod. He pulls out a slab of pork belly and slices it into gossamer strips. Stephanie knows more French than me, and they rattle off a conversation while he slices. He is affable; his laugh reminds me of John in Kenya.

He hands me the bacon and asks, "*Rien d'autre?*"

I point at a row of chickens behind the glass, then slice my neck with my hand. The butcher finds this hilarious. He pulls out a chicken, lays it on the counter, and whacks off its head with a thud.

Stephanie orders her meat checklist; then we pay, say, "*Merci, au revoir!*" and head out.

He runs to the door, says, "*Attendez une minute!*" and points to a notice taped to the glass window. We look at him in confusion, and he explains its meaning in rapid-fire French.

"Got that?" I ask Stephanie.

"Nope," she answers.

I take a photo of the paper, nod, and smile, say *merci*. I am doing a lot of smiling and nodding. When we return to the Langfords' house, I look up the words. The sign reads, *We will be closed next week. We'll be in Chamonix, skiing.*

Our regular small town is devoid of guidebook features, so we immerse ourselves into life in a working community. These days in southern France begin with school and work, then in the afternoon, daily trips to various stores and markets to replenish supplies. If we're at our friends' house, the kids walk to the park together and pop in the bakery for pain au chocolat. If they're at our house, they explore the orchards and creek.

After schoolwork, the kids are free to wander outside the olive mill, so long as they stay together and don't bother the crops or farm equipment. Over several afternoons, the seven kids create a village along the creek bed, various trees landmarking each of their houses— leaves, grass, and sticks as walls, floors, and roofs. They dedicate a mayor, doctor, teacher, and mailman, and over long afternoon hours hold town meetings to discuss events and air grievances. The town is christened Terabithia.

Terabithia is freedom, permission to play. Their afternoon agenda is sticks and mud, imagining the orchard is the Daintree; the creek is the Nile. Each evening, our friends' kids go home and our kids take showers to wash off the French dirt. We eat roasted chicken and vegetables for dinner, then read in bed until sleep takes over. There is no Little League, no ballet lessons, no school playgrounds or trips to the arcade. There are books and blocks inside and nature outside. There are ingredients to sample at the farmers' market. There's French cuisine, the local bakery, and day after day, there is always Terabithia.

It becomes a third second home for them, a home away from home away from home.

Even though we're quite content to never leave Cadenet, it'd be a mistake to not explore her surroundings. When we make shopping trips into Aix-en-Provence, we pull over and investigate Roman ruins marked by official signs like scenic overlooks in America. We ride a Ferris wheel along the waterfront in Marseille and eat more Quick burgers. I leave for a weeklong work trip to Israel, and Kyle takes the kids to the Ochre Trail in Roussillon.

When I return, we drive two hours east to Monaco for the day, the world's second smallest country and the wealthiest per capita. It's a playground for the über-rich and full of parked cars when they're not hosting the Grand Prix; we debate the merits of bringing seven children, but decide to try anyway. Fiats and Peugeots mingle with Ferraris and Bentleys, and our younger kids gallop and zigzag around mailboxes, lampposts, and luxury vehicles. All afternoon, I say things like "Stay away from the Lamborghini!" and "Don't touch the Aston Martin!" Car journalist Doug DeMuro says, "Exotic cars are everywhere in Monaco. And I mean everywhere. You can't walk down a street without seeing a Ferrari 458 Spider. You can't turn the corner without hearing the roar of a Lamborghini Aventador."[1]

We stroll to the legendary Casino de Monte-Carlo because Kyle and Ryan want a peek inside. It costs ten euro to enter the lobby *before* the casino, and they tuck in their shirts, smooth down their travel-ridden hair, and gallivant inside. Stephanie and I distract the kids outside on the sidewalk. A row of Lamborghinis are parked on the right and a crowd of Russian elite mingle on the left. There's nothing for us to do but stand and wait. Stephanie rolls her stroller back and forth to lull Kepler to sleep, and I keep an eye on the squirming boys and say, "Please stop lying across the sidewalk." Three women in gowns walk by.

I look in desperation for a distraction to amuse the minors and ask Tate and Abbie to see if they can spot a park. They come back in ten minutes and say, "All we can find are stores named Donna Karan and Estée Lauder."

Late afternoon, we hike up the hill past docks parked with titanic yachts overlooking Prince Albert's palace. The kids ooh and aah over boats, and I imagine the interior of the one named *Nirvana*.

Reed says, "I wish we were traveling around the world in *that*." Kyle and I haven't revealed to the kids our harbored secret dream of circumnavigating the globe in a boat as empty nesters. We don't even know how to sail.

"You know what? I don't," I say. "I'm sure it's cool in those, but think of everything we've done *because* we have to be tight with money. We've stayed with friends instead of fancy hotels. We visited Abubeker's family instead of spending money on a longer safari. We've lived in neighborhoods instead of touristy parts of towns."

"We ate cheese and crackers in our campervan in New Zealand," Tate adds.

"We're eating cheese and crackers in France too," Reed says.

"Remember the tarantula in Sri Lanka?" Finn tosses into the conversation.

"Yeah," Tate says, looking out at the yachts. "I like living like regular people."

This evening, after our drive back to Cadenet, we pull our dusty rented Toyota Yaris into the gravel driveway at the moulin à huile d'olive and feast on more roast chicken and salad for dinner.

We tuck the kids into bed, and Reed sleepily asks, "Mom, do you think yachts are a lot of work?"

———

Morocco was cold, but southern France is even colder. We buy knitted hats and gloves at Cadenet's farmers' market and find sweaters in Marseille and Aix. I buy Moroccan mint tea at a market and make several cups a day. Provençal mistrals are violent, freezing winds that rush through southern France during the crossover between winter and spring. They have become our uninvited guests. We leave the house under a cloudless bright sky, and while we're sampling pistachios with the farmer at the Tuesday market, mistrals whip through Cadenet's narrow alleyways like the angel of death. Just when it feels like we've settled in as long-term residents, I zip up my lightweight windbreaker and remember we're here as pilgrims. Our plan for spring in Europe is to layer, layer, layer; soon, we will wear our paltry outerwear into the Balkans, and later, the Alps. I wonder how I'll feel about my sartorial options come Paris and London.

———

Aside from the pleasure of good company, a benefit to living near friends is trustworthy child care. Kyle and I have gone on two dates in the previous six months (one in Sydney, thanks to Adriel, and one in Kampala under the mango tree, thanks to Joy), and one evening, after Ryan and Stephanie go on a date and leave the hordes of offspring under our care, it is our turn.

We drive four kilometers north through winding French country farm roads to Lourmarin, the next village over. It's home to the gravestone of Albert Camus and the still-living British writer Peter Mayle, famous for his books on Provence. It's a bigger town, a thousand years old and a magnet for tourists in search of a Renaissance castle and medieval farmhouses—and therefore offers more restaurants than humble Cadenet. We lace our fingers and walk through Lourmarin's quiet, dark streets; puddles of rain shimmer on asphalt and fog hovers on top of streetlamps. The mistrals bite through my market hat and windbreaker, whip my hair like a scarf around my neck. My teeth chatter, and we lean into the violent wind. We sprint past art galleries and closed patisseries and duck into an open brasserie; it is seven-thirty in the evening, early for dinner in France, and the place is nearly empty.

A teenage boy walks up with menus. "*Bonsoir—table pour deux?*"

"*Oui,*" answers Kyle, and my heart flutters at the sound of the French word for two. It's a rarity this year.

We sit by a large fireplace with a roaring fire under way, and my numb cheeks begin to thaw. We split orders of roast duck and asparagus pizza, and we share a bottle of wine. The marinated meat slides off the bone. We spoon velvety creme brûlée for dessert and order a round of espresso. The food is earthy and clean, like a farm in early spring. It is a meal for the books.

The brasserie fills with more patrons, but it's still pin-drop quiet. We update each other on thoughts about the kids, news from our parents back home, our opinions on Provence, the novels we're reading. Our time is spent side by side 24/7, but our thoughts catch up to us at night while we sleep, and it's an effort to disclose them when the kids are never elsewhere. We laugh at bad inside jokes. We hide our laughter at the four old men who've come in wearing black turtlenecks and mustaches, as French men do. There is a reason people fall in love in France.

A few weeks ago, we risked a double date with Ryan and Stephanie, leaving our kids in charge of themselves in our friends' house. We were four blocks away at a local brasserie. The oldest two were put in charge, and they were armed with half our phones so they could text in an emergency. This practice is not uncommon in these parts. We fed them a simple dinner and set them up with a new movie, and the four of us ducked out.

The waitress poured the wine; Ryan forked a hunk of bread into fondue, and asked with the bluntness of a hammer, "So—how's your marriage holding up to the trip?"

"Excuse me?" I asked.

"I mean, how are you guys doing? Has it been rough?"

I knew what he was asking. Stephanie and I had talked on the phone a few years ago when they were on a year-long global trip, and she had confessed that the family togetherness had taken a toll on her sanity. They ultimately powered through to the other side with a marriage stronger than before their travels, but it wasn't without a lot of work. That evening I had hung up the phone and vowed that when we started our journey in a few years, we'd remember their struggle and what it took for them to make it out alive. We weren't immune.

Four months ago in Chiang Mai, Kyle and I spent hours walking up and down our neighborhood street while the kids watched a movie. We confessed grievances about each other's personalities, our struggles working together, day in and day out for years, and what would be our mutual dream scenario with the kids and our careers back in the real world. That night became the impetus for a collection of chats—marriage intimacy while navigating slippery New Zealand roads, a particular child's speech delay while on a Ugandan porch swing, vocational unhappiness over wine in Kenya, theology in Singapore.

Passport stamps became icons for gathered wisdom. Every time we crossed political borders, we collected more conversations, more honesty, more willingness to take risks. Each heft of our backpacks marked commitment for one more day married through congested markets and frenetic metro stations. Our affection has been dirt under fingernails, translating foreign maps for the one in the driver's seat, late-night dripping clotheslines in guesthouse bathrooms.

"Here's the truth," I told Ryan. "We're actually doing well. No one's more surprised than us. Your experience has stayed on our minds constantly. And it's made a difference. So thanks for that."

"Glad to be of service," Ryan laughed. He put his arm around Stephanie and kissed her forehead.

The French are known for their sensuality, but tonight we pay for our roast duck and asparagus pizza, we walk to our car parked under Lourmarin's fog through mistral winds, and I think of that conversation last week with Ryan and Stephanie. I think of people who think we're crazy for traveling the world with a gaggle of kids. I think of our long talk in that Thai neighborhood. The French writer Antoine de Saint-Exupéry once said, "Love doesn't mean gazing at each other, but looking, together, in the same direction."

Kyle stops me before he unlocks the car, and he kisses me, newlywed-style, under a lamppost on a foggy night in Provence.

16

ITALY

It is hard to leave France, but it means being in Italy, a handsome exchange. We cross the French-Italian border via train and watch chiaroscuro shadows dance on Tuscan hills. Barreling through the countryside at 223 miles per hour in an aluminum tube is a spectacular way to remember how loud a herd of traveling children can be, particularly when the only seats left are in the business carriage. The train stops in Milan, and men board in smart-cut suits, cross their legs, slip on tortoiseshell glasses, snap open the morning's issue of *Corriere della Sera*. I pull Reed onto my lap. We are surrounded by class. A painting whirs by out the windows.

Both of our families, all eleven of us, will share an oversize apartment in Rome. We leave the train station and walk six blocks to our apartment, a trail of adults and children in backpacks, several of them crying and gnashing their teeth at the weight they carry. Our apartment is on a Roman side street in an ordinary neighborhood, but still a stone's throw from the density of it all: Colosseum, Pantheon, Piazza Navona, Vatican City. Ryan and Stephanie already explored the city with their kids several years ago, so we plan to divide and conquer for most of the week.

Our apartment's owner is waiting inside when we arrive, and she laughs at the sight of us.

"Che bello! Bambini che viaggiano!" she says, clasping her hands and pinching our kids' cheeks.

We feed our kids cheap pizza we picked up from the neighborhood street for dinner, and it tastes like fare from our favorite artisan restaurant in Bend. The next morning, the five of us walk down our gray street to hop on a tram. We are meeting friends we first met when we visited Italy last summer, an American family who lives in nearby Perugia.

They know of a public park where we can picnic on pizza. I sense we will eat a lot of pizza this week. But when in Rome . . .

We enter a family-run *pizzerie*, and Dan rattles off an order for the lot of us while I inspect the options behind the glass. This pizza is rectangular and thick, like focaccia bread, with toppings like prosciutto, peppers, and fig. The man behind the counter slices oblong hunks, weighs them on a scale, and wraps them in paper.

"You pay by the gram," explains Dan.

Traditional Roman pizza is paper-thin and charred on the edges, but this is *pizza al taglio*, thick, rustic, and handheld. Although Italians dispute which city invented this style, it is popular throughout the country as an easy takeaway fast food. Dan says it's his favorite because he grew up in Venice. I'm not sure what this means.

Dan and Bethany, his wife, and their two young girls have skipped a day of school and work to show us their favorite Roman spots, so we walk toward the Circus Maximus, now a public park, to start our day with lunch.

We pass a *caffé*, and Bethany asks, "Would anyone like a quick coffee before lunch?"

"I'm always up for coffee," I say. We walk into the coffee bar and I order a *macchiato*, an espresso served in a small demitasse cup with a layer of foamed milk on top. Unlike the giant American chain's counterpart, a true Italian macchiato is a cross between a straight espresso and a cappuccino. And unlike American coffee shops, Italian coffee bars aren't filled with patrons who stay for hours to chat, let alone work from their laptops.

Coffee bars have a literal bar—people quaff their coffees standing elbow to elbow at the counter, debating the latest neighborhood news. They can also opt for soft drinks or alcohol, and everything is consumed quickly, a hit of caffeine or a buzz before moving on with the day. Most caffés have a few tables for patrons, and they charge extra for the seat.

We swig our coffee and, as we leave the bar, Dan says, "Don't worry, we'll get more coffee in a few hours."

The nine of us settle on a grassy hill overlooking the Circus Maximus, a decaying stadium built around 50 BCE and last used in 549 CE; it was quarried for building materials soon after and eventually morphed into a market garden in the 1500s. At the turn of this millennium, it was still being used for public events—the Rolling Stones played here in 2014. We munch on blocks of pizza and talk about expat life while the kids roll their bodies down the hill toward the Circus.

"They'll want to watch out for old stones," Bethany warns.

"What—like ancient Roman Empire stuff?" I joke.

"Well—yeah," she says.

Kyle asks Dan about Italian culture. Yes, it really is run by the Mafia in certain pockets. Yes, Italians communicate with their hands, and each gesture has its own distinct meaning (point your finger into your cheek to tell a waiter your food was delicious; brush the tops of your fingers underneath your chin to tell your friend *I don't care*). Except for university years in Texas, where he met Bethany, Dan has lived his entire life in Italy, growing up in the outskirts of Venice. His parents live in Milan and another brother lives elsewhere in the country. I ask Bethany if it was hard to follow him back to Italy when they married.

"It was hard at first," she says. "But we've lived here so long now, it's home. The States feel foreign."

They share their upcoming family travel plans: once the school year ends, they'll take their girls camping through Scotland and explore Paris and London. They'll drive through Tuscany, the Alps, the French countryside with camping gear in the trunk. This is their road trip to the Grand Canyon, their visit to Chicago and New York.

Before we left for our year of travels, we received a smattering of criticism when we announced our trip around the world. Most people we told found it an amazing idea, but a few wondered why we'd invest money in something the kids wouldn't remember later in life. For a split second, I'd second-guess our sanity, wonder if we should wait until the kids were older.

"I'd say the best thing my parents did for my brothers and me was raising us with a normal family life and traveling a lot," Dan says. "We didn't have much money, but we always went on family vacations. *Always*. We'd go to the Alps in Switzerland or Austria every summer, and we did normal family stuff."

I think of our expat friends who feel guilty about traveling because of the cost. They live somewhere exotic, they deduce, so why should they still feel the need to travel?

"My parents got a lot of flak for taking time off, mostly from the other expats in town," Dan explains. "But they chose not to worry about them and do what was best for our family anyway. To this day, we all still get along great."

The act of travel, the constant moving and shuffling of our bodies and backpacks, our dotted lines across the map, the simplicity of owning less to see more—these small acts are weaving our family's tapestry. Threads of pliable spirits when the train is delayed, rubbing sweaty shoulders with people of different races, sleeping in close quarters, converting new currency every week—these fibers are becoming the heft of our ancestral fabric, the patterns we will show our grand-children and say, "Here—this corner of the tapestry. This is why you are who you are." We are learning presence, how to delight in each other's mere existence, muster affection in spite of our quirks. As Hemingway says, "Never go on trips with anyone you do not love."[1]

Dan and Bethany lead us to the Pantheon and we spend a few minutes sampling a troubadour's cello. The kids drop euros into his instrument case, then we find another caffé and another macchiato. Dan takes us to his favorite *gelateria* nearby, and I spoon lemon cream into my mouth and imagine the summer afternoon when the fruit was plucked from its tree. I taste sunshine.

We will not be in Rome as long as it insists, with its infinite arched alley-ways and timeworn landmarks. Its trams lead us to places on a postcard; we survey the Colosseum and imagine gladiators and lions and bloody Christians. We walk through the Vatican and scratch the smallest coun-try in the world off our list, spin around and gaze at the 140 saints carved as statues standing guard along the balustrade columns. We overwhelm our senses in the Vatican museum, gawk in wonder at Renaissance art-istry and gape at Michelangelo's offering to the Sistine Chapel. The boys keep asking about chapels one through fifteen.

I want my kids to understand the magnitude of this history but I don't think I understand it myself. My brain, not yet forty, cannot compute the immensity of human talent, the red-letter vigor for con-tributing art to a broken and beautiful world. Raphael, Caravaggio, and da Vinci have painted operas with oils and have given us the gift of seeing them. We sample more gelato by the papal residence and marvel at our midday dessert's opulence, its simplicity of milk, cream, sugar that mingle into a song.

Anthony Doerr says, "Rome is beautiful, Rome is ugly." It is "American before coffee was 'to go,' when a playground was a patch of gravel, some cigarette butts, and an uninspected swing set; when everybody smoked; when businesses in your neighborhood were owned by people who lived in your neighborhood; when children still stood on the front seats of moving cars and spread their fingers across the dash."[2] It is the crumbling walls of the Roman Forum, and it's a model in a see-through dress plastered on a wall down our street. It's murky tobacco shops on every corner, and it's strangers who smile at our children. It's a fountainhead of historic innovation, and it's 40 percent of the population in their thirties who still live with their parents. It is the world's magnificence of architecture and divine devotion. It is throngs of Vespas, with drivers flicking each other off.

A trio of musicians play jazz outside the Roman Forum at sunset, pealing sounds more apropos on Bourbon Street in New Orleans. We toss euros into their upturned hats, then find a bar for dinner. There are four tables, and we sit at the empty one.

The *cameriere* takes our order—pasta, sparkling water—and when the table next to us clears, he takes a seat.

"It's *bellissimo* to see children on holiday with mamas and papas," he says, kissing his fingers like an Italian stereotype. "Usually in here it's couples without kids. Or it's *grandissimo* groups of kids from school." He shakes his head at the chaos of the thought.

After our meal we say *Grazie, ciao*, and he waves, says, "Families, they are nice. It's good to do things while they are young." He winks at Finn. "They don't stay so small. Mine are here." He points to an imaginary spot next to him, above his head. "They grow big."

Tonight, as I lie in bed in our Roman apartment, I scroll through photos from Beijing at the beginning of our trip. All three kids look like they've grown a foot and have lost some pudge from their cheeks.

If all roads lead to Rome, those same roads can lead you away. We take the one that leads us one hundred miles north to Assisi. There's not much in minuscule Assisi, but that's its charm. Narrow roads, impassable by cars, spiral up a hillside and cradle limestone houses connected as one long, multiwindowed facade. As a known settlement from a thousand years before Christ, the entire town is declared a UNESCO World Heritage Site. People still live in the village and worship at the Basilica Papale di San Francesco d'Assisi, built in 1228. After Rome, we spend a day here with Dan and Bethany to wander shops of wood-carved trinkets and ogle frescoes of its favorite citizen, Saint Francis. The kids run with glee down carless streets and Finn chases pigeons through the Piazza del Comune. We sample *fragola* and *stracciatella* gelato. The sun falls asleep behind farmhouses in fields, and we witness the spectacle from Assisi's pinnacle. The sky transmutes from powder to amaranth and St. Francis's six bells knell its ominous, warbling song on the hour. The moment is sacred, and it is earthy. Francis would be pleased.

We commute ten minutes downhill on a bus to the nearby twenty-first-century town of Santa Maria degli Angeli, where our guesthouse perches above a store on the main street. Dan knows of a pizzerie named Penny Lane where the menu options are named after Beatles songs. Kyle orders Sexy Sadie; I order Ob-La-Di, Ob-La-Da. The kids split Get Back. After dinner, we stroll a few blocks to the Papal Basilica of Saint Mary of the Angels, where an evening service has begun.

The kids are amused for two minutes, then beg to leave. In Kenya and Australia, flamboyant animals are hyperbole, yet safari drives and zoo excursions become commonplace, predictable. In Italy, every gilded chapel is a pageant of legendary art. Visit them in abundance at rapid-fire pace, and they might become banal, monotonous even. We want to guard the kids from the danger of renowned artistry becoming sidewalk art. Kyle agrees to watch them play in the piazza so I can stay a few more minutes.

The service in session isn't technically in the basilica; it's in the Porziuncola, a miniscule chapel erected in 1211 and parked inside this standard-size basilica. Its location marks where Saint Francis established his order and where he was brought to die in 1226. It's a chapel plonked in the middle of a grand cathedral, built with rough stones hewn by the saint himself, and eventually covered with frescoes in the fourteenth through nineteenth centuries. The newer cathedral, built in the seventeenth century, pulses light through its windows and ricochets through chandeliers above while Francis's humble church prostrates, dark, with a few flickering candles scintillating a yellow-lit altar. The entire structure is ten by eighteen feet, squeezing the crowd inside. I join them, cross myself, and let an Italian homily wash over me.

This is a Catholic service, and as a low-church Protestant my entire life, I am personally in the midst of walking the Canterbury trail of Anglicanism. With some intention, we aren't visiting local church services this year, keeping near instead our Bibles and our Book of Common Prayer. Neither Kyle nor I doubt the tenets of our faith, but we are on a spiritual pilgrimage, desperate for freedom to question, brood, and venerate, without the necessities of ecclesiastical culture. We went to church twice in Chiang Mai, and it was enough.

Tonight, in the flush glimmer of Santa Maria degli Angeli's tapers, I hear a merciful, moored voice. The priest prays in Italian, and a voice in English whispers, *It's time for you to return.*

God, I never left, I reply.

Neither have I, says the whisper.

I think of Nora in Chiang Mai. There in her office, I would stare at my own bitterness, turn it over and over in my hands, beg God to reveal its purpose. I would sit in silence and hear God say, *Your bitterness is not about me. It is about your brokenness, the weight of this world from which I've already set you free.* I tell Nora what I hear. She would put her hand under mine, help me unclench and release the bitterness, throw it away, wash my hands. She would pray a blessing over me, then tell me to go write a poem.

I stare at the yellow candles at the altar.

Where do I return? I ask. The priest speaks, and people stand. I copy. *Community. To the order of humanity and neighbors. Home.*

God, I ask, *where is home?*

Silence. The answer I hear every time I ask this question. This silence has grown louder on our travels. Tonight, however, my shoulders slack and my spirit loosens; some of my frustration releases into the candlelight. My question still lacks an answer. I resolve that perhaps I'm not yet to know.

People of the earth make home all over its crust, but their particular whereabouts aren't the chief concern. These people cluster together, huddle into families, and flock into parishes, neighborhoods, precincts, villages. Saint Francis gathered twelve men to break bread and live in the mountains near birds and trees. He made his home wherever; the whereabouts weren't the issue. He lived in community.

It's getting late, and Kyle is still outside with the kids. I cross myself, leave the chapel-in-a-chapel, and walk to the main doors. As I leave, I notice leaflets in a basket, blessings from Saint Francis typed out and offered for passersby. I snag one. It reads:

May the Lord bless you.

May the Lord keep you.

May He show His face to you and have mercy.

May He turn to you His countenance and give you peace.

The Lord bless you.

I slide the blessing into my pocket and slip out of the church.

Venice has an unfair reputation. When we planned our trip, American friends swarmed us with unsolicited advice to avoid Venice—it's touristy, smelly, not as impressive as you'd think. We go anyway. It's one of my favorite places.

It's March, low on tourists, and the mildewy canal odor is divorced from summer's heat and humidity. Boats hug winding sidewalks, bobbing in waterways and parked like carpool pickup lines. Row houses share laundry lines, pristine sheets and shirts hanging brave, spanning canals like a tightrope. Venetians have an odd obsession with pocket-size dogs; most stride the sidewalks dressed up in sweaters and hoodies as if they own the place. Why a city with no actual grass and plentiful opportunities to descend into dark waters is a haven for miniature canines, I'll never know.

It is a city of art and architecture, ancient maritime power and home of Titian and Tintoretto, Bellini, and Vivaldi. Its Renaissance nickname was the Republic of Music. It is Constantinople's medieval wartime foe, a curious haven for eighteenth-century Jews, and was left largely intact by World War II. An official Disney Store is now parked in one of its cavernous fifteenth-century storefronts.

This is Dan's hometown, and he has given us a laundry list of Venice's greatest hits off the beaten path. Wind whips through cramped alleyways, but sunrays splay past rooftops and bullet our faces. It is a beautiful day. *Vaporettos* are Venice's buses, water ferries with service lines as detailed as London's Tube and twice as expensive. The kids beg to ride one. We are back traveling with Ryan and Stephanie's family, so that means there are eleven of us, which also means eleven tickets.

"We will eventually," Kyle says. "But we're gonna walk most of this city." Venice is a floating city two and a half miles from dry land; during high tide pilgrims must walk on wooden platforms in

St. Mark's Square. There are miles of alleys in which to get lost. This is our plan for the weekend.

Dan's directions guide us to the best gelato in town, and we patronize it twice a day. He leads us to a dock for a coveted gondola-riding photo for two euro per adult—a 175-foot ride across the Grand Canal, where four strokes of the oar commutes Venetians to their homes. Dan's savviness saves our budget in this costly city.

He also hints how to find a glassblower happy to show loud foreign children a behind-the-scenes look at his talent on Murano, an island in the Venice lagoon. We ride a vaporetto to the islet and tuck past touristed streets of shops selling glass vases, jewelry, and statues to an unremarkable shop with a warehouse door in the back. We push the door and walk into a concrete room with stacks of cardboard boxes on storage shelves, and find a man blowing into a length of steel pipe, molten orange and red ballooning on the opposite end. A teenage girl with a fauxhawk opens a fireplace with burning embers, and he shoves the tip of his pipe into fire to reheat liquid glass. He spins as he shapes with heavy-duty pliers, blows, spins, bends melted glass to his will. He makes a miniature horse and we burst into applause.

We hop back on the vaporetto and head to Burano, a lesser-known island than its counterpart. A swath of grass reminds me I haven't seen it since we've been in Venice, and its halcyon allure calls the kids to run wild. They've tiptoed through narrow concrete walkways and mildewed waterways for days. Finn climbs a statue of naked women, innocent and unaware.

Burano is humble fishermen's houses and squinting lace makers, and shops beckon us with delicate lace wholly out of our budgets. Row houses are walls shared but separate with distinct hues: raspberry, lime, blueberry, and mango. Looking at them from a canal bridge is like peering through a glass case at a gelato shop. The kids call out their favorites and claim houses as theirs.

Late afternoon is macchiato time for adults, and we sit at a caffè alfresco on the piazza while the kids sit in a circle and play hand games. We wait for our return vaporetto, slurping seafood and pasta at a tiny corner café overlooking the water, and watch the sun dip into the Laguna Veneta.

The next day is our last in Venice and, therefore, Italy. We have work to do, but our hearts are heavy at departing Italy and so we leave work on our laptops for twenty-four more hours. The five of us play hide-and-seek in the dark bowels of Venice and we chase one another through three-foot-wide passageways. At one of its entryways, I snap a photo of an unidentified saint etched in stone, cracked and graffitied, barely noticed on the brick wall. It has stood guard over this alley for centuries and watched medieval and Renaissance children dart and dash through its shabby hallowed halls. I wonder how long it's been there. I wonder how long the graffiti has been there.

Italy is art. Italians carve their farmland, their marble, and their dingy alleyways as artisans. I think of Rome a few days ago with Dan and Bethany, when he took us to a pub offering twenty kinds of beer.

"Does Italy have good beer?" Kyle asked, assuming the answer.

"Actually, they have fantastic beer," Dan replied.

"Really? I thought it was all wine here," I said.

"Because there are no expectations for beer," he explained, "it's excellent. Belgium has strict regulations as to what makes a beer Belgian. There are no cultural rules for Italian beer, and Italians look at everything as art. They're free to take risks, and they know it will sell because Italians are curious and are usually willing to try something new. For the art of it."

We all leave Venice the next morning, and we pass a piano parked in the train station, free for anyone to play. There is always someone there, tapping the keys as Beethoven, Busoni, or Porter vibrate through hollow train platforms. It's empty this morning. Ryan sits down and plays while we bide time for our train. We are heading through Slovenia next and onward to our last country together.

The train arrives, we board, and I settle into my window seat. Tate sits next to me, and we work on fractions for a while, then stop to pay homage to the bucolic, earth-shattering scenery sprinting past our window. We blow kisses to Italy as we cross the border.

The sun blazes noon, and Tate rests her head on my shoulder, closes her eyes. I open the book I'm currently reading and find this:

He who works with his hands is a laborer.

He who works with his hands and his head is a craftsman.

He who works with his hands and his head and his heart is an artist.[3]

17

CROATIA

The bus pulls out onto country Croatian roads, and the driver starts playing Taylor Swift's *Red* album. Reed begins singing along in the seat behind me, and I tell him to lower the volume.

"Are you American?" a girl asks from the seat across the aisle.

"Yep. You too?" I ask.

"Yeah, we both are," she says, leaning back to show the guy next to her. I introduce myself and Tate sitting next to me.

"I'm Megan; this is Charlie," she says. They look road weary.

"You backpacking around Europe?"

"Eastern Europe," Charlie says. "We're about to start grad school, so we thought we better travel while we can, get it out of our system."

"So you're heading to Split? Whereabouts after that?" I ask.

"Bucharest, then Budapest. After that, not sure. We might be out of money then, so we'll just go back to Montana."

I nod. Reed is still singing behind me, sitting next to Ryan and Stephanie's oldest son, Caden, and Finn is asleep on Kyle's lap a seat back. Tate's listening to our conversation.

"You know," I say, "you probably won't ever get it out of your system."

"I see that," Megan says, looking at our collection of kids. "Are they all yours?"

211

I laugh. "Three of them are. The other four belong to those guys," I say, pointing to Ryan and Stephanie.

"You're all just traveling, then?" she asks. I explain our year around the world and our friends' few months in Europe.

"Wow, so you're just—taking them with you," Charlie says, surprised.

"Well, we tried to leave them, but they never got the hang of driving to the store on their own," I answer.

"Seriously, though," Megan says. "That's cool. I mean, you didn't let kids stop you from traveling. You're just taking them with you instead of waiting till they're out of the house."

I think for a minute. "Yes. True. But . . . they're honestly one of the main reasons we are traveling now. We want to show them the world while they're young. The earlier they see the world, the more normal it is for them. And the younger they start traveling, the better travelers they become."

"Man, that's the truth," Stephanie says from the seat in front of me.

"That's supercool," Charlie says. "Man, what I would have given to get to do this when I was younger. What an education, you know?"

"Yep," I say. "I know."

Charlie leans over to look at Tate. "Appreciate this, okay?" he says to her. "Not many kids get to do this at your age." Tate gives a shy smile and nods.

The bus pulls into the station and we board the next train. It's older, with more rattles, and it herky-jerkies down the tracks. It's nearly empty, so we spread out to sleep across seats. I dream of New Zealand, mint tea, and Turkish delight.

We arrive in Split under a dark sky, black waves licking a dock right outside the train station. It smells like fish and saltwater, coffee and ice cream. Fishing boats wave from their parking spots along the concrete barrier. It's a few blocks' walk to our apartment in the historic part of the city, and the kids are a mess of exhaustion. I pick up Finn and his backpack; Kyle picks up Reed.

Our guesthouse host, Marin, has given instructions for us to meet him "at the palace entrance. You'll see it." We trudge past closed cafés and ice cream shops facing the water, then out of nowhere, a white marble walkway under a stone-hewn arch. It leads down a marble path, worn smooth from eons of footsteps and gleaming white from streetlights. A young man leans against the wall, scrolling his phone.

"Marin?" Kyle asks.

Marin looks up and smiles. "Yes, that's me. Looks like you found the palace," he says, and takes Reed's and Finn's backpacks to carry. We follow him farther down the marble walking path.

"You really live in a palace?" I ask.

"Did," he says. "I used to. This apartment is where I grew up. I now live not far from here."

"So, what do you mean, though?" I say. "This is really a palace then?"

"Yep," Marin says, "It's Diocletian's palace. It's pretty old. A while ago, they divided it up into lots of apartments, and this is where I grew up."

By "pretty old," Marin means 300 CE.

We stop at a narrow wooden door next to a closed restaurant, and he unlocks it with a skeleton key, ducks as he enters, and motions us to follow suit. A twentysomething Croat, Marin fits the type I see lingering around the marble palace grounds: broad-shouldered, olive-skinned, tall. Taller than Kyle, who is over six feet.

Spiral stairs thread a narrow staircase, stone steps are six inches too high to pass modern building code; a three-foot gap between the stairs and the handrail threaten the most careful of sober adults without awkward backpacks and sleepy children. Finn can't reach the handrail, and we have three flights to climb. I move him to the wall side of the staircase and tell him to keep his shoulder touching the wall as he climbs. When we reach the third floor, I look down and my stomach drops. The minuscule landing pad hosts another tiny door. Marin unlocks it with a second skeleton key and ducks inside his apartment.

Beijing is the only guesthouse smaller than this one. Our slice of Diocletian's palace is a kitchen-dining-room combo fit for two adults, a bathroom and standing shower just past the kitchen sink, and two small bedrooms down a tapering hall. The best thing about the place, aside from its history and location, is the price. For thirty dollars a night, this is just fine. I'm glad Ryan and Stephanie's family have found their own apartment here.

The size of our place doesn't matter much, because in Croatia, we'll mostly be outside. This land is glorious.

Split is like Southern California with ancient buildings and cheaper prices. The sky here is cobalt and cloudless; the sea air left its humidity farther south. People here are young and beautiful. We drink cappuccinos at tables along the waterfront while the kids eat ice cream, and I feel like a slipshod American tourist. The palace is chock-full of trendy clothing shops, and we buy Finn a new jacket (his was stolen outside a train station in Zagreb) and me some new jeans. Ryan and Kyle tag team with Stephanie and me, trading kid time with work time, and we're surprised that most cafés have fast, free Wi-Fi, unlike the more Western countries we've traveled through, like Australia and France. The kids' playground is archaic alleyways and derelict columns. They run across open marble plazas and slide until their feet give way.

I text a friend back in Austin to tell her I felt like I keep seeing her husband in a crowd, with all the men resembling his brawny build and coloring. "I've always thought of him as part Eastern European," she says, "What with his body type and his penchant for beer and philosophy." Kyle says on day three in Croatia, "Of all the nationalities we've been around, these are the sort of men I wouldn't want to run into in a dark alley." The women keep their hair long and wear stilettos with their jeans. Nearly everyone speaks English.

After the hallowed museum-like cities of Venice, Assisi, and Rome, and because we're living in a veritable archaeological site, we pine for a bit of God's country. The kids are clamoring to get dirty and we are surrounded by marble and deep ocean harbor. For our last full day in Split, we rent a car and drive two hours away to waterfalls named Krka, picnic lunch packed in the trunk.

The falls require a benign hike on a wooden boardwalk through the forest. We stroll through trees and I breathe in the smell of dirt, stream water, and grass. It smells just as April should, and I remember that as much as I admire humanity's architectural and artistic endeavors, there is nothing quite as sweet as being near the Creator's original artwork. I think back to Saint Francis and his love for the birds, and I sympathize with his preference for grass and trees.

Like Victoria Falls, we hear these before we see them, a cleansing rush of water collecting in a pool. Seven waterfalls spill into a murky-blue lake, smaller than Zimbabwe's but just as dignified. Croats cover the fields next to the lake, dining on picnic tables, lighting grills, playing Frisbee and volleyball. Our seven kids disappear into the trees and rocks along the lake and begin creating another imaginary land of their own, crafted from sticks, rocks, and mud. These sticks look identical to their counterparts in southern France, and the mud reminds me of the same stuff that collected in our campervan in New Zealand. The kids seem unable to not build another Terabithia, a

Pavlovian response to being thrust into nature. Tate and Abbie swing from vines and squeal with delight over the risk of falling into the lake. I watch from a boulder, a bit sad that tomorrow they will say farewell. One family heads east to Kosovo, and the other heads farther north to Norway.

Reed asks me to help him find the bathroom, and on the way, we bump into Charlie and Megan.

"Hey, guys!" I say. "We're from the bus."

"Hi, yes, of course," Megan says. "Beautiful day, right?" We squint up at another pristine sky.

"Where are the rest of the kids?" asks Charlie. I point to the waterfalls, where our gaggle's exuberant hijinks can be spotted half a mile away.

"Man, that's so great," he says. "Seriously. What an education."

We say good-bye, and I wish them luck in grad school. In life. With kids. Without. I hope they'll nurture their own wanderlust.

On our way back to our car, we pass a surprising chapel tucked in the woods, made of stone with a simple wooden door. A cross fashioned from nearby sticks hangs above the door, and the few small windows are shuttered closed. The structure is about the size of Francis's Porziuncola in Santa Maria degli Angeli, but it's bare of any medieval or Renaissance frescoes. It's a simple stone place of worship. I wonder if the Croats picnicking by the falls even know of its existence.

I stop walking and stand in silence, soaking in the chapel's abrupt presence. Everyone else pays more interest to a small waterfall a few feet away, and for a moment, I'm alone. This chapel seems to be carved out of the woods where it rests, as though its parishioners are the birds and deer, perhaps a wandering pilgrim taking the long way back. The incense burned here would be rainwater and new grass; the Eucharist a hunk of bread in a vagabond's backpack, saved from an earlier stop in a village bakery. The door is locked, so I walk around its perimeter and find a sign. It reads:

IN LONG AGO 1761, THIS CHURCH WAS BUILT AND
DEDICATED TO ST. NICHOLAS, THE PROTECTOR OF
TRAVELERS AND SEAFARERS. THE CHURCH HAS A SIMPLE
PLAN AND NO PARTICULAR STYLISTIC TRAITS. ITS CLAIM
TO FAME IS THAT IT IS MOSTLY BUILT OF DRIPSTONE,
A NATURAL MATERIAL THAT IS EASY TO FORM, BUT AT
THE SAME TIME SUFFICIENTLY LASTS A LONG TIME.

I know St. Nicholas's story, the man our family recognizes each December with gold coins in our shoes, the saint we paid homage to back in Queensland with sweaty summertime sandals. But I had forgotten he is also the patron saint of travelers, the person entrusted to watch over nomads wandering the earth.

Over two-hundred-fifty years ago, people fashioned a simple chapel and dedicated it to Nicholas, the watchful protector of people like us. I think of him the next morning as we say good-bye to our friends, and as we hug the Croatian coastline heading south in our car. We listen to Mat Kearney and Josh Garrells, retell our favorite stories from our time with friends, and watch the sun slide between boulders bursting from the Adriatic Sea.

Tonight, I fall asleep in another guesthouse, waiting for another flight, grateful for God's reminder of first Francis, and now, Nick.

18

KOSOVO

It was the year 2000, and Kyle and I were working for separate humanitarian organizations in Kosovo, a diminutive crumb of land that had been fought over for centuries in former Yugoslavia. He was rebuilding houses, while I was teaching English to Albanian teenagers, taking the summer to decide whether I wanted to work abroad full-time. I was with my team of volunteers, sitting inside in the heat of the day, parked next to oscillating fans and misting our foreheads with water. That's when we heard there was a new American in town.

I was located in a village of a thousand people, two kilometers from the Serbian border. It usually doesn't show up on maps, even the local ones. Nobody knows about the village unless you're from the area. It was more than a little strange that an American would move here, alone. Still, we thought we should welcome our new neighbor with an invitation to dinner.

But it was broiling and I was sticky, and moving required getting out in the non-air-conditioned world, where walking down the lone dirt road meant a show for the elderly villagers as they peeked behind their curtains for the latest news.

I literally drew the short straw. Postwar technology being in short supply, a girl in my group cut a drinking straw and added it to the rest in her hands to determine who was lucky. I sometimes wonder whether I'd have a different life if I hadn't drawn the short one.

I sighed, put on my shoes, and crept into the blazing heat. There was a high likelihood of running into everyone in this village by walking up and down the main dirt road, so this was my plan. Twenty seconds into my search, I saw a mirage, hazy atmospheric waves blurring what appeared to be an American gait. The body was coming toward me about a hundred feet away. This was my Mr. Darcy moment, though Balkan dirt road instead of pastoral British pond, dusty blue T-shirt instead of a white peasant blouse.

Kyle and I met in the middle of that dirt road.

"So, you're the new American," I said and instantly felt foolish.

He said, "Um . . . yep."

I invited him to dinner that night, and he joined our group at the one restaurant in town. I noticed he made an effort to sit next to me.

A few weeks passed, and I left Kosovo, saved up money waiting tables in Austin, then returned to the village six months later. By then, Kyle had moved to a different village, but Kosovo is small and there aren't many English speakers. We became fast friends, upgraded to dating, then married a little over two years from the day we met.

Fifteen years later, we look back at our meet cute on a dirty Balkan farm road on August 1, and we admit to *knowing* that afternoon. I was a spry college graduate, rosy future before me, and I looked at him and thought, *I'm going to marry him.* He says the same thing, standing at that spot on the road next to the ramshackle market with cheap cookies and cold Fanta. He just knew.

Fifteen years have passed, and we want to show our three children the spot on the road.

It's been more than twelve years since either Kyle or I have set foot here in Kosovo, and we've heard continual rumors about its changes since the early postwar era. We can only hope so. When we met in Kosovo, it was riddled with bullet holes, and backup generators compensated for spotty electricity. Now we've booked a guesthouse online in the capital city of Pristina, an indication that people actually visit. Some of my village students now live in the city, having left rural life for urban jobs and apartments where they can raise children near schools. They are all adults now.

The city air smells like mountains, chilled and unrefined, and I still breathe in secondhand smoke. The forecast calls for snow this weekend, and I debate trawling the market for faux leather jackets, the same one I shopped at fifteen years ago (the last time I bought a jacket at the market, it melted when I set it on a radiator). A high-rise that once lost a wall and revealed a grid of Soviet-era flats has now been razed and replaced with a gleaming glass building. A bustling coffee shop stands where I used to buy pirated CDs. On Wednesday nights, Kyle and I would ride buses into this city and listen to jazz music at a bar. I wonder if it's still there. I doubt I could find it again.

We park the car in downtown Pristina and walk pink-nosed to where we'll meet our Albanian friends.

"It's so cold here!" Tate says between chattering teeth.

"I can't believe I remember this, but want to know how you say that in Albanian?" I ask, speeding up to ward off the chill.

"How?"

I laugh before I can get it out. *"Unë jamë ftöhtë!"* I shout, and the kids peal with laughter. I remember now that this was my favorite Albanian phrase for its onomatopoeian quality.

"What else do you remember?" Reed asks. I look at Kyle and raise my eyebrows.

"Don't look at me," he says. "I don't remember a thing."

We turn the corner into the wind. I shiver and say, "Hmm, let's see . . . I remember how to say 'I'm full.' That one's fun."

"How?" Reed says, giggling.

"*Unë jamë plotë.*" The kids howl, then start to practice the phrase.

We turn another corner and Kyle says, "Whoa. This wasn't here." Our friends told us to meet them on the walking street, but the last time we were here, it was a potholed thoroughfare for cars. It's been transformed to a cobblestone boulevard where pedestrians now stroll in the early spring evening.

Skender is waiting for us on the street with his new wife, Jackie, an American English teacher. They met at an English-speaking high school in Pristina started by my former coworkers. Skender and Jackie now help run the place.

"Tsh! Kyle!" He waves us over.

We cross the street to hug Skender and shake Jackie's hand. He looks like the same kid with a few extra laugh lines and gray hairs. Fifteen years ago he would sit at my kitchen table and recite *her* and *hair*, unable to hear the difference. I remember him walking in on a hot day and proudly declaring, "I am a sweater!" I affectionately nicknamed him Smiling Skender.

I hear footsteps, and a familiar voice says, "*Mirëmbrëma, shoqet.*" Beqir, Kyle's old roommate, is standing behind him.

"Beq! What in the world!" Kyle says.

"Skender texted me and let me know you were here," he says. He looks unchanged as well. The postwar years have been kind to our friends.

We walk to a trendy brick restaurant off the walking street, and we dine on wine and memories. The electricity never once blacks out and the Italian food is delicious. Skender tells us stories about a recent trip to Washington, DC. We can't possibly be in Kosovo.

"The changes here are really remarkable," Kyle says between bites.

Skender and Beq nod. "It's not even the same country, right?" Beq says.

"I really can't believe it," I say.

"It's not all perfect," adds Skender. "Unemployment is huge here. Young people are all leaving for Germany because they can't find jobs." Earlier this morning I read something about this, about Kosovo's growing pains as Europe's youngest country.

"Well, looks like you guys lucked out," Kyle says.

"It helps enormously to know English," Skender says. His eyes are grateful. He now teaches in English at a school he helped found.

———

The next morning, we drive our rental car to the village. Kyle remembers the bends in the road and I remember the terra-cotta tiles on the roofs we pass, the same ones we passed countless times when we took the bus into the city and wondered whether our future included each other. The car curves around the lake embedded in the rolling hills that always marked our proximity to the village. We're almost there.

Kyle pulls into the parking lot of the lakeside restaurant where we had our first meal, where we had dozens of meals afterward. Distorted music blares indoors, as usual, but the gazebo near the water is open and quiet. A waiter seats us, and he's sporting the same white dress shirt and black tie uniform as before, better suited for a four-star establishment instead of an esplanade café.

We order our usual—chicken, a plate of fries sprinkled with feta cheese, sparkling water, wine. I'm disappointed that *lake crap* is no longer on the menu, but I'm glad they still proudly serve *beefsteak in hell*. The food tastes the same—hearty, simple, eastern European. The kids play on the restaurant playground after they eat and we sip cappuccinos. I don't recall the playground's existence in 2000, but it wasn't on my radar then.

We pay our bill, then drive over a bridge that didn't exist fifteen years ago (Milošević had bombed the original nineteenth-century bridge, so villagers built a wooden overpass, like a playground suspension bridge, only poorly constructed). I show the kids where I once lived—a kitchen window and balcony on the second floor of a Soviet-era concrete building, where I would check to see if Kyle was driving down the road.

The official spot on the road where we met was outside my kitchen window. We put our rental car in park, walk to the spot, and take a family photo with our hair flying in the wind. This is it. We made it back. These three kids exist because of this patch of concrete.

The kids are freezing and beg to return to the car, so they leave the two of us on the road. We kiss, and I imagine old ladies peeking from behind their curtains. Albanian children giggle around us. I want to high-five my twenty-four-year-old self, whisper in her ear that everything would work out with the lanky Oregon boy with the derelict Volkswagen van.

19

TURKEY

Our kids had never been to Kosovo, but they'd heard of it for years, their parents regaling them with romantic tales of a war-torn land as the backdrop for our family's origin. Touching Kosovar soil meant connecting them to an important piece of their existence, context for future conversations. Turkey, on the other hand—they remember this place on their own.

Finn is the only one who hasn't crossed the border to Turkey; we returned to the United States when I was five months pregnant with him.

Though we can't stay in Turkey long, we need to be here. Reed took his first breath here, Tate grew from a toddler to schoolgirl here, and Finn was conceived here. This place is in our family blood. We lived here for three years and made a home for ourselves, five stories up in an apartment high-rise overlooking the Aegean Sea. We'd watch cruise ships glide past as we ate our breakfast on the patio, made friends with the man down the street who sold the best rotisserie chicken, and learned the back routes to avoid traffic during rush hour. We were making plans for Tate to start kindergarten in Izmir when, due to health reasons, we suddenly needed to relocate to the States. We've long made peace with that abrupt transition in our lives, but we made an oath to keep Turkey a significant part of our life. It is good to step on its soil again.

It's the first full morning in Izmir, city of four million, and I am nursing a latte from a park bench where I've sat many times before. The kids are playing on the playground as though five years haven't passed. Our neighborhood grocery store is on the right, and I've just bought two of my favorite cooking staples from our life here—*kaşar*, a substitute for cheddar, and Milka bars for chocolate chips. Five years ago, I was annoyed that common American commodities were nowhere to be found, but this morning it is charming. *How resourceful this made me*, I ponder. *How outside-the-box I had to think*. My past self is rolling her eyes at me with contempt.

In the last hour, I have surprised myself. As if on autopilot, I knew the exact whereabouts of canned tomatoes, toothpaste, and *gözleme*. Those grocery aisles are hallowed. It's where I learned to get over myself. Pity parties got me nowhere.

It's hard to live far away from home, but Turkey can be breathtaking.

I curl my sleeves over my fists, shivering from wind whipping in from the Aegean a mile away. Snow pours over Kosovar hills seven hundred miles to the north, and two days ago we kissed good-bye to our Albanian friends from fifteen years ago, when I was a college graduate and in love with a boy. Now, I'm on a Turkish bench in the throes of young motherhood, thanks to the same boy.

"Hey, Mom, I remember this slide!" Tate yells from the playground.

"Yep. You'd go careening so fast you'd slam your bottom to the ground with a thud." I'd have to scoop her in my arms with a peck on the cheek because of that steep slide.

"And I remember this swing set, how it's so low to the ground, your feet drag!" she yells, running to the merry-go-round with the tacky ducks and bears, paint chipped and worn.

"That's it," Kyle declares, handing me his coffee. "I'm going in."

He climbs a ladder to a slide, spooks the kids, and they shriek with delight. Parents on benches next to me wide-eye him, incredulous a grown man would scale a plaything. *Just the same*, I think, recalling the familiar response to our parenting here. I smile and dig out my camera, and an old woman points at my youngest and shakes her head. I know she's appalled he's not wearing a winter hat. The temperature is sixty-five degrees.

Turkey is complicated, chock-full of paradoxes. It's a delightful place to sightsee, with vividly colored rugs and ceramics, stunning beaches, otherworldly food, and more historic sights than you could explore in a lifetime. I remember one of my earliest visits, standing on a balcony overlooking the bay and someone saying, "Archaeologists have unearthed at least twenty layers of civilization underneath the surface. There's a reason it's taken so long to build a decent metro system here—every time we dig, we find something important."

After two visits to Turkey ten years ago, Kyle and I knew we wanted to live here. But living here, raising a family and working as a foreigner, is different from being a tourist. Cultural mores are confusing—when company comes to dinner, when do we serve the *çay* and when do we present the bowl of fruit without being rude? Sexism is rampant—even in secular Izmir, women still cannot sign their own housing contracts. Schools are tough—the mathematics curriculum is impressive, but pint-sized bullies tend to run the place. The language takes years to conquer, a lifetime to master—the longest word in Turkish is *Muvaffakiyetsizleştiricileştiriveremeyebileceklerimizdenmişsinizcesine*. Thankfully, it's not very useful (it means "As though you are from those whom we may not be able to easily make into a maker of unsuccessful ones").

But . . . Turkey. Turkey has a sizable portion of the world's best landscapes, historical sites, food, and humanity. For personal reasons, it's for the best we no longer live here. But we'll never tire of coming back.

High on our Turkish agenda: eating. I crave Turkish food on gray, drizzly afternoons—*mercimek çorbasi*, a creamy, tomato-based lentil soup, followed by a steaming cup of çay. I crave Turkish food when the summer sun is relentless—*tavuk dürüm*, a chicken wrap, chased with a chocolaty Magnum ice cream bar. God gave the Turks an extra dose of culinary prowess.

We make a list in our notebooks of the must-have provisions during our week: gözleme (several flavors), *kiremitte, iskender, pide* of various sorts—*tavuklu, kuşbaşılı kaşarlı, kıymalı*; tavuk dürüm, *döner kebap*, mercimek çorbasi, *köfte, manti, lahmacun, baklava*, and a traditional Turkish breakfast. There aren't enough meals on our calendar, but we'll try. Our gastronomical jaunt takes high priority.

Pide is Turkish pizza, long and narrow, edges folded to encrust melted sheep's cheese and toppings like minced lamb, or my preference, chicken. Baked in a wood-fire oven, it's served piping hot with a side of arugula, sliced tomato and lemon, and *biber salçası*, a cool, piquant red pepper paste. Pile on veggies, smear the paste, fold the pide in half, turn your head, and feast. We have this delivered to our apartment three times.

I stop for a quick gözleme whenever we're out because it's my favorite. One afternoon I'm having çay with an American friend who still lives here while my kids join hers for a community art class, and I order a pumpkin gözleme. This savory pastry is filled with anything from ground beef to spinach to feta to potato, but pumpkin takes me back.

"Oh, my gosh, I think the last time I had pumpkin gözleme was at the water park," I tell my friend Andie.

"The water park? That's weird," she says.

"Yeah, but Turkey," I reply, and she nods.

While the kids would swim in the neighborhood water park, I'd order this unconventional poolside lounge fare. Paper-thin circles of yufka dough are seared atop a large, round griddle; filling is then added and pressed into a half circle and folded again in thirds to create a triangular pocket. It's Turkey's answer to a French crêpe. In the urban areas of Istanbul and Izmir, you can find trendy gözleme toppings like orange zest, walnut, and smoked salmon served on a busy street corner, the line of hip, hungry patrons wrapping the block.

Nothing is as quintessentially Turkish as iskender kebap, named after its nineteenth-century inventor, İskender Efendi; it's as commonplace as barbecue in Texas. Tonight, we take the kids to a restaurant with nothing on the menu but iskender kebap.

We walk through the doors, and the restaurant is packed with boisterous families. It's a school night, and several kids wear school and soccer uniforms. IKEA is next door, and there is a sea of blue bags slung over chairs. A waiter cleans a booth, leads us to it, and sets down one menu. There is iskender kebap, there are sides of fries, and there are drinks.

"*Iyi akşamlar,*" the waiter says. "*Ne yemek istersiniz?*"

Kyle looks at me. "Well, I guess our choices are iskender or iskender."

"I think we should order iskender," I say. The waiter looks at me. "*Iskender kebap alabalirmiyiz,*" I say.

"*Tamam. Aile için?*" he says, pointing to all of us. One for all of us?

"Um . . . *evet,*" Kyle says. Why not?

A few minutes pass, and the waiter returns with a colossal platter of iskender kebap, sizzling strips of thin meat piled high on top of chunks of flatbread soaked in tomato sauce and yogurt. I can't imagine us eating all this.

A younger waiter approaches with a ladle and tureen and asks, "*Tereyağı?*" Would we like butter?

"*Evet, evet,*" Kyle answers. The boy dips the ladle in his tureen and pours bubbling melted butter over our meat. The gold liquid crackles. Before we can stop him, he pours a second round.

"*Daha?*" he asks, ready for a third helping.

"*Hayır, hayır!*" I say, covering the platter with my arm. If he pours it again, he'll sear my skin. The meat is swimming in butter, intermingling with the tomato sauce and tangy yogurt.

We pass out forks and dig in.

"Whoa," Tate says after she swallows. "This is really good." She has forgotten the taste of this.

"Mm-hmm," Kyle answers, mouth full.

I don't like gamey meat in the States, but I love lamb here—somehow, the nostrily punch of wet earth found in lamb meat feels more apropos on the streets of Turkey. It's grilled for hours vertically on a spit, and its juices marinate each slice cut fresh per order. The taste is fresh, simple, hot, and succulent, with just a hint of cumin. The sweetness of pureed tomatoes and the surprising tang of cold yogurt is an impeccable pairing with lamb. The bread is seared directly on a grill, burned with perfection.

We order honey-sweet baklava for dessert and wonder why we ever left this country. We lick the platter clean.

Several years ago, two-year-old Tate pitched a fit one afternoon crossing the Aegean Sea bay, stamping her foot in protest on the ferryboat taking us to the north side of town for a playdate. The sun striped the deck and sparkled the gray-green waves; seagulls circled and scooped the water for lunch. The weather was sublime and I had successfully used my Turkish to navigate the two of us onto a bus and then the boat. I was in my second trimester with Reed, so queasiness had quelled and ferryboats were feasible at last. Tate was splayed on the deck at the front of the boat, throwing a toddler tantrum. I sat on the bench and ignored her, denying her attention so as to defuse the outburst, employing my remaining energy to ignore the staring multitude of commuters.

A *caycı*, the man who serves tea to ferryboat passengers, rushed over and offered her the last thing I wanted her to have: a sugar cube. Turkish toddler parenting called for more indulgence, a more laissez-faire way than my American style; plus, her blonde hair and blue eyes granted her local adoration. I snatched the sugar cube out of Tate's hand before she could pop it in her mouth, her tantrum ensued, and I paid the well-meaning *caycı* for a tulip-shaped glass of çay. It wasn't any better than a sugar cube, but I let my two-year-old have a sip. And another. And another. She loved tea. She left her tantrum on the ferryboat deck.

There might not be dessert after a Turkish meal, but there will always—*always*—be çay. In a diminutive, handleless, tulip-shaped glass, you lift it by the rim, careful not to burn your fingers, and slurp as a sign of satisfaction. Some say leaving the teaspoon inside the glass signals a call for seconds, and resting it facedown across the top means you've had enough (typically after thirds). Adding two sugar cubes is normal, though I personally take mine black, much to the chagrin of Turks (and Albanians; çay—or *çaj*, as it's spelled in Kosovo—is just as essential to daily life there).

Black-leaf tea from Trabzon or Rize along the Black Sea is best, brewed loosely in a double-decker kettle over a gas stove. Pour a few tablespoons of concentrated tea into your tulip glass, fill the rest with the boiling water, and let sugar cubes dissolve with a clink-clank swirl of the teaspoon. Then sip. It's chock-full of caffeine, but it's culturally appropriate to drink it at ten in the evening.

When çay no longer stifles your yawns, you'll tap off with a whole clove, sucking the flavor clean off the seed. This cleanses the palate, freshens your breath, and tastes like Thanksgiving. Pop a clove in your mouth, and suck until the flavor dissipates, then put the remnant spice on the saucer. Do it over the years, and it'll taste like Turkey.

———

Near the end of our week, we make a spur-of-the-moment trip a few hours east to see some ancient ruins. We'd been to Ephesus, Pergamon, and Smyrna while we lived in Turkey, and we want to check off a few more sites. If we swing through Philadelphia en route to Laodicea, we'll have six of the seven ancient churches mentioned in St. John's book of Revelation to our name. All of them are near Izmir.

We dash north to Manisa and drive by the scant Philadelphian ruins, which are now sandwiched between two modern apartment complexes; then we veer southeast to Laodicea, where the archaic city displays a vast acreage of crumbling marble columns, derelict roads, and piles of stone blocks. While we're here, we visit cotton-white calcified pools of Pamukkale and the ancient ruins of Hierapolis, a spa town from the Roman Empire.

The kids play tag next to ancient marble columns while Kyle plays with his camera and I journal.

"Aaaaaaaaaaah!" I hear in Tate's voice. I look up, and she's holding her face, bent over and crumbling in pain. Reed stands next to her, apologizing and worried. We rush over.

"What happened?" Kyle asks, pulling Tate's hands away from her face. She's in crying hysterics, unable to answer.

"We were playing tag, and my head bonked her mouth," explains Reed. "I'm so sorry. Tate, are you okay? I'm so sorry." He's holding his head in pain.

Her bottom two teeth have chipped off their tops. We search the grass in vain—they've flung who knows where, mingling with pebbles and ancient rubble. There might be teeth a thousand years old here too. We're near the end of our trip, so close to finishing without needing medical attention, but alas, we did not succeed. My role shifts from explorer to parent; my afternoon's focus is now how to handle missing teeth bits. I am awakened from the dreamlike state that comes from wandering ancient ruins.

We find a dentist in Izmir who speaks English and can see a new patient at a moment's notice. The next morning, we're at his office, filling out medical forms and answering dental history questions.

A man in jeans and a white doctor's jacket walks into the waiting room, hand out to shake ours. "Hi—my name's Trent. Come on back."

Tate, Kyle, and I follow him, and the front receptionist promises to entertain the boys with toys. Tate settles into the dentist's chair, and he peers into her mouth.

"You guys traveling?" he asks.

"Yes," I answer. "But we used to live here."

"Where are you from?"

"The States. Oregon, mostly."

"I'm from Washington!" he says. "Been here for a few years now, though."

He raises the dental chair and stands up for a better look.

"What brings you to Turkey?" Kyle asks.

"My wife's Turkish," Trent says, "and she missed home. We lived in Spokane for a while, but American culture just got too hectic for her."

He presses a button on a phone. "Hey, babe, mind bringing back some çay?" He looks at us. "Want some çay?"

"Uh, sure," I answer.

A few minutes later, a woman comes in with a tray holding four tulip glasses of çay and introduces herself as Trent's wife.

"She's filling in for my assistant," he says, as he slides over a tray of tools to begin work in Tate's mouth. "She's out again somewhere.

Where is she, honey?" "She's protesting something downtown," his wife says. "She says she'll be in tomorrow."

He laughs. "She's always protesting something." He takes a sip of çay and continues working.

"Do you want Kyle and me to . . . leave?" I ask.

"Oh no, you're fine," Trent says. "It's way more laid-back here. Just hang out, keep me company. Tell me about your travels."

We tell him about our family, our work, where we've been.

"So great. What a great experience." He lights up a screen above Tate's head and shows us a photo of her teeth, before and after. "Almost done."

"Wow, you're quick," Kyle says.

"Well, I have a light day, so you caught me at a good time."

He cleans up, gives us a card for his brother, a dentist in Washington, and tells us to call him if we ever need dental work in his area.

"Do you miss working in the States?" Kyle asks him. Trent laughs.

"Nah, no way. It's so much easier being a dentist here. Almost no red tape. My work is straightforward. I get paid less, but it means I don't have to charge patients out the wazoo for my work. Means I sleep better at night."

We thank him for his pristine work on Tate's teeth and for his astoundingly low rates.

"Anytime," he says. "Hey—I got a question. Has the tooth fairy visited your family on the trip? What kind of money did she bring you?"

We laugh, and we tell him how often she's visited us. Between Tate and Reed, she's brought Chinese *quai*, Thai *baht* twice, Australian dollars, South African *rand*, euros from France, and, as of yesterday morning, Turkish *lira*.

"That's amazing. And amazing she knew where to find your teeth. I guess she knows home is wherever you are."

Five years ago, we made a home in Turkey. It's not home now, but

I like to think she's somewhere in the mix—together with my twenty-two other homes. She is a part of the foundation, a stud, perhaps a rafter. She is a small part of the sticks and bricks of home, a home taking shape somewhere in the world. Home—impossible to locate on a map.

20

GERMANY

Like many Americans, Kyle and I have German blood running thick through our veins. *Oxenreider* means more or less what you'd think it means: someone who clears fields with oxen. I'm told my maiden name, Henegar, evolved long ago from Heineken, and it finds its origins in a keg of German beer (there's a Henninger lager, another derivative of the name). My father is full-blooded German, and my grandfather's mother's maiden name was even the word *German*. Sausage and sauerkraut are coded into our DNA.

We land in Munich after a quick flight from Izmir, pick up a new rental car, then pick up Kyle's parents, who have jumped the pond for a visit.

It's our first morning in Bavaria, and five seconds after gathering my things out of the car to head down the squeaky-clean streets of Munich, Finn has disappeared. Panic sets in. He was just here; he can't have gone far. I find him ten feet down the road, standing on a windowsill four feet off the ground.

"Dude! How on earth did you get up there?" I say. "And get down—you're not supposed to be staring in people's windows." The window's shutters are open, and he's peering into the house.

"It's okay," I hear in German-accented English from the other side. Four teenage boys are playing foosball. "He's just watching. We don't mind."

They continue playing and pay him no attention. We watch a few more seconds, say *Auf Wiedersehen*, then head to the science museum with the grandparents.

Bavaria is Germany's most German province. Lederhosen, glock-enspiel, the mammoth clock celebrating the wedding of the duke who founded the nearby famous Hofbrauhaus, Oktoberfest—all these hail from here. We walk Munich's cobblestone streets, climb church towers, and sample giant pretzels for two days, then leave town for the countryside.

While in Italy, Dan and Bethany recommended a theme park in Bavaria. I balked at the idea, shuddering at the thought of com-mercialized, concrete-ridden parks full of overstimulating noise and movement. I'm a poor poker player, and my face tipped Bethany off. She smiled, said, "Oh no, it's not like a regular American theme park. Trust me—this is a good one."

"Is it worth the money?" I asked her. For much less money, we could have an *actual* local experience, and not a manicured, prepackaged, branded one trapped in a theme park.

"It's only like ten euro each," she said. "Totally reasonable. And the food is really good too. Just trust me."

Fifty bucks for our entire family is a steal, and Dan and Bethany haven't yet steered us wrong. We decide to visit Freizeitpark Ruhpolding.

Kyle drives us through idyllic Alps-infused Bavarian countryside to a little town hugging the Austrian border, GPS charting a rural route with no theme park in sight, and I'm fairly sure we're lost. Then I see it—a wooden sign swinging on a pole. A gravel parking lot is tucked into the hillside, and a narrow hiking path disappears into the hills. Arrows on the path point to the park. We zip our jackets and trek uphill, panting to the entrance.

Devoid of primary colors, rubbery walkways, and the stripped natural landscape so common in American theme parks, Freizeitpark Ruhpolding is hewn out of these Bavarian hills. Trees canopy the play areas and slides copy the ebb and flow of the land, resting on hills and letting nature dictate their downward course. I breathe in forest air and exhale worry. Bethany was right.

There are vintage carnival rides and a roller coaster, but the park is mostly wooden climbing structures, monstrous tire swings, zip lines, and merry-go-round discs set at an angle on a hillside, devoid of handles and safety rails. The kids jump with abandon in a ball pit crammed full of other kids. I haven't seen a ball pit in the States outside a therapy clinic in years.

"This place is the best!" Finn trills as he whips down a slide in a felted toboggan.

Some parents are playing with their children, zipping in tree houses and besting them at skeeball and tin can–shooting games. Many more are seated on decks outside cafés, sipping beer and coffee and quietly chatting. All kids are free to wander. Ours join them.

We play with the kids at first, whooshing down precipitous metal slides and screaming with them. We spin in a ride that whirls backward at such breakneck speeds that I make my body a seat belt for Finn for fear he'll careen out of our shared seat. Later, when Kyle and I tire, we soak in Bavarian sunshine on the wooden deck, nursing drinks and watching the kids gallivant.

We leave at closing time and make the hillside stroll downward. On the way, I instinctively grab Reed's hand. He's my wild child, a boy who prefers to sit upside down to hear a story, who dances down the sidewalk and spins circles in the produce aisle.

"Hey, Mom," Reed says, voice quivering, "did you notice you're always grabbing my hand?"

"Well, I just want you to be safe," I say, loosening my grip. I am called out.

"But I'm seven now. I know I'm a kid, but sometimes when you hold my hand like this, it feels like you don't trust me." His face crumples with tears.

Last week in Turkey, Tate and I were waiting in the car while Kyle and Reed ran across the street to take a photo of him in front of the hospital where he was born. We were reminiscing about the trip, the freedom she felt to go alone to the bakery in Cadenet, to swim by herself in the community pool across the street from our Thai guesthouse, to stroll the acreage of the Pasignano farmhouse in Italy with Abbie.

"If we were still living in Turkey, would I be allowed to run errands on my own?" she asked.

"Yep," I answered her. I remembered watching eight-year-olds run into the corner store from our apartment balcony, three-year-old Tate begging me to let her join them. *Soon enough, you will*, I'd answer.

Tate sighed. "I really wish kids were allowed to do that kind of stuff in America. We should tell the president to make it a law so that kids have more freedom and adults aren't so nervous all the time."

I remember this conversation, and stop on the Bavarian trail back to the parking lot and look Reed in the eye. "I don't mean to treat you like you're little. I want to show you that I trust you. Because you are a good kid. You're a *fantastic* kid."

"Mom—I have something to tell you," Reed says. He breathes deep and wipes tears running down his face. "I've been almost around the whole world now, and I've done a good job. I haven't gotten lost or gotten hurt. I feel like I'm growing up." He pauses. "Do you think you can stop holding my hand so much?"

I look down at our hands; I'm still holding on and Reed is cupping his palm free. I release my fingers and he slides his hand in his jacket.

"I love you, bud," I say, messing his hair.

"Love you too," he replies, and runs ahead.

Uhldingen-Mühlhofen is so difficult for us to say, that between Kyle and me, we default to a butchered nickname: Uberlingen-Dinglehopper. We snicker childishly at the highway exit and entrance signs declaring *Ausfahrt* and *Einfahrt*. I love that the word for airplane is *flugzeug*, which literally translates to "fly-thing." The word for speed limit is *geschwindigkeitsbegrenzung*. German amuses.

We want to revel in more Bavarian countryside, so at the last second, we book a guesthouse in Uhldingen-Mühlhofen, the miniature village along the Bodensee lake. Along the way, we take ausfahrts to villages that sound even mildly interesting, soaking up our rental car before returning it in Paris. We need coffee this morning, having spent a day at Freizeitpark Ruhpolding yesterday, and Uhldingen-Mühlhofen is still two hours away. We approach a road sign for the village of Landsberg am Lech, and it looks pleasant enough from a distance. Italy is less than two hundred miles south, but it's no small feat to find a decent cup of brew in Germany. We cross our fingers, hope for the best, and make the exit.

I find directions to an open bakery on my phone app, and as Kyle searches for a parking spot, I read about this unassuming village.

"Oh, my goodness," I gasp.

"What?" Kyle asks.

"This is where Hitler wrote *Mein Kampf*," I say, scrolling *Wikipedia*.

"Whoa. Are you serious?"

"And this is said to be where the Hitler Youth first formed." I survey the village's town square, with its innocent houses and pink-tinted shops. One of the vilest persons born into this human experience wrote his foundational ideas in this pocket-sized place. I see no signs commemorating this history.

I scroll through my phone and read more as I wait for our coffee order at the bakery. Landsberg am Lech is also where the United States Army liberated a concentration camp with the help of one of their soldiers named Tony Bennett, and it's where Johnny Cash was stationed with the air force. The village's medieval wall is still erect, cannonball still stuck on one side.

I return to the car, coffees in hand, and I think about the world's other Landsberg am Lechs. How many random villages down this street hold the weight of history in their annals? How many layers of civilization are we driving over, roads so old they're too deep to unearth? Twenty, like Izmir's? What other ausfahrts hold secrets, hinges that alter the trajectory of global saga—not just in Germany, but in Italy, Croatia, Morocco, even in the States? How many shoulders do I stand on, their spirits whispering around me as I walk through Venetian alleys, Cadenet's market, Kenyan fields, and little, unpredictable Landsberg am Lech?

Tonight we tuck the kids in at our new guesthouse in Uhldingen-Mühlhofen, where we watch the sun set from our backyard over the Bodensee, Switzerland waving from the other side. We have no agenda here, other than one final week to catch up on school and work before heading northwest, into northern France and onward to London. The last time we stopped for any length of time was in Cadenet, almost two months ago now. We need a breather before our journey's final push. I can already see a pinhole-sized light at the end of the tunnel.

The kids' grandparents are with us, and it's our duty to let them watch the kids while we go on a much-needed date. The last time we went out was Lourmarin, eight weeks ago. Kyle opens the gate in the backyard, and we cross the street, walk hand in hand along the Bodensee. Earlier today we spotted a pub with outdoor seating in the microscopic town square, overlooking the waterfront. Our kids played in the grass while German teenagers ate picnic lunches nearby, and we eyed the pub like a beacon of light.

Tonight, we stroll down the darkened street that leads to the town square, order lagers from the smoky bar, and zip our jackets as we cradle drinks and wind whips our hair.

"Babe—we've done it," Kyle says, taking a slug of beer.

"We did it," I answer. I clink his glass in cheer.

"Around the world in one direction. Who'da thought?"

"That it was doable?" I ask.

"No," he says. "That we'd do it without killing each other."

"A worthy endeavor," I answer. We clink glasses again.

He pauses. "Well, we're not done yet. I guess there are still a few weeks to kill each other."

Tonight, we decide it's time to begin landing the plane. In three weeks, we'll be back in the United States, still undecided about where to call home. We don't have our answers yet about home, work, and postnomadic life, but we know they'll come when we need them. Right now, we are still vagabonds. I think of the hat I wanted to exchange with Nora, and I wonder where I finally tossed it into the wind. We're still crawling the earth and chipping away parts of us that no longer fit, but we're molding new clay, fresh stuff we gathered on the road. The trip has changed us, but we're so fully present, here in this Bavarian forest, we don't yet know how.

I want to write a rough plan on how, exactly, we'll debrief the kids as our plane descends. We've chatted with each of them throughout our year, asking about their favorite and worst moments of a day, what they think about nonstop travel, what they miss about normal life, their favorite things about different countries. Debriefing well is to unpack a backpack and name what's inside. It doesn't prevent rough reentries back to a home culture—we know this from personal experience—but it can certainly help smooth the bumps. Tate and Reed are already thinking about a return to American life, but Finn has a limited grasp of time. We need to break the news to him soon: our trip is almost over.

Kyle and I slurp our lagers and hash out what the kids will need to process: people they met, places they already miss, the aftermath and beauty of dividing your heart and leaving it in infinite places. The surprising and inevitable challenge of returning to life in one location looms. These are things we need to process as adults.

We know one kid needs to hash out thoughts about friends, and another needs his own room. One kid needs to catch up on math, and we need a heart-to-heart about continuing school during the summer. All three need serious sleep. This is the stuff of parenting. Traveling never gave us a free pass.

We toast to our three kids and marvel at their growth because of traveling, not in spite of it. We scroll back to photos from the Great Wall in China and witness how much they've grown, discuss how they've matured. Reed hardly needs his hand held anymore. Tate is solidly in tweendom. Finn outgrew shoes midway through the trip, and is already outgrowing his second pair.

We walk home when the pub closes with a game plan to start preparing for a return home in the next few days. Just before I turn out the light on my nightstand, Kyle already snoring, I pull out a pencil and add to my journal: *I need to work through every bit of this too.*

A few days later, we're on our way to the French border town of Strasbourg and we slink down one last ausfahrt, this one for the town of Gengenbach. We know nothing about it, but it's our last chance to walk on German soil. I've grown a fast affection for this country. Barely on the western edge of the Black Forest region, Gengenbach's medieval town square hosts the world's largest Advent calendar through its town hall's twenty-four windows. It also has some bang-up lemon gelato by the main fountain. It's home to the second labyrinth of our trip.

The kids play in the park that afternoon in Gengenbach, and Kyle watches them from the bench while he chats with his parents. I have a few quiet minutes alone.

Shoes tossed aside, I step into the labyrinth and begin my prayer from Chiang Mai: *Christ be with me, Christ within me, Christ behind me, Christ before me.* I have questions for God. What has this epically long family road trip taught me about myself? How have I changed? How am I still the same? How is God speaking to me through the sheer act of travel? I remember St. Nicholas, the patron saint of vagabonds.

I know, in my soul, that a love for travel is a gift and not a hindrance. It feels like a burden when the bucket list is bigger than the bank account, but a thirst for more of the world is not something to apologize for. Denying its presence feels like denying something good in me, something God put there. Wanderlust has a reputation as the epitome of unrequited love, something the young and naive chase after because they don't yet realize it's as futile as a dog chasing its tail. Turns out, ever-burning wanderlust is a good thing.

I step deeper into the labyrinth, one more step, two steps, one foot in front of the other.

Even so, my innards ache for home. My heart has a magnetic pull toward an earthly center, a place of permanence. I want passport stamps, so long as I have a drawer to keep that passport in at the end of a trip. Giving up a home this year felt like swinging on a netless trapeze. The kids are eager for a home, to be in their own beds with blankets and stuffed animals. Kyle is eager to dust off his tools and get back to woodworking. I pine for my books, splayed on a shelf instead of an e-reader. My soul feels pulled in two directions: toward home, and toward another unknown road in another town.

God, why do I have both wanderlust and *a yearning for home?* I step deeper, closer to the center. This labyrinthine path, a circular back-and-forth toward a central ebenezer, resembles our family's year. It zigzags, rambles out farther then returns closer, takes the long road to its destination. The rock stays unchanged. No matter how many times I'd try to rewalk this path, I'll wind up at the same rock.

Wanderlust and my longing for home are birthed from the same place: a desire to find the ultimate spot this side of heaven. When I stir soup at my stove, I drift to a distant island. When I'm on the road with my backpack, my heart wanders back to my couch, my favorite coffee cup. My equal pull between both are fueled by my hardwired desire for heaven on earth. And I know I'll never find it.

I stop at the labyrinth center, and I think of the stanza to one of my favorite poems, from Elizabeth Barrett Browning:

> Earth's crammed with heaven,
> And every common bush afire with God:
> But only he who sees, takes off his shoes,
> The rest sit round it, and pluck blackberries. . . .

I've seen an earth crammed with heaven. Hints of its existence are dropped all over the place, even in the birthplace of Hitler. If I could see to the fathoms beneath the surface, I'd see the secret behind all these common bushes, the roots of Thai banana trees and the avocado trees of Uganda. They'd wink at me, sharing their secret and nodding in affirmation at my bare feet. I press my naked toes into the labyrinth's gravel path.

I love finding one more new place to explore, I love showing it to my kids, and I love wandering those new streets with Kyle. But unless the flickering bushes compel me to remove my shoes, traveling the world will never satisfy. Neither will the daily liturgy of normal life back home. The laundry folding and bill paying would do me in. I'd resign myself to plucking blackberries.

The way to reconcile my wanderlust with life back home is to lean in to the tension, to extol life's haunting inability to ever fully satisfy. Life's full of paradoxes, after all. Why shouldn't this be one more of them?

21

ENGLAND

We spend a week in Normandy and Paris, showing my in-laws my second-favorite European city and touching the sacred sands of Omaha Beach. Daily gelatos are replaced by daily crêpes. We climb the steps up the Eiffel Tower, devour a box of macarons from Lauderée on the Champs-Élysées, and wander the Pompidou and Louvre. I queue at Shakespeare and Company while the family sips cappuccinos and sodas in a crowded café across the street from Notre Dame, and we take a family selfie underneath the Arc de Triomphe. We pack all of Paris into a few short days, then hop on a puddle-jumper to my first-favorite European city.

I've been to London at least five times before, but it's been a while, and the kids have never been. Kyle's only been once, when we were engaged, and it was such a short jaunt and we were so poor, we did almost nothing. I am eager to show my favorite people my favorite city.

Ending in London isn't an accident. Except for Australia, now more than ten thousand miles away, its culture is most similar to our own. There are differences, of course, but the disparities between the United States and Britain, and the United States and, say, China? There's no comparison.

Our primary agenda is togetherness. We walk by Big Ben, the

London Eye, the Globe Theatre, the Tower Bridge, and they form the backdrop for family chats about what life will soon look like. We sigh with relief at the lack of a language barrier, and we make heavy use of the cleanest metro system in the world. I also want to find a souvenir of my own.

We've been collecting art this year, rolling up prints and tea towels in a travel tube, grateful for lightweight mobility. I'd eye a ceramic tea set in Sri Lanka or a gumwood bench in Australia, yet our lengthy backpack living couldn't justify them. But London is our last stop. I want to find something.

I reckon I'll find what I'm looking for on Portobello Road in one of London's most iconic markets. It's in Notting Hill, one of my favorite areas. Every Saturday, the street and surrounding alleys of Notting Hill fill with throngs of booths offering antiques, books, vintage clothing, and records, with even more hordes of people eager to browse and buy. It's a collector's dream, it's a Highly Sensitive Person's nightmare, and if you want something British besides a Union Jack magnet or snow globe, it's worth the overwhelm.

All morning, we skirt the alleys and main street, weave through crowds, and stop at booths to eye old-fashioned cameras, teacups honoring the queen's jubilee, and forty-year-old double-decker bus toys. I drool over old copies of *Peter Pan* and *Winnie-the-Pooh*, but nothing is priced well enough for my few precious pounds, so by lunch, I resign myself to fish and chips. From Notting Hill, we head toward the Tube station, and on the way, I see precisely what I want. It's nothing special—a silver pitcher, part of a long-gone tea set, now orphaned and priced to move. Eight inches tall, tarnished, and boxy shaped with a flip-top lid, it's not worth much to anyone. But I want it. It could be used for tea, or it could house flowers as a vase. Probably, though, it'll sit on top of a stack of books, high on my bookshelf, as a reminder of our year around the world. It is lovely.

Engraved on the front, in plain-set typography, are the words *Rosebery Felixstowe*. I have no idea what this means, so I ask the booth's vendor, who's busy making change for other buyers.

"No idea, love. It's old and missing its set, so it's hard to say. But it's yours for ten pounds," he says. He returns to haggling a price on a set of teaspoons. I toss the man a ten-pound note, wave thanks, and tuck my new silver pitcher into my backpack.

When we return to our flat I search for Rosebery Felixstowe on the Internet, and I discover that Rosebery is a short neighborhood street in the seaside town of Felixstowe, not far from Ipswich. I've never been there, I have to find its whereabouts on a map, and until now, I've had little interest in visiting that part of England.

I'm a confessed Anglophile, my loyalty second only to Europe as a whole. When I graduated college, I backpacked around the United Kingdom with a girlfriend, and a year later, I returned with a group of friends for two more weeks. I love English gardens, my favorite movies and books tend to be set somewhere in the British Empire, and of course, I still dream of a white owl delivering an acceptance letter to Hogwarts. High on my travel list is a month in a rental car, winding backcountry roads in summertime with the family. I want to visit the Cotswolds, Brighton, and Yorkshire, head up to Scotland's Isle of Skye and the Shetland Islands, touch base in the Welsh town of Hay-on-Wye. I want to nibble on scones in Canterbury. And now? I want to visit unassuming, unknown Felixstowe.

Back home, wherever that is, I'll display my heavyweight silver pitcher. Its engraving, front and center, will equally remind me that I'll never see it all, all the places people call home, where they shop for bread and what they eat for dinner. Rosebery Felixstowe is home to someone else, and I'd like to see it, firsthand. What's the street of Rosebery like? My pitcher will be in my American home, waving its English flag and reminding me to get back out.

Two days before our flight back to the States, we spend the afternoon in Hyde Park, a green haven in the midst of the city. The kids need to run, Kyle and I need to rest, and we all need to chat, one last time, about our trip's end. The kids play for hours on the pirate ship at the Diana, Princess of Wales Memorial Playground, and Kyle and I take turns napping. Near dinnertime, we gather our jackets for a final stroll through the grass.

"All right, kids," Kyle says as they climb up a log, "favorite park you played at this year?"

"This one!" declares Finn, little thought beyond the present.

"Hmm . . ." Tate pauses for a moment. "I think the park in Germany, the one with the supersteep slides."

"Oh yeah—that's my favorite!" Finn says.

"Where was that one park with all the tree logs stuck together, like a jungle gym treehouse?" Reed asks.

"That was Strasbourg, in France," I say.

"Okay. Then that one's my favorite," he decides.

We can mark time on the trip by playgrounds. Princess Di's memorial playground is our last stop, and before this, there was the creative conglomeration of logs in Strasbourg, France, more art than child's plaything. Before that was the modern decagon in the court-yard of our apartment in Innsbruck, Austria. There was the Bavarian theme park in the woods, of course, and before that, our well-loved neighborhood park in Turkey, where the swings still dragged too close to the ground. The kids played in the microscopic play space at the restaurant in Kosovo, where Kyle and I first flirted many years ago, and the Zagreb airport's outdoor playground was a surprise during a layover in Croatia. In Jinja, Uganda, the kids climbed the wooden fort at Sole Hope's guesthouse, and back in Queensland, Australia, they splashed in a park of hoses and sprinklers to soak off December sweat. The airport in Singapore had several playgrounds worthy of awards, naturally, and in Chiang Mai, we lived by a play structure full of old tires and chains, perfect for climbing. Before that, in Hong Kong, we wandered a park with an aquarium and a bamboo-hungry panda, and at our friend's apartment in Xi'an, China, the neighborhood kids met in the courtyard to climb monkey bars while elderly neighbors made laps on the sidewalk.

"Hey—do you remember all that exercise equipment on the streets in Beijing?" Tate asks as we head back to our guesthouse in Camden Town, where we'll start packing for the last time.

"What exercise equipment?" Reed asks.

"You remember. All those twisty machines and stuff we played on," she says.

"That was for exercising?" Reed says, surprised. "I thought those were playgrounds." China has a penchant for exercise machines, free to the public and lined along urban sidewalks.

"That was a long time ago, at the beginning of our trip," Kyle muses, picking up a rock in the grass. "Back when we were still getting over jet lag. We've done a ton of stuff since then."

"Oh yeah, remember how Finn woke up in the middle of the night, looking through the empty fridge in Beijing?" Tate asks. "And how he was so tired he was talking in his sleep?"

"I don't remember that!" Finn says. "What did I say?"

"Bananas!" Reed says. They double over with laughter.

"Come on guys," I say, grabbing Kyle's hand. "We've got a big flight coming up. Let's go make dinner so we can get a decent bedtime."

Turkish Dust

Twenty layers of civilization park beneath parking lots,
Each dusted by feet of descendants.
You've played on the broken-free columns
Sarcophagus in shambles, a keen spot for play
We dance on the dead, we're alive longer and stronger.
Take this, all this,
And take none of it for granted.
We walk hallowed halls and
You play on Corinthian columns
And soon we are like them.
Dust.
Art, marble, music worldwide splay glory in remembrance
That this, this too, shall all pass, as with us
Collected into glory like them.
Renewed.
We set out one day more,
One foot in front of another
And another, and another,
Around the bend, in awe of it all.
Earth is, after all,
crammed with heaven.

PART VI

Once you have traveled, the voyage never ends,
but is played out over and over again in the quietest
chambers. The mind can never break off from the journey.

—Pat Conroy

22

RETURNING

Benedictine monks take, among other vows, a vow of stability. In it, they promise to stay in the monastic community in which they enter, and to not move unless they're sent elsewhere by their superiors. They stay put. If this idea was so radical during Benedict's sixth-century Italian life that it called for a monastic vow, imagine how utterly antithetical this idea is to our frenetic, whirlwind twenty-first-century society. I can't imagine the possibility of this kind of rootedness.

Six in ten adults move to a new community at least once in their lives, and the average length of a job is only 4.4 years now. Smartphones, Wi-Fi, toll roads, and commuter jets make it a cinch for modern-day nomads to work from anywhere and take their lives on the road. This isn't a bad thing, necessarily; the average Western adult has a range and reach that Benedict and his followers could not fathom a thousand years ago. We can visit lifesaving doctors the next state over; we can surprise our mother on her birthday across the country; we can interview for a new job stationed a thousand miles away before we say yes to it.

For those of us who can take our work wherever we go, contemporary infrastructure paves the road to geographical freedom. We can check e-mail from a chaise longue on a Thai beach. We can Skype with our boss from an Austrian coffee shop. Our work deadlines are dependent only on a decent Internet connection and foresight to calculate the time difference. Add worldschooling to the mix, and the whole family can be anywhere, together.

Modern conveniences make for grand adventures. But they don't always cultivate stability.

Because flight patterns and passports make it possible to be literally anywhere in the world, it's tempting to dream of being there. By *there*, I mean anywhere. I can be in a hammock hovering over powder-white sand on the Mediterranean, and suddenly I'll wish I were in a mountain cabin in the Southern Alps. I'll be in my favorite megacity, and while I sway in tandem to the other bodies around me on the London Underground, I'll drift in daydream to a plebeian village in the Swiss countryside, preferably one I've not yet visited. My kids and I will be canoeing down the Deschutes River in central Oregon, and I'll crave insatiably for food-truck tacos in downtown Austin.

Traveling means touching, tasting, smelling the world. It means the chance to explore hamlets and boroughs that citizens the world over call home. Through travel, you can know, firsthand, the difference in taste between the bread in Sri Lanka and Turkey. You'll add years to your life with more layers, thicker skin, and a softer heart because of it. Travel is a gift.

But travel doesn't provide stability. And isn't it in stability that we find home?

Twentieth-century Trappist monk Thomas Merton explains the vow of stability this way: "By making a vow of stability the monk renounces the vain hope of wandering off to find a 'perfect monastery.' This implies a deep act of faith: the recognition that it does not much matter where we are or whom we live with."

Choosing stability over volatility means staying put when life throws a curveball. It means digging in your heels when the economy sends your housing price crashing, or when community crime rates skyrocket. Possibly even harder, stability means staying put when life gets boring.

I find it fascinating that in all our exploring of the world's nooks and crannies, my three kids most loved the times we settled down and stayed somewhere awhile. A year after we returned to the States, I can ask one of them their favorite part of our year, and their answer is usually "the month we lived in Sydney and fed chickens in the backyard," or "the month we lived in France and built Terabithia." We bring up memories from the Great Wall of China, the Daintree Rainforest in Queensland, and the Eiffel Tower, and after a few minutes of reminiscence, they turn the conversation, preferring to talk about the houses that accompanied them:

Remember that loft in France with the Star Wars chess set?

I loved Chiang Mai—we each got our own bed.

Remember the triple bunks beds in Uganda?

I totally wish we could have chickens like in Sydney.

I didn't travel around the world with my family to "find myself," but I was curious what I'd learn about home. Can home be anywhere? Is home where I'm originally from? Where I've lived longest? Do we even *need* a place to call home, so long as we have each other? Some people live "location independent," making the entire world their home—they'll park for a while in one neck of the woods; then when the wanderlust itch needs scratching, they'll pack up again and move to a new spot. Could this be a feasible way of life for us?

The single most significant thing we gained when we paused in Thailand, Australia, and France was community. By staying in one place for a month or longer on our travels, we burrowed into our surroundings and invested in neighbors, even if only for a little while. We stayed put—in a nomadic sense, anyway—long enough to cultivate relationships unshielded by the next great thing to see, the next place on our itinerary.

The nuns at Our Lady of Mississippi Abbey say that by taking a vow of stability, they are "resisting all temptation to escape the truth about ourselves by restless movement from one place to the next." Resisting all temptation to escape the truth about ourselves. That's an easy thing to do in our rapid-fire world.

Just for fun, I snapped photos of mailboxes around the world. The aim was at least one per country, and I almost made my goal. I had no ulterior motive for this; I simply wanted a side project as we filled our days with train-hopping, worldschooling, and scoring coffee by whatever means necessary (which sometimes meant fashioning a pour-over from a soda can, a paper airline cup, and a stolen coffee filter from the previous guesthouse). I've always admired mailboxes, seen them as a focal point in a house's curb appeal, and have lowered my enthusiasm for a potential home if it had a boring street-side gray metal box with locked cubbies.

Before my mailbox photos, I don't think I noticed that the majority of the world's mailboxes are red. At least they are in the countries we visited. Many were impressive—intricate ironwork painted a vibrant cardinal, impossible to miss and oozing with charm. Others were less so—a simple, rusted box with a lid, available to the public and wired to a pipe on an apartment building. One in Sri Lanka was derelict, strapped on a fence and so faded I'm not sure it's justifiably considered red.

All of them, no matter how picturesque, meant one thing: people lived there. Citizens needed to mail stuff to another address that had, presumably, a mailbox as well.

Mailboxes are portals to the rest of the world, where, with just a few stamps, we have access to almost anywhere on the globe. This was a marvel before the Internet, and if you think about it, it's still astonishing that we could send a postcard halfway around the world in just a few days. If we wanted to reach back in reply, all we'd need is an envelope, something to say, and a few more stamps. We have access to the whole world, right where we call home.

————

Where we call home in the world matters.

When our travels ended, no one was more surprised than I that we decided to move back to Austin, Texas, my birthplace. Because of our life in Turkey and then Oregon, it had been almost a decade since we'd lived here, and the kids mostly knew of it as a city where we visited people. It was always fun, and we'd return to either Turkey or Oregon with full bellies and happy hearts, grateful for the people who provided our excuse to visit. But Kyle and I routinely bemoaned the thought of daily life here:

Can you imagine dealing with this traffic every single day?

Oh my gosh, I'd die in this heat, and it's only May—I don't know how I endured August here for thirty years.

It's gotten so hip and trendy to live here; let's vow to not be one of "them."

We preferred to live where landscapes were magnificent, streets weren't as congested, and crowds didn't flock like lemmings to wherever the latest publication listed as the Top Ten Most Exciting Places to Live. We wanted freedom to explore our surroundings, and we preferred to do it where mountains were tall and humidity was low, and preferably where it didn't take all the live-long day to get out of town.

This is why we stunned ourselves by moving back to Austin.

On our trip around the world, Kyle and I kept the question of home in the backs of our minds and the forefront of our conversations. When a locale proved itself pleasing enough, we'd ask each other—*Could we move here? Could this be home?* If nowhere pulled strong enough, our default was a return to central Oregon. That was our assumption, in fact, until the last month of our journey.

In Uhldingen-Mühlhofen, Germany, Kyle and I went on that date to that pub, and along with talking about the kids and their year of nonstop travel, we talked about home. I don't remember who brought it up first, but we shocked ourselves with a mutual admittance that of all the places in the world, we thought Austin might be calling us back. Late that night, we listened to drunk Germans sing in the background and we stared at lights reflecting over an inky-black Bodensee while we brainstormed what a return to Texas would look like.

Kyle said, "I don't know why, but no matter where we are in the world, Austin has this magnetic pull. It's like we're supposed to be there."

A month later, we got rid of another handful of our belongings waiting for us in a central Oregon storage unit, packed the rest in a truck, and signed a rental agreement in the north Austin suburbs.

We don't know how long we'll be here. We're not Benedictine monks, and twenty-first-century life is what it is. But as our kids get older, we're surprising ourselves with our unassuming, quiet draw to stability.

Austin's traffic has only gotten worse, and all the queso in the world doesn't quell my hatred for the refracting heat waves in the steaming summer air. Turns out, we didn't move here for convenience, culture, or our taste buds. We moved here because of people. There were just enough old friends and just enough family to pull us back here, and together with the Anglican church we now attend with ardor (we've even been confirmed as official Anglicans), we've unearthed what we found in a sliver of a fraction in Thailand, Australia, and France: community.

This isn't to say we didn't make friends in Oregon. We managed to meet lovely people that we still enjoy visiting when we're in the Pacific Northwest, and we hope to know them for a long time. We have family who live several hours' drive away from our former central Oregon home, and we miss living in closer proximity to them too. But for whatever reason, it never became *home*. We loved living there, but our souls remained restless.

Author Terry Pratchett wrote, "Coming back to where you started is not the same as never leaving." This comforts me, here in Texas.

We will always travel. In fact, we've got more trips on the horizon, both scribbled on calendar squares and in daydreams for the kids' teenage years. Our move to Texas was on the condition that we'd spend a sizable chunk of our summer months in Oregon, as much as we could help it.

Wanderlust is never truly quenched—as C. S. Lewis famously penned, "If we find ourselves with a desire that nothing in this world can satisfy, the most probable explanation is that we were made for another world."

The more I travel, the more I'm at peace with the unslakable satisfaction of wanderlust. Its very nature exists on the promise of something better around the bend, and the stamps in my passport have proved to me my heart will always yearn for something better. And better. And better, yet. It's as though I were made for another world.

Am I at home in the world? Yes. Its waters and forests, megacities and villages, bus lines and bicycles make it feasible to find a reasonable escapade anywhere. When I travel, I'm at home in the world, so long as I'm with the people I love most.

But I still need a home in the world. I'll backpack with gusto until my back gives out, but at the end of the day, I need to hang up that backpack in a closet, check my mail, and sip a drink with my next-door neighbor, watching the sun set from the backyard. I need to water my neighbor's plant when it's her turn to travel. I need to pick up my husband's prescription refill from the pharmacy that already knows his needs. I need to harp on my kids to clean their rooms for the third day in a row. I need to lose my phone in the same couch, and stir soup simmering on the same stove in the same pot.

Merton continues about the Benedictine monks: "Stability becomes difficult for a man whose monastic ideal contains some note, some element of the extraordinary. All monasteries are more or less ordinary. Its ordinariness is one of its greatest blessings."

Travel has taught me the blessing of ordinariness, of rootedness and stability. It can be found anywhere on the globe. It's courageous to walk out the front door and embrace earth's great adventures, but the real act of courage is to return to that door, turn the knob, walk through, unpack the bags, and start the kettle for a cup of tea. In our rituals of bread making and wine tasting, tucking our kids into bed and watching stars flicker from a chair on the back patio, we are all daring to find ourselves at home, somewhere in the world.

EPILOGUE

Today it has been about a year since we've returned from London; nine months since we unpacked the last box at our cookie-cutter suburban rental in Austin. We felt it prudent to rent a house for our first year back, in order to better decide into which neighborhood we should establish permanence. It had been some time since we lived here, and rapid change has settled in, made itself at home. I grew up here, but much of it is unfamiliar.

We've decided to call central Texas home, to do what Thomas Merton advises and call its ordinariness one of its greatest blessings. The kids are adjusting to a commonplace routine of school at the same place every day, and the five of us have neighborhood pool passes.

We are also going to buy a house.

This afternoon, Saturday and muggy already for early May, we pull into the driveway of a house for sale—a complete fixer-upper, which is just what we want, to take advantage of Kyle's carpentry prowess. The five of us walk in and greet a woman named Gillian, who is the childhood friend of my aunt Jan, and who is selling the house on behalf of her elderly mother.

We start the polite but awkward investigation of envisioning our family meals in a stranger's kitchen, arranging our shelves of toys in these different bedrooms. I want to peek in the closets without feeling like a snoop. It is a good house, and it would serve us well. But this is Austin, and the price we can offer is a long shot for this neighborhood.

The five of us head out to the backyard, a weeded-over swath of grass and dandelions, and the kids start claiming specific spots for our things: *Here's where our picnic table can go; this can be a vegetable garden; maybe Dad can build us a treehouse here.* I spy something standing near a fledgling tree, lopsided in the corner, perhaps a forgotten gardening tool left long ago. I walk over and inspect.

It is a garden statue of Saint Francis, buried in the dirt up to his waist and caked with dried mud. It looks as though he's been keeping watch over this corner of a suburban backyard for decades, with nary a witness to give substance to his quiet work. I smile, remembering some of the wisdom Francis imparted on me in Italy: "We have been called to heal wounds, to unite what has fallen apart, and to bring home those who have lost their way." And now he's here, in a potential home of ours.

I follow my family back toward the house's sun porch, where Kyle has started chatting with Gillian. I walk through the screen door and spot an unexpected army of oil paintings leaned against the screened walls, stacked in twos and threes behind one another, some mounted in chipped gilded frames, others unframed as undressed canvases.

"Was your mother an art collector?" I ask Gillian.

"No," she replies, "She was a painter." My eyes gaze over the stacks of paintings.

"Are all these hers?" I ask.

"Yes, they were. She was just an amateur, but she loved doing it."

I walk slowly around the screened porch to admire this layperson's ability to wield a paintbrush in oil; her subjects seemed to be everything from bowls of fruit, to children, to fields of Texas wildflowers, to busy city streets. She was gifted.

"Hey—we've been here!" I hear Finn exclaim. He is pointing at a painting in the corner.

We all walk to where he stands as he continues. "See? That town is where we lost my red sweatshirt! Remember?" He jumps up and down in excitement. I squint my eyes to scrutinize the painting. It is lovely enough, but to me it looks like a nondescript corner of a European village—stone-colored buildings with awnings covering doors on the bottom floor, vendors selling flowers, patrons being served coffee on outdoor bistro tables.

"Actually—Finn, I think you're right. That does look like Assisi," Kyle says.

"It does?" I ask. I don't notice details with nearly the aptitude as Kyle.

"By any chance, did your mom spend any time in Assisi?" he asks Gillian.

"I'm pretty sure she did, now that you ask," she answers. "If I remember, I think she went there, then came back and painted this."

"See? I told you," says Finn. "It's Assisi!"

"That's remarkable he would notice that," Gillian says.

"It really is!" I laugh. To me the painting still looks like customary old buildings pervasive all over the continent, but I suppose there is a razor-thin hint of familiarity to those cobblestone roads. I shake my head in wonder—first, Francis hanging out in the backyard. Now, Assisi saying *ciao* to me when I least expect it.

It's tempting to play mind games and tell myself, *It's a sign! This is the house for us!* But I know better. The highest price we can offer for this house is lower than the going rate in this part of Austin, and Gillian needs a solid bounty for her mother's sake. We make our offer, cross our fingers, and shrug our shoulders in disappointed understanding when we find out she has to decline.

Our family eventually pinpoints the just-right fixer-upper for us, in a town just outside Austin I've admired since I was a young girl. We find a slice of land to, Lord willing, start burying deep roots; a foundation supporting four walls that will house our backpacks when we're not out in the world exploring. This is a small town, too, and during our year in Austin, we've come to remember how much we love small towns—like Bend, Cadenet, and Assisi.

One afternoon a few weeks later, my aunt Jan texts me to ask if I'd like to go to lunch. We make our plans, and I end with a reply that I'll see her soon.

"Oh, and I have something for you," she adds as an afterthought a few minutes later. "Gillian wanted you to have this one painting of a European street scene, so she dropped it off here at my house. I guess you know something about it?"

I smile, and my eyes water. I know something about it.

<hr />

A painting of a quotidian street corner in Assisi is mounted on the wall, humble and dignified, in our fixer-upper home next to a pile of Kyle's tools and a plastic cup of nails waiting to be used. Her happy scene greets me when I walk in from the library and start the kettle for a cup of tea, winks *ciao* after I tuck the kids into bed at night and collapse onto the couch with the day's exhaustion behind me. Even though she was collecting dust in a ramshackle Texas home while we were out there, she reminds me of my family's adventures.

She is now part of our home in the world.

ACKNOWLEDGMENTS

When I think that I was given the task to pen a journey that really included hundreds of souls sprinkled around the globe, I want to cower in the corner because I know I can't thank by name that one kind taxi driver in Hong Kong, the delightful *boulanger* in Provence, or the gracious waiter in Pristina who let us use the restaurant Wi-Fi for hours even though we only ordered an espresso.

To the many, many nameless folk who made our experience magical—I hope one day you know who you are. *Faleminderit, grazie, teşekkür ederim, danke, asante, hvala ti,* and *xièxiè.*

I can, however, thank by name Soup. Thank you, Soup, for leading the way to our guesthouse in Phuket.

Many, many thanks to my brilliant agent-friend, Jenni Burke. I wouldn't want to be in this business with anyone else—someday let's braid each other's hair on the steps of the Cattedrale di Santa Maria del Fiore in Florence, shall we? I'm indebted to your wisdom and kindness, and I plan to stay that way. Also grateful for your Italian connections.

Seth Haines, you have a remarkable way with words—thank you for imparting that way to the words between these covers. I'm grateful for both your red pen and for your friendship, and Amber's too. You two are salt of the earth, and Kyle and I are deeply glad to know you both.

Many thanks to Angela Scheff, who, once again, made a book of mine even better. Jessica Wong, Brigitta Nortker, Aryn Van Dyke, Tiffany Sawyer, and the rest of the kind folks in the HarperCollins/ Thomas Nelson offices—it's a pleasure to work with you. Thank you for your partnership.

Words aren't enough to thank our friends around the world who showed us hospitality, poured us a glass of wine, or let our kids play with your toys—Dave and Karen, Ashley and Giff Ransom, Joan and Tim Peagam, Laura and Matt Parker, Darren and Vanessa Rowse, Ben and Brooke McAlary, Beryl and Pete, Adriel and Ryan Booker, Dave and Joy Forney, Asher and Dru Collie, Heidi Wright, Eric and Kristi, Dan and Bethany Bassett, Ruth and John Chestnut, Skender and Jackie Zeqiri, Beqir Dema, Bekim and Fikrie Lushaku, Albina Haliti, Ernie and Suzy Penner, Andie and Chuck Wade, and Murat and Nilüfer Talu. Thanks to the myriad guesthouse owners who opened their front doors and handed us their keys. Thank you to The Well in Chiang Mai for your significant, sacred work. And thank you to Ryan and Stephanie Langford, delightful travelers-in-crime and fantastic friends—we love any time we spend with you on any dot on the map.

Mad grateful for good friends, especially those who understand the weird world of what we do—you know who you are. Overflowing with thanks for the many friends who love us, even when they think we're a question mark. *Saluti* . . . a round of drinks are on us, with every one of you, one day, in the same room.

I have so much supportive family, it almost doesn't seem fair— thank you and much love to Josh, Joan, Holden, Nellie, AJ, Karisa, Kylie, Nathan, Ashton, Carsyn, Carly, Darren, Owen, and Olive, as well as the umpteen-jillion cousins, aunts, uncles, and grandparents of mine that I count an honor to call family. Of course, thank you to my in-laws, Ed and Linda, and to my own parents, Rod and Karen— love you all to Vacoas-Phoenix, Mauritius, and back approximately eighteen times, and thanks for praying for us as we cart your grand-children to the four corners of the world.

And finally, to my favorite people in the entire world . . . I can't believe God's great blessing in letting me live life with you, Kyle. Thank you for hailing that taxi and telling it to chase that bus across the Macedonian border, and for pulling up old floor planks to lay down new ones. I'll make a home and ride rickety buses with you anywhere. Here's to many more adventures.

To Tate, Reed, and Finn, who are truly my greatest adventure yet—these travels, these words, this home—they're all for you to find your place in the world. I'm honored you call me Mom, and I love you so. Rudyard Kipling once said, "God gave all men all earth to love, but since our hearts are small, ordained for each, one spot should prove beloved over all." You guys, along with your dad, are the one spot on earth beloved to me over all.

ABOUT THE AUTHOR

Tsh Oxenreider is the author of *Notes from a Blue Bike* and *Organized Simplicity*, and is the top-ranked podcaster of *The Simple Show*. She is the founder of the community blog *The Art of Simple*, and her writing has been featured in the *Washington Post*, *CNN*, *Real Simple* magazine, and other venues. A graduate of the University of Texas, where she studied English and anthropology, Tsh currently lives with her family in Georgetown, Texas, and eats tacos several times a week.

NOTES

Chapter 2: China

1. *Wikipedia*, s.v. "List of Chinese Inventions," accessed October 31, 2016, https://en.wikipedia.org/wiki/List_of_Chinese_inventions.
2. "History of Umbrella and Parasol," *Umbrella History*, accessed November 2, 2016, http://www.umbrellahistory.net/.
3. Sky Canaves, "Earthquake Detection Past and Present," *China Real Time Report* (blog), *Wall Street Journal*, June 5, 2008, http://blogs.wsj.com /chinarealtime/2008/06/05/earthquake-detection-past-and-present/.
4. *Wikipedia*, s.v. "History of Rockets," accessed November 1, 2016, https://en.wikipedia.org/wiki/History_of_rockets.

Chapter 4: Thailand

1. Eugene H. Peterson, *Eat This Book: A Conversation in the Art of Spiritual Reading* (Grand Rapids: Eerdmans, 2009), 43.

Chapter 8: Australia, Again

1. Mary Oliver, *White Pine: Poems and Prose* (San Diego: Harcourt, 1994), 8.

Chapter 10: Uganda

1. See http://www.atlasobscura.com/places/source-of-the-nile-at-jinja.

Chapter 12: Zimbabwe

1. Marquess Curzon of Kedleston, *Tales of Travel* (London: Hodder and Stoughton, 1923; digitized by Internet Archive, 2014), chap. 5, https:// archive.org/stream/talesoftravel00curz_0/talesoftravel00curz_0_djvu.txt.

Chapter 14: Morocco

1. Nigel Tisdell, "Fes, Morocco: A Flavour of the Nation," *Telegraph* (UK), February 10, 2015, http://www.telegraph.co.uk/travel/destinations /africa/morocco/Fes/articles/Fes-Morocco-A-flavour-of-the-nation/.

Chapter 15: France

1. Doug DeMuro, "Here's Why Monaco Is the World's Best Place for Car Enthusiasts," *Jalopnik*, July 23, 2014, http://jalopnik.com/here -s-why-monaco-is-the-world-s-best-place-for-car-ent-1609741707.

Chapter 16: Italy

1. Ernest Hemingway, *A Moveable Feast: The Restored Edition* (New York: Simon & Schuster, 2014), 175.
2. Anthony Doerr, *Four Seasons in Rome: On Twins, Insomnia, and the Biggest Funeral in the History of the World* (New York: Scribner, 2007), 140–41.
3. Attributed to Louis Nizer in *Between You and Me*.